United Nations
Educational, Scientific and
Cultural Organization

Holocaust Education
in a Global Context

Edited by Karel Fracapane and Matthias Haß
In collaboration with the Topography of Terror Foundation, Berlin

Published in 2014 by the United Nations Educational, Scientific and Cultural Organization,
7, place de Fontenoy, 75352 Paris 07 SP, France

© UNESCO 2014

ISBN 978-92-3-100042-3

Particular appreciation is due to Thomas Lutz, Topography of Terror Foundation, for his major contribution to
this publication.

Special thanks also go to Hannah Marek for her assistance in editing the draft, and to all those who reviewed the
manuscript.

Edited by Karel Fracapane and Matthias Haß
In collaboration with the Topography of Terror Foundation, Berlin

Cover photo: Wall of Names at Shoah Memorial, Paris ©Mémorial de la Shoah/Nathalie Darbellay
Graphic design: UNESCO
Printed by: UNESCO

Printed in France

Contents

Foreword

How did the Holocaust happen? How was it possible?

Answering these questions means addressing complex and troubling chapters of the past. It means unpacking the history of a fundamentally racist and antisemitic project that led to genocide. Teaching about the Holocaust can raise challenges for educators, because the stories they must tell will leave leaners struggling with disturbing ethical questions.

This is precisely why Holocaust education is so important. Teaching and learning about the Holocaust, and the history of genocide, provides an opportunity to engage students in deep reflection on the origins and mechanisms of violence, so that they can better understand the past and the world they live in. This education is essential today, to raise awareness about a shared history, to promote human rights everywhere and eliminate all forms of discrimination and intolerance.

UNESCO believes in the transformative power of education. Taking up this challenging subject provides a way for all to learn how to welcome difference and diversity on the basis of respect and tolerance. Whether in Europe, or in Africa, Latin America or anywhere else in the world, education about this common history will help young people to understand better how mass violence can be prevented and to reinforce their own role today in fostering respect for the rights and dignity of all.

Holocaust education is a responsibility – to face the reality of crimes perpetrated, to commemorate the victims and to sustain a meaningful dialogue between history and memory. Many people risked everything to leave a trace of what happened to themselves, their families and their communities, so that their story would not be forgotten. We have an obligation to the victims and their legacy, as well as to the survivors who speak for them, to ensure that their stories are heard and will be studied for generations to come.

These are the goals guiding this volume, which explores the opportunities that arise from educating about the Holocaust in various cultural contexts and educational settings. With this publication, educators will have at their fingertips an up-to-date account of the most salient issues discussed in the field of Holocaust education. This volume will also help policy-makers grasp more clearly the objectives and the implications of dealing with this complex subject. All of this is essential to our efforts to deepen mutual understanding and respect today, in societies undergoing deep transformation, across a world changing quickly.

I wish to thank the **Topography of Terror Foundation** for their contribution to this publication, which draws on the 2012 experts meeting we organised jointly in Paris on "Holocaust Education in a Global Context". I am deeply grateful to each of the authors who contributed to this work, sharing a wealth of experience, teaching rationales and diverse points of view on a subject that is essential and universally relevant.

Irina Bokova
Director-General of UNESCO

From the ashes of the Shoah

Seven decades ago, the Soviets liberated Auschwitz and the Americans liberated Dachau. Today, for one of the last living survivors of these two infernos to be still alive and well, with a new and happy family that has recreated the one I lost, seems almost unreal. When I entered Eichmann and Mengele's gruesome universe at the age of thirteen, I measured my life expectancy in weeks or months at the most.

During the winter of 1944, as the Second World War was coming to an end, we in the camps knew nothing. We were wondering: What is happening in the world outside? Where is God? Where is the Pope? Does anyone out there know what is happening here to us? Do they care? Russia was on the edge of defeat. England was resisting with her back against the wall. And America? She was so far away, so divided, so isolationist. How could she be expected to save the sinking barge of civilization from the seemingly invincible forces of darkness?

It took a long time for the news of the Normandy landings to reach us. There were also rumours that the Red Army was advancing on the Eastern front. The Nazis' nervousness was also becoming palpable. The gas chambers were now spewing fire and smoke as never before, killing innocent men, women and children at the rate of 10,000 per day. One grey, frosty morning, our guards lined us up and marched us out through Auschwitz-Birkenau's main gate with its perverse sign: 'Arbeit Macht Frei' (Work Brings Freedom). Those of us who could still be used as slave labourers would be shunted westward, deep into Germany.

I was beside myself with excitement and apprehension. Salvation seemed so near, and yet so far away. At the last moment our jailors will surely slaughter us. The 'Final Solution' must be completed to the last Jew. All living witnesses must be wiped out. Oh, to hang on, to hang on a little longer... I was sixteen years old, and I wanted to live.

Our death marches from camp to camp continued day and night, until we, and the guards, became aware that we were hearing distant explosions of artillery shells. One afternoon, on the outskirts of Dachau, we were strafed by a squadron of Allied fighter planes, which mistook our column for Wehrmacht troops. As the SS men hit the dirt, their machine guns blazing in all directions, someone near me yelled: 'Run for it!' I kicked off my wooden clogs and made a desperate sprint, with a few other fellow prisoners, into the thick of a nearby Bavarian forest. There we lay low in daytime and walked in the direction of the Western Front after dark, until an armoured regiment of American G.I.'s brought us life and freedom.

Now we, the few living witnesses of the greatest catastrophe ever perpetrated by man against man, are disappearing one by one. Soon, history will speak about our cruel fate at best with the impersonal voice of researchers and novelists; at worst in the malevolent register of falsifiers and demagogues who call the Holocaust a 'myth'. That process has already begun...

This is why we have a sacred duty to transmit to our fellow humans the memory of what we have endured in body and soul; to alert younger generations of every race, colour and faith that the fanaticism, bigotry and xenophobia that are spreading again in our newly enflamed and destabilized world could destroy their universe as they once destroyed ours.

UNESCO's noble initiative to promote global education and knowledge about the Shoah has never been more relevant and timely than now, in the currently deteriorating economic and geopolitical climate that breeds hatred, prejudice and fear on all continents. For the genocides, ethnic cleansings and other mass atrocities humanity has experienced during and since the Second World War are, in the words of its Director-General, Irina Bokova, 'living history that concerns us all, regardless of our backgrounds, cultures or religions'. Indeed, their awesome legacy can, and must, mobilize the common core of universal values shared by all great creeds – religious and secular – lest the nightmares of the past return with a vengeance to doom our chances for a better future.

Dr Samuel Pisar
UNESCO Honorary Ambassador and Special Envoy
for Holocaust and Genocide Education

Introduction

International interest in Holocaust education has reached new heights in recent years. This historic event has long been central to cultures of remembrance in those countries where the genocide of the Jewish people occurred. But other parts of the world have now begun to recognize the history of the Holocaust as an effective means to teach about mass violence and to promote human rights and civic duty, testifying to the emergence of this pivotal historical event as a universal frame of reference. In this new, globalized context, how is the Holocaust represented and taught? How do teachers handle this excessively complex and emotionally loaded subject in fast-changing multicultural European societies still haunted by the crimes perpetrated by the Nazis and their collaborators? Why and how is it taught in other areas of the world that have only little if any connection with the history of the Jewish people? *Holocaust Education in a Global Context* will explore these questions.

Teaching and learning about the Holocaust from an international perspective

The word *Holocaust* – widely used, together with the Hebrew word *Shoah* (catastrophe) – refers to 'the systematic, bureaucratic, state-sponsored persecution and murder of approximately six million Jews by the Nazi regime and its collaborators'[1]. The Holocaust Encyclopaedia of the United States Holocaust Memorial Museum further indicates:

> *'Holocaust' is a word of Greek origin meaning 'sacrifice by fire'. The Nazis, who came to power in Germany in January 1933, believed that Germans were 'racially superior' and that the Jews, deemed 'inferior', were an alien threat to the so-called German racial community.*
>
> *During the era of the Holocaust, German authorities also targeted other groups because of their perceived 'racial inferiority':Roma (Gypsies), the disabled, and some of the Slavic peoples (Poles, Russians, and others). Other groups were persecuted on political, ideological, and behavioral grounds, among them Communists, Socialists, Jehovah's Witnesses, and homosexuals.*

The Holocaust was not the first or the last genocide in the history of humanity, but it was unprecedented in many ways and is still the most radical attempt to destroy every member of a group without exception. It also gave rise to a new international legal instrument that tackles this specific and extreme type of mass atrocity: the United Nations Convention on the Prevention and Punishment of Genocide, adopted by the United Nations General Assembly on 9 December 1948. It is indeed against the background of the Holocaust that the Polish lawyer Raphael Lemkin, in his book *Axis Rule in Occupied Europe* published in 1944, defined the concept of genocide, a 'crime committed with the intent to destroy, in whole or in part, a national, ethnic, racial or religious group, as such'.

---

1   *Holocaust Encyclopedia*, United States Holocaust Memorial Museum
    (http://www.ushmm.org/wlc/en/)

By 'genocide' we mean the destruction of a nation or of an ethnic group. This new word, coined by the author to denote an old practice in its modern development, is made from the ancient Greek word genos (race, tribe) and the Latin cide (killing).... Generally speaking, genocide does not necessarily mean the immediate destruction of a nation, except when accomplished by mass killings of all members of a nation. It is intended rather to signify a coordinated plan of different actions aiming at the destruction of essential foundations of the life of national groups, with the aim of annihilating the groups themselves. Genocide is directed against the national group as an entity, and the actions involved are directed against individuals, not in their individual capacity, but as members of the national group.

In the context of a globalized world, the genocide of the Jewish people is often presented as a paradigmatic event, providing a methodological background against which other occurrences of mass violence can be understood. Although of course the history of the Holocaust cannot serve as the only framework to understand events that must be apprehended in the specific context in which they unfolded, it can however be seen as a starting point to reflect upon other cases of mass atrocities and human rights violations, and to examine the mechanisms that may lead to future violence. From that perspective, the Holocaust is studied and taught through the double lens of the promotion of human rights and the prevention of genocide.

This trend is encouraged by the 2005 United Nations General Assembly Resolution on Holocaust Remembrance, which designates 27 January as an annual International Day of Commemoration in memory of the victims of the Holocaust and urges 'Member States to inculcate future generations with the lessons of the Holocaust in order to help prevent future acts of genocide'. This resolution presents the Holocaust as a global reference point for education that has both particular historical significance and universal meaning. This perspective corresponds to a change of paradigm in how the Holocaust is studied. Indeed, until recently, the Holocaust was mostly taught as part of the national history of countries of Western Europe that were directly affected by it, as well as the United States and Israel, and it was studied strictly in the context of Second World War history. The fall of the Berlin wall and the integration of the former communist countries in the European Union allowed for the memory of the Holocaust – and all its consequences in terms of commemoration, research and education – to be 'Europeanised' and, subsequently, internationalized. This process of globalization has far-reaching implications.

First, the goal of commemorating the Holocaust, and of teaching about it, is broadened to universal considerations related to peace and human rights. As a matter of international interest, the Holocaust is an historical reference now shared by many people across the world, evoking the worst of state violence, serving as a universal reminder and stimulating a common sense of responsibility in the face of human rights violations and dangers of genocide in today's world.

Second, beyond this universal, human rights-oriented approach, it could be expected that introducing the Holocaust as a shared global reference might in turn have consequences in local contexts. Holocaust remembrance is charged emotionally and politically. It is often enmeshed in geopolitical considerations and it stirs national debates about painful memories, and brings to light a legacy of victimization and guilt. Teaching and learning about the history of the Holocaust is seldom an emotionally neutral process, because it arouses feelings and attitudes related to one's identity and perceptions of the past. It touches upon the core of remembrance processes that affect individuals as well as societies, and may challenge their historical narratives. This dynamic naturally holds true for all countries of Europe in which, behind the long-standing and apparently consensual commitment to deal with the subject, a multiplicity of sometimes competing narratives continue to co-exist. But it may also affect remembrance processes in other societies in which the subject is taught, thus raising new challenges for educators and policy-makers: What are the implications of teaching about the Holocaust in a country that has gone through crimes against humanity or conflict? How do these societies deal with the subject, and for what purpose? To help students comprehend the magnitude and the unprecedented nature of the Holocaust is in itself an exceptional challenge for educators. But the mere fact that it is now being taught significantly in countries with no direct connection to this historical event opens a whole new space for research and reflection about the practices, methods and objectives of educating about the Holocaust.

However, this process of internationalizing Holocaust remembrance also has a downside, clearly visible in the inflationary use, often for political or moral purposes, of the terms *Holocaust* and *genocide* to characterize crimes or abuses of a totally different nature. The increasing use of the Holocaust as a symbolic reference in public discourse, functioning as a rhetorical device to address all sorts of issues of the present, does not necessarily reflect an increasing knowledge of what the Holocaust really was and how it occurred. In fact, if there are lessons to be learnt from the Holocaust, then these lessons will shift according to time and place and will reveal a variety of ideological and historical perspectives. The 'lessons from the past' are shaped by the political and social agendas of the time, and may change according to the audience. We should remain aware – and concerned – that this globalization of Holocaust memory and the increasingly prominent place that the genocide of the Jewish people is taking in the consciousness of our contemporaries also leads to the oversimplification or the distortion of historical facts, with possibly serious consequences: the 'banalization' or 'relativization' of the events evoked and of the victims' suffering.

As the event recedes in time, this trivialization is probably the greatest didactical challenge educators must be prepared to handle when dealing with the history of the Holocaust in a global context. Holocaust education has great potential, in many areas of the world, and there are a great many reasons to encourage its dissemination as a powerful vehicle for critical thinking and for encouraging more active citizenship. But it also entails possible pitfalls, of which educators and policy-makers should be aware when engaging with this academically arduous, politically perilous and morally unsettling subject.

Focus and overview of the book

This volume came out of a seminar entitled *Holocaust Education in a Global Context*, organized at UNESCO on 27 April 2012, in partnership with the German foundation Topography of Terror. This gathering of Holocaust and genocide educators and historians representing every region of the world provided the backbone of this volume. The book gathers some of the most remarkable presentations made during the seminar; it is enriched with additional contributions bringing other views on issues highlighted by the experts invited by UNESCO.

This publication does not provide guidelines for teaching about the Holocaust. It is our understanding that specific national or regional contexts raise specific questions and thus call for different answers. But it displays a variety of approaches to Holocaust education, and explores diverse methodologies and experiences. Our purpose is to discuss these different perspectives on Holocaust education for the benefit of a wide, global audience. The book therefore presents to policy-makers and educators wishing to engage with this subject some of the most important challenges being debated by researchers and educators, from a point of view that may be relevant in multiple educational settings. In addition to presenting current practices and challenges in the field, it outlines in particular the role Holocaust education can play in tackling difficult issues of the past in diverse national and cultural contexts.

A book about Holocaust education from international perspectives should begin by examining the situation in Europe, where the genocide took place and where it is taught most extensively. Obviously, Holocaust education is first and foremost an opportunity for European societies to reflect on their own past. The first chapter therefore focuses on how the transmission of Holocaust history, which is greatly emphasized by the educational institutions of Europe, affects the formation of cultures of remembrance in the region. It explores how Germany, the society that initiated and has primary responsibility for perpetrating the crimes, finds new ways to address its own sense of guilt and its responsibilities more than two generations after the Holocaust took place, in a changing societal and cultural environment. The case of France provides another perspective, which may resonate with the situation of other western European societies. Seven decades after the events, the memory of the Holocaust is a central cultural feature of the country; it stirs vivid debate about various contemporary issues and is entangled with new memorial claims. This continuously changing situation creates difficult new challenges for teachers and requires permanent adjustment and creativity on the part of education stakeholders. Poland is different, and more representative of the cultures of remembrance in former Eastern Europe, because it struggles with a dual sense of victimhood related to the crimes perpetrated by the Communist and the Nazi regimes. But it is also very specific, being the 'core' geographical space where the Holocaust took place and where two divergent memorial perspectives, a Jewish and a Polish one, must find a way to coexist peaceably.

A third chapter addresses a series of issues related to education policies and methods: research in the field of pedagogy, current trends in textbook design, contemporary challenges of managing education in historic sites of persecution and the introduction of new perspectives, such as the lens of gender in education about Nazi crimes. It also emphasizes opportunities related to the development of Genocide Studies, and shows how such educational and research approaches, if handled with particular care, can have great relevance in a global context.

Indeed, beyond Europe, educating about the Holocaust is inevitably less rooted in local history and therefore can reflect other educational agendas that do not have a direct connection with the historical events discussed in the classroom. Through a variety of case studies, the fourth chapter shows how, sometimes very successfully, the universal reference of the Holocaust can become a starting point from which other historical traumas – and therefore contentious aspects of the past – can be dealt with. In the cases of Argentina and South Africa, Holocaust education can provide a safe environment to address local traumatic issues and thus contribute to the articulation of more inclusive national cultures of remembrance. In China, it familiarizes students with new concepts, on the basis of which they can address their country's own past of suffering and persecutions. In the case of Rwanda, it helps bring the local history of genocide into a larger perspective, making it easier for historians and educators to approach recent events. The chapter then focuses on the role of non-European institutions with international reach that seek to put strong emphasis on the link between Holocaust history and the promotion of human rights and the values of democracy, such as Facing History and Ourselves, the United States Holocaust Memorial Museum or, in a more contentious environment, the Centre for Humanistic Education of the Warsaw Ghetto Fighters House in Israel.

The book's conclusions, prepared by two prominent thinkers and historians of the Holocaust, Georges Bensoussan and Yehuda Bauer, underline what the 'centrality' of the Holocaust in modern cultures entails for our present, highlighting why teaching about this historical event is so relevant in today's world.

We hope that this collection of essays written by some of the leading experts in Holocaust education will help educators see the exceptional value of addressing the history of the Holocaust and mass atrocities. We are confident that it will encourage them to create opportunities to develop new programmes and contribute to the enhancement of best practices in a very rich, enlightening and vibrant area of education.

Karel Fracapane and Matthias Haß

1

1903 • Rohan ATLAN 1915 • Jean ASZERMAN 1898 • Gisèle ATL
1914 • Estellé ATTAS 1921 • Lucien ATLANI 1911 • Germaine ATTAL
ATTYASSE 1898 • Guy AUBER 1925 • Irmgard AUBRY 1909 • Pessia AUFLEGER 18
914 • Léon AUSCHER 1900 • Eda Henriette AUSIEFF 1931 • Geneviève AUSIEFF
USTERER 1907 • Maurice AUSTERLITZ 1887 • Rebecca AUTOFAGE 1893 • Claire AVID
AVIDOR 1929 • David AVIGDOR 1880 • Lydia AVIGDOR 1887 • Nissim AVIMELEK 1
AVISSAY 1925 • Donna AVLAGON 1871 • Estelle AVLAGON 1907 • Nissim AVLAGO
M 1927 • Léon AVRAM 1905 • Mireille AVRAM 1924 • Nissim AVRAM 1904 • Pierre AV
le AVRUTIK 1939 • Esther AVSIPOFF 1876 • Moïse AVSIPOFF 1877 • Berthe AXELRAD
rges AYACHE 1911 • Jules AYACHE 1902 • Léonie AYACHE 1870 • Reine AYACHE 190
eph AZARIA 1900 • Fanny AZENSTARCK 1921 • Dora AZIZA 1911 • Charles AZOULAY
uliette AZOULAY 1897 • Moïse AZOULAY 1916 • Simone AZOULAY 1899 • Victorine
hel BAACH 1942 • René BAACH 1941 • Sally BAACH 1901 • Perez BABAN
BABANI 1920 • Moyem BABIC 1896
rona BACHNER

Teaching about
the Holocaust
in contemporary Europe

During the past two decades, western European countries have developed a consensus about the need to commemorate the Holocaust and to transmit its history to new generations. The post-war narratives and national myths of victimhood and heroism have been progressively replaced by a more self-critical vision of history. This understanding includes at its core the fate of these societies' Jewish minorities, and therefore the explicit recognition of collaboration of local government in the perpetration of genocide.

Countries formerly under the influence of the Soviet Union have followed a different path. A consensus on how the Holocaust should be remembered has not yet been reached in this part of Europe where most of the European Jews lived and where most of the killings took place. Civilian populations and national groups were targeted with extreme brutality by the Nazi and Soviet regimes, leaving countries such as Poland, Ukraine and others totally devastated. The atrocities perpetrated claimed the lives of tens of millions in the region, and for half a century, when they were acknowledged at all, they were taught as part of a broader anti-fascist and anti-capitalist struggle, according to the communist propaganda of the time. Later on, following the collapse of the Soviet Union, the typical Western celebration of the victory over Nazi Germany was expected to coexist with a new narrative, focused on decades of communist persecutions and less eager to put emphasis on the 'liberation' of Europe. These societies had been freed from the grasp of Nazi Germany only to endure fifty years of Soviet hegemony, a period of such trauma in itself that unravelling its history of suffering became a primary focus. Not much space was left therefore for remembering the Jewish victims, either during the communist or the post-communist periods, especially if this implied also recognizing the participation of members of one's own national community in destroying this particular minority.

Societies remember first and foremost the crimes that were committed against themselves. Victimization is at the centre of remembrance processes and serves to create national identities as well as collective identities of smaller social groups. In a context where the Jewish minority has been in large part, if not entirely, destroyed, and its voice has not been represented over time or has been silenced, the emergence of a new, Holocaust-focused narrative signifies a meaningful and important break from the traditional monolithic forms of remembrance. These new perspectives on history, however, can become all the more problematic when victims of Nazism or Communism or both were themselves involved in the destruction of European Jewry or other crimes perpetrated during this period.

Holocaust education, by definition, is embedded in these discourses about the past. The following essays, focusing on three very different cases, show the role of Holocaust education in furthering the emergence of inclusive forms of remembrance, in which historical narratives do not compete with each other by seeking recognition by minimizing others' sufferings. They argue in favour of a 'conjoint vision of contested history' (Konstanty Gebert) or a 'multi-perspective approach' in pedagogy (Wolf Kaiser): in other words, shared historical consciousness based on mutual acknowledgement and open historical debate.

Teaching about perpetrators of the Holocaust in Germany

Wolf Kaiser

The Holocaust is a collective trauma, above all for Jews, but also for the German nation that gave birth to the perpetrators of this genocide. At the same time it has become a global topic because of its ramifications and the universally relevant lessons to be learned.

The development of international criminal law is closely linked to the prosecution of Nazi perpetrators by the victorious allies after the Second World War. The International Military Tribunal in Nuremberg sentenced Nazi leaders not only for aggression and war crimes, but also for crimes against humanity. The Holocaust was not mentioned as such in Nuremberg, but the systematic murder of the European Jews was obviously a major part of the crimes against humanity committed by the Nazi state. The Tribunal was instrumental in establishing international criminal justice. Since then, international courts were created that can prosecute perpetrators of mass crimes even if they were acting as government members of sovereign states. This development culminated in the foundation of the International Criminal Court, which can act whenever the national judiciary is not able or not willing to press charges against such people. The goal is not only atonement for mass atrocities, but also prevention. All people in power – even heads of state – should be aware they can be held responsible for mass crimes committed by the army, police or other state agencies.

But prevention needs more than the threat of punishment. Mass crimes are not simply a result of the viciousness of powerful people. Under certain preconditions, developments can lead to atrocities in dimensions that even the perpetrators may not have foreseen. Prevention therefore requires a comprehensive analysis of the factors and dynamics that can form a constellation that allows perpetrators to deny certain groups of human beings the right to live. This happened to the European Jews when Nazi Germany began a war of destruction in Eastern Europe and initiated the genocide of all Jews on the continent, which we now call the Holocaust. It did not happen out of the blue; it was the climax of a process of radicalization of antisemitic politics that became official state policy when Adolf Hitler was appointed chancellor in 1933.

The Holocaust is certainly the mass crime in modern history that has been explored in the most detailed and comprehensive way. Historians, political scientists, sociologists, psychologists, theologians and other scholars from all over the world have contributed to this research. Their findings are also widely used to design research concepts for the analysis of other genocides. This is why the Holocaust has been called the 'paradigmatic genocide'.

In Germany, however, the Holocaust cannot be considered as a paradigmatic event in the first place. It is the greatest moral catastrophe in German history. This crime could never be denied by any serious person, but during the first decades after the end of the Second World War most Germans blamed the Holocaust on Hitler and the Nazi leadership only. They ignored the involvement of large segments of the German state and society in the planning, the organization and the implementation of the genocide. Later – with progressing generations – the attitude of the majority of Germans changed fundamentally. A culture of remembrance developed that focuses on the most negative period in the history of the nation: Nazi rule and the persecution and murder of European Jewry. In contrast to the traditional 'culture of national pride', this has been called a 'cathartic memorial culture' due to the expectation that, by facing the darkest part of its history, the nation may be able to cope with the burden of its past and to shape a better future.

There is an official consensus in Germany that the history of Nazi crimes, in particular the Holocaust, must be taught and remembered[2]. This consensus encourages teachers to confront the Holocaust in depth in the classroom, but it also puts a great burden on them. Teaching about the Holocaust is often seen as a moral duty, not just as a chapter in history. Many history teachers consider lessons on the Holocaust as their most important but also most challenging task. Most students are interested in learning about the Holocaust, but react with discomfort to moral pressure. Teachers must avoid expecting students to develop feelings of guilt. At the same time they must insist on the special responsibility people living in Germany have, Germany being a country that fought a war of destruction in most European territories and

---

2   Yet the prominence of this topic is not unchallenged. Recently it has been competing with references to injustice and crimes under communist rule and to positive events, in particular the overcoming of Germany's partition into two states through the 1990 reunification.

committed unprecedented crimes. This responsibility is not based on ethnicity, but on citizenship. People who emigrate to a country and become citizens accept its legacy. Young people who are brought up in an individualist society do not easily understand why they have to take responsibility for the legacy of former generations. It can be helpful to point out that the legacy of the Holocaust is not only a burden; it can also stimulate self-reflection and commitment.

Confronting the history of the Holocaust is an emotional challenge, and it requires knowledge and historical analysis. The crucial questions that lessons on this topic in German schools must attempt to answer are why the Holocaust happened and why it was planned, organized and implemented by hundreds of thousands of Germans and tolerated by the majority of the population. These questions are aimed at the perpetrators and the society from which they originated. This does not mean, however, that the victims' perspective should be neglected. The motivation to explore the Holocaust will be stronger if the students are interested in and moved by the fate of the victims. Students should study the experiences of Jews under Nazi rule. By reading letters, stories and diaries of Jews and listening to survivor testimonies, the students get an impression of the suffering. Students can thus feel empathy with the victims, which can reinforce their readiness to explore the roots of the genocide. The Holocaust can and should be taught with a multi-perspective approach. Most German textbooks contain sources from both sides, victims and perpetrators. Some also address the attitude of bystanders and the actions of helpers and rescuers. In this case multi-perspectivity does not imply moral relativism. Teachers will encourage students to form their own opinions when they listen to a report of a survivor or analyse documents issued by perpetrators. Doing this, students are not only obliged to respect the well-established rules of reading sources critically, but are also expected to be aware of the fundamental values of democratic societies.

The various elements of history lessons on the Holocaust refer to different categories of sources and have different functions in the learning process. In order to analyze and understand the process of radicalization of anti-Jewish politics that led to the Holocaust, students must study documents that offer information about the motivations and activities of the perpetrators, who initiated and controlled this process. The victims had very little influence, if any, on the process of radicalization.

Dealing with the perpetrators and trying to explain their actions does not only require studying acts of persecution and biographies of Nazi leaders. Students need information about the structural changes in German legislation, politics and society that allowed perpetrators to act the way they did. Before Nazi dictatorship was established, Germany was a state under the rule of law. Every citizen had the right to appeal to the courts whenever he or she felt that actions of the state were not in line with the constitution and the laws. Nobody could be imprisoned without a trial. The power of the police was strictly limited and, according to the constitution, all citizens had equal rights regardless of their religious affiliation, ethnicity, political opinion or social status. But after Hitler had come to power, all checks and balances, fundamental individual rights and equality before the law were suspended or abolished within a few months. The police were authorized to take political opponents into 'protective custody', which meant they were sent to concentration camps. Jews were officially treated as second-class citizens, thus paving the way for their total exclusion from society, allowing anti-Semites to take action against them without fearing sanctions. Freedom of speech no longer existed, so that Germans who opposed these developments could not stand up in public without taking great risks. Anyway, a large part of the population supported the so-called 'German Revolution', hoping it would overcome the economic and political crisis and re-establish a powerful German state. Injustice and cruelties were accepted as inevitable side-effects or tolerated as transitional provisions. They were even welcomed by some as measures taken against people they hated, namely communists and Jews.

Students must be aware of these fundamental changes in Germany in order to understand the process that brought about mass murder and genocide. But they must also learn this was not an automatic process or inevitable development. It was a result of decisions and actions taken by people who should be called perpetrators even if they could not be prosecuted on the basis of the existing criminal code after the collapse of the Nazi regime. A broad concept of the term *perpetrator* is required for historical analysis. Perpetrators of the Holocaust were not only Nazi leaders like Hitler and Heinrich Himmler (chief of the SS paramilitary party organization and also head of the German police), and not only the SS and policemen who committed mass murder in the camps and at the shooting ditches. Bureaucrats in many state bodies, in municipalities and in the Nazi Party also contributed in many ways to the process of destruction. They were involved in the discrimination against and isolation of Jews, in their systematic expropriation and the organization of their deportation to their deaths.

How certain perpetrators behaved and why they took part in the persecution and murder of Jews can only be explored through examples. However, studying biographies of perpetrators presents teachers and students with great methodological challenges. We often rely on statements made by perpetrators after the end of the Nazi regime, mostly in the context of investigations or trials against them. Such statements tend to be apologetic and distorting, as the defendants would have incriminated themselves by telling the truth. German law differentiates between manslaughter and murder, and one of the criteria for murder is base motive. Since antisemitism counts as base motive, whereas obedience does not, defendants would always argue they followed orders without any antisemitic motivation of their own. Obviously, we cannot conclude they were indeed free of antisemitism.

Contemporary sources that allow a closer look at the perpetrators' way of thinking are rare. Only a few of them wrote diaries. Only in some cases were collections of letters kept, and not many were published. Such documents also confront us with methodological challenges. Some examples[3] illustrate the difficulties but also the potential insights.

Police secretary Walter Mattner from Vienna, who served as an administrative officer of the German police at Mogilev in occupied Belarus, wrote several letters to his wife between 22 September 1941 and 19 April 1942.[4] These letters give us an authentic impression of the deeds and the mentality of this committed and professed Nazi. He describes how quickly he gets accustomed to the participation in mass killings: 'When it came to the tenth van [that had brought Jewish victims to the pits] I already aimed calmly and fired surely at the many women, children and babies. ... Newborn babies were flying high through the air and we picked them off in flight, before they even fell into the pit or the water.'[5] He tries to justify the mass murder by quoting from one of Hitler's notorious speeches and repeating Nazi propaganda stock phrases: 'Asian hordes'[6], 'this brood that has thrown all of Europe into war'[7]. There can hardly be any doubt that he is convinced of what he writes. But do these letters reflect the mentality of all policemen involved in mass killings? Were they all eager to become mass murderers like Mattner, or were they too craven to refuse the orders to kill defenceless human beings, even though such an insubordination would not have put their own life at risk? Can we find Germans in uniform who refused to

---

3   For other examples see W. Kaiser, 2010, Nazi perpetrators in Holocaust education, *Teaching History 141*, pp. 34–39.

4   The letters were published in German in the 2003 document collection *Deutscher Osten 1939-1945* edited by Klaus-Michael Mallmann, Volker Rieß and Wolfram Pyta, pp. 27 28. Translation into English: http://holocaustcontroversies.blogspot.de/2010/06/otherwise-youll-think-that-im.html (26 Oct. 2012)

5   Op. cit., p. 28

6   Op. cit., p. 28

7   Op. cit., p. 27

follow criminal orders? Did some of them even try to protect Jews? There is indeed evidence that policemen and soldiers responded very differently to the murderous mission given to them. While Walter Mattner represents the unscrupulous Nazi mass murderer, on the other side of the spectrum we find the Austrian sergeant Anton Schmid, a rescuer of Jews and active supporter of Jewish resistance. Abba Kovner, leader of a Jewish resistance group in the Vilna region, mentioned him during the trial against Adolf Eichmann in Jerusalem.[8] Between October 1941 and February 1942 Schmid did everything in his power to save Jews. He brought almost 300 Jews by truck from occupied Vilna to places more secure at the time. He provided Jews with false documents that could protect them, and supported the Jewish resistance movement.[9] While policemen or soldiers who refused to kill Jews were never sentenced to death, because Nazi leaders considered them simply too weak to take part in this 'very difficult command' – as Heinrich Himmler called it – Anton Schmid was executed when his deeds of active support to Jewish partisans became known.

When students explore the different kinds of behaviour, they may ask for a quantitative analysis. Unfortunately, this cannot be provided because the necessary data is not available. Undoubtedly there were only very few Germans who risked their lives to save Jews, but they deserve to be mentioned, not only because of their humaneness and courage, but also because they prove that even people of lower ranks had options. We can only estimate the number of policemen who avoided taking part in killing actions, in spite of the orders given to them. The American historian Christopher Browning, who investigated the behaviour of men serving in a police reserve unit, assumes that fewer than 20 per cent of them avoided participation in executions.[10] In other words, more than 80 per cent committed mass murder. We cannot know how many of them were eager to participate for ideological or other reasons like sadism or greed, and how many of them were more or less reluctant but opted for conformity and obedience though they did not believe in Nazi propaganda. Unfortunately, Anton Schmid's deep sigh in a letter to his wife expressed nothing but a dream: 'If every honest Christian tried to save only one

---

8   Kovner's testimony during the 27th session of the trial was recorded.(See: http://www. youtube.com/watch?v=LcN9UimX32E , 28 Oct. 2012)

9   Hannah Arendt wrote about Sergeant Schmid's story in her book about the Eichmann trial, first published in 1983: '... how utterly different everything would be today in this courtroom, in Israel, in Germany, in all of Europe, and perhaps in all countries of the world, if only more such stories could have been told.' H. Arendt, 2006, *Eichmann in Jerusalem. A report on the banality of evil*, London, Penguin, p. 231.

10 C. Browning,1992, *Ordinary men. Reserve Police Battalion 101 and the Final Solution in Poland*, New York, HarperCollins, p. 168.

Jew, our Party dudes would get into damned trouble.'[11] There were always enough executioners ready to realize the negative utopia of the Nazi leaders: a Europe 'free of Jews'.

Obviously, attempts to explain the Holocaust cannot ignore these leaders. We are well informed about the mentality of one of them: Joseph Goebbels, a fanatical anti-Semite who had great influence as the Reich propaganda minister and leader of the Nazi party in Germany's capital, Berlin. Goebbels wrote diaries almost obsessively. Twenty-nine volumes, each between 400 and more than 700 pages long, were published.[12] These represent an important source of information about Nazi history and about the actions and thoughts of an influential Nazi leader. But due to the vast amount of material it can only be used very selectively in the classroom. The most effective way is probably to juxtapose excerpts from Goebbels's diaries with diary entries regarding the same events written by people who were persecuted by the Nazis. One good example of this is the labelling of German Jews with the Yellow Star in the fall of 1941. Goebbels was the driving force behind this measure and described his intentions and expectations in his diary. Victor Klemperer, a German-Jewish literature professor who risked his life by keeping a journal almost every day and hiding the booklets, provides information about responses of Jews and non-Jews to the infamous Nazi ordinance.[13] Here we learn that public reactions did not always work according to the intentions of the perpetrators. This puts the ideological impression conveyed by Goebbels' diary into perspective: he was not in full control of the situation as his diary conveys.

When dealing with Nazi perpetrators, educators must make sure students will not be overwhelmed by the propagandistic self-dramatization of the regime. They should be aware of the possible attraction emanating from the power and ruthlessness of Nazi perpetrators. This is nurtured by sensationalist publications in various media that exploit and satisfy a morbid fascination with powerful villains. The

---

11   Quote from the radio broadcast *Der Feldwebel Anton Schmid – Eine Begegnung im Wilnaer Getto. Erzählt von Hermann Adler*. First transmission: Südwestfunk 9 March1967, cited in W. Wette, Zivilcourage unter extremen Bedingungen. Empörte, Helfer und Retter in der Wehrmacht, Freiburger Rundbrief 1/2004 (http://www.hrb.at/bzt/doc/zgt/b11/dokumente/zivilcourage_w_wette.pdf ,30 Oct. 2012).

12   Cf. *Die Tagebücher von Joseph Goebbels*, Elke Fröhlich (ed), Part1: Aufzeichnungen [notations] 1923-1941, München, Saur, 1998 ff.; Part 2: Diktate [dictations] 1941-1945. München, Saur, 1993.

13   Cf. The Klemperer diaries 1933–1945, *I shall bear witness to the bitter end*. Abridged and translated from the German,Martin Chalmers (ed), 2000, London, Phoenix Press , pp. 410, 411, 415, 418, 419, 423.

Nazis are the most popular example. Fascination for Nazi leaders is a widespread phenomenon, not only in Germany and other European countries. Educators will not be able to eliminate it, but they should be aware of the related psychological pitfall. Young people, in particular boys, tend to admire strength and power. Developing sympathy for people who are powerless and seem to be weak can be difficult for some. 'Victim' is not used as a term of insult in German schoolyards by coincidence. It is understandable if a teacher expresses disgust about such attitudes and calls for empathy for people who are suffering. But it might not be very successful. There are more promising ways than applying moral pressure. Students can learn that victims of the Nazis – though powerless - were often mentally and morally much stronger than the perpetrators. The organizers and contributors to the Ringelblum-Archive can be mentioned as an example. Jews imprisoned in the Warsaw ghetto who knew what to expect from the Nazi regime decided in spite of their desperate situation to collect and hide as much material about life and death in the ghetto as they could. They methodically counteracted the intention of the Nazis to extinguish all traces of Jewish existence. One of the most remarkable contributors to the archive was Avram Jakub Krzepicki , who escaped from the Treblinka death camp and returned to the Warsaw ghetto in order to warn its inhabitants[14]. The courage of Krzepicki, who lost his life in the Warsaw ghetto uprising, can be contrasted with the whining self-pity in the memoirs of the former commander of Auschwitz Rudolf Höss, which he wrote after his imprisonment[15].

Focusing on perpetrators does not imply a neglect of other perspectives. But even history lessons that manage to present a complex picture will not be able to provide ultimately satisfying answers to the question of why the Holocaust happened. If they succeed, however, in providing knowledge and provoking thoughts that at least partially explain it, they contribute to the awareness of threats that are no less troubling today than they were when the Nazis were defeated.

---

14   Cf. O. Schabbat, 2003, *Das Untergrundarchiv des Warschauer Ghettos*, Ringelblum-Archiv. 3rd edition. Warszawa, Zydowski Instytut Historyczny, p. 60.

15   Cf. *Commandant of Auschwitz. The autobiography of Rudolf Hoess*, 2000, Trans. Constantine FitzGibbon. London, Phoenix, and *Death Dealer. The memoirs of the SS Kommandant at Auschwitz. Rudolf Hoess*, 1992, Steven Paskuly (ed), trans. Andrew Pollinger, Buffalo, N.Y., Prometheus Books.

Conflicting memories: Polish and Jewish perceptions of the Shoah

Konstanty Gebert

On May 1, 1943, Simcha Rotem, an activist of the Jewish Fighting Organization (ŻOB) in the Warsaw ghetto, together with another underground fighter, was smuggled through the sewers into the 'Aryan' part of Warsaw, in a desperate attempt to get in touch with the Polish resistance. The uprising in the ghetto had started two weeks earlier, and the fighters were desperately short of everything: guns, ammunition and hope. Only a coordinated action on the other side of the wall could delay the impending defeat. Years later, speaking to French movie-maker Claude Lanzmann in his film **Shoah**, Rotem described his first impressions:

'Early in the morning we suddenly found ourselves in the street in broad daylight. Imagine [us on] this sunny day of May 1st, stunned to find ourselves among normal people, in the street. We were coming from another planet. ... On the Aryan side of Warsaw life continued in a quite natural and normal fashion. The coffee-shops worked normally, the restaurants, the buses and the trams, the cinemas were open. The ghetto was an isolated island in the middle of normal life.'[16]

Rotem's mission ended in failure, but his words open a valuable perspective on one of the reasons why Poles and Jews have such different perceptions of the events of the Second World War in Poland. Apart from the well-known and important, mainly conscious distortions motivated by self-interest, essentially on the Polish side (about which more below), there is the very important issue of differences of perception caused by the very different circumstances affecting the two groups. The Jews in Poland, as elsewhere in German-occupied Europe, were to be totally exterminated, down to the last child hiding in the woods, and the plan was largely implemented. The Poles, on the other hand, were to be reduced to slave labour, and even this goal was not largely achieved. These differences in circumstances account for the differences in perspective: Not for the first time it turned out that sharing geography does not necessarily mean sharing a history. Polish and Jewish narratives of the Second World War differ significantly.

---

16   C. Lanzmann,1985, **Shoah**, Paris, Fayard. All translations mine.

The Jewish underground fighters, emerging onto a sunlit Warsaw street, came from just several hundred metres away – but indeed, as Rotem himself says, he could have come from a different planet. The fighting triggered by the uprising had turned the Warsaw ghetto into an inferno of death and flames; yet the two and a half years preceding the uprising, ever since the Germans had created and sealed the misnamed 'Jewish residential district' in the Polish capital, had been a steady descent into that inferno. Famished and lacking the most basic medical services, surviving in unheated apartments during the bitter Polish winters, subjected to constant violence at the hands of the occupying authorities, the inmates of the Warsaw ghetto experienced a fate much closer to that of concentration camp prisoners than of the non-Jewish inhabitants of the city, on the other side of the wall that divided them as of November 1940. In fact, it can be argued that the difference in the fates of Warsaw's Jewish and Polish inhabitants was greater than that which separated the latter's experience and, for example, that of the inhabitants of the French capital, where the occupation regime was much milder, or even of the residents of unoccupied parts of Europe. This statement holds true even before we consider the two most traumatic moments in the ghetto's brief history: the uprising itself, and the *Großaktion* of the summer of 1942, in which in a matter of weeks a quarter of a million Jews were transported from the ghetto to their deaths in the extermination camp at Treblinka. Again, Rotem's metaphor rings true: the ghetto was an island, belonging not to the 'normal world', but to the archipelago of the camps.

But was the 'Aryan side' of Warsaw itself part of that 'normal world'? For Rotem, definitely. Coffee shops were open, trams were running, dead bodies did not lie on the sidewalks. From the perspective of someone who had just emerged from the inferno of the ghetto, 'Aryan' Warsaw was to all intents and purposes a city at peace. Yet, to have that perspective, one indeed needed to have come from the other side of the wall. For its non-Jewish residents, the 'Aryan side', coffee shops and all, was experiencing the most brutal occupation regime in the Polish capital's long history of suffering oppression. The German forces routinely conducted roundups of people on the streets in order to prevent underground activity, but mainly to capture slave labourers for work in Germany; some fifteen thousand people were captured that way in a series of roundups from 5 to 7 January 1943, though most were subsequently allowed to return to their homes. The occupation authorities also routinely took hostages, to be executed in retaliation for acts of violence against German soldiers; on 9 January a German poster announced that two hundred 'Polish activists' had been arrested and would be subject to 'severe measures' – meaning execution – if the attacks continued. In a mass execution on 12 February, seventy people were killed in retaliation for a Polish underground shootout with the German police six days earlier, including all the arrested inhabitants of the building in which the shootout had taken place[17]. These were but the first actions taken in 1943, a year during which the brutality of the occupation regime would only escalate. So was Warsaw part of the 'normal world'? Hardly. And yet one should not be surprised that Rotem, with his experience of a nightmare incomparably greater than what the Polish residents of the capital were enduring, thought otherwise.

More puzzling is the seeming indifference of some Poles to the immensity of Jewish suffering. The merry-go-round that stood by the wall of the Warsaw ghetto in April 1943 was a case in point; it continued to provide entertainment to many Varsovians as the insurgents fought on the other side of the wall and the ghetto was engulfed in flames. Even more shocking, perhaps, is the sole reference to the ghetto in a book of wartime memoirs by Agnieszka Hulewicz Feillowa, daughter of a prominent musician and underground activist sentenced to death by the Germans. Describing the day of her marriage in 1941, she notes: 'We made a mistake en route to the church and entered the ghetto. The German police wanted to arrest us. It was very nerve-wracking and we were late for church.'[18] This is all – in a book of over two hundred pages. Though obviously it would be wrong to make generalizations on the basis of single quotes – both for Hulewicz and for Rotem – these do have illustrative value to represent segments of Polish and Jewish opinion. In both cases, the emphasis is on the suffering these groups had themselves gone through; there is much less interest, bordering on indifference, regarding the suffering of others.

We tend to find this shocking, because we would like to see the opposite be true, in accordance with the maxim that suffering ennobles. Yet, as William Somerset Maugham had already pointed out in **The Moon and Sixpence**: 'It is not true that suffering ennobles the character; happiness does that sometimes, but suffering, for the most part, makes men petty and vindictive.' Without going as far as the eminent English author, it would seem fair to argue that suffering makes many people less, and not more, inclined to notice the suffering of others, let alone to take action to alleviate it. In other words suffering alters perception. The examples provided above give fair illustration of that. But, coming as they do from eye-witnesses of the most atrocious crime in history, they represent not only the exemplification of a counter-intuitive human psychological trait. They are part of the basic foundations

---

17   W. Bartoszewski, 1974, *1859 dni Warszawy*. Kraków,, Wydawnictwo Znak.

18   A. Hulewicz Feillowa, 1988, *Rodem z Kościanek*., Kraków, Wydawnictwo Literackie, quoted in F. Tych, 1999, *Długi cień Zagłady*, Warszawa, Żydowski Instytut Historyczny.

of collective memory, which itself provides the building blocks of history. In other words, the way that Poles and Jews remembered the events they witnessed in German-occupied Warsaw shaped the way the history of these events would be written, yet it seems clear that, in some cases at least, very important elements of that history were, for psychological reasons, omitted in the original accounts. What we read today, then, might be a faithful account of what the eye-witnesses remembered – but their memory of the events might be substantially flawed.

None of this is new, of course; historians and lawyers have learned to treat eyewitnesses with mistrust, not only in cases where they might be suspected of intentionally distorting their depositions (such distortions are also easier to detect), but where the eyewitnesses themselves are not aware of any selectivity in their accounts. Yet both Polish and Jewish historiography, at least until recently, had largely been consistent with this selectivity, by not paying much attention to the suffering of the other group. This was not only due to the nature of the documentary record itself, but also to the fact that both groups engage in a kind of competition of suffering, and often tend to perceive it as a zero-sum game, with the amount of recognition granted to the suffering of the others supposedly detracting from that granted to our own pain. There is some truth to such fears: certain Polish authors do try to promote the awareness of the immensity of the disaster that befell their country in the Second World War (6 million dead, of which half were non-Jewish Poles) by subtly undermining the importance of Jewish suffering. Polish public opinion – possibly on the grounds of the above casualty figures, which do not take into account the scope and impact of the separate persecutions Poles and Jews suffered – tends to believe, as shown in public opinion polls, that both groups suffered equally in the Second World War. Sensing this trend, some Jewish authors see in the recognition of Polish suffering a tacit encouragement given to this kind of historical revisionism. Jewish public opinion in Israel – at least as represented through statements often made by visitors to Shoah sites in Poland – seems barely aware of the fact that Poles, too, were victims. If anything, they are seen as accomplices of the perpetrators.

This belief – though offensive to many Poles – is well rooted in the historical record, even if the extent of participation by Poles (though not by Polish state institutions – there was never a Polish Quisling) in the German extermination of the Jews cannot be assessed with historical accuracy. Eyewitness reports, however, both by Jews and also by many Poles, clearly show that all Jews hiding on the 'Aryan side' were at all times in danger of denunciation by some Poles to the Germans, and subject to the no less permanent threat of blackmail. This is in no way invalidated by the fact that Polish saviours of Jews are the single biggest national group among the Righteous Among

Nations, awarded by Yad Vashem; we are talking about two different minorities among the Polish population, though certainly the numbers of the denunciators were larger. The historical consensus indicates the overwhelming majority of the Poles were simply busy surviving. They did not give assistance to Jews in need of it, but neither did they go out of their way to hinder them.

This, however, sits very uneasily with Polish self-perceptions. Even more important, from the Polish perspective, are perceptions of third parties. For both Jews and Poles, their suffering in the Second World War is a central element in their self-narrative – and in the way they want to be seen by the world. Both nations tend to believe their suffering – in each case truly atrocious, even if not equal – qualifies them for special attention from the post-war international community. They both want to enjoy the moral high ground that seems to come with the status of victim – and to use this status to demand both compensation, at least moral, and protection, at least political. The world, having betrayed them and having allowed them to suffer and die, now owes them at least the reassurance it will not allow the suffering to be repeated. Never again.

Yet, as the American writer David Rieff wrote after witnessing first-hand the horrors of Sarajevo under siege, we have to realize that 'never again' only means 'never again will Germans kill Jews in Europe in the 1940s.' The guarantee of security this solemn plea seemed to imply in the immediate post-war era is gone. And if so, the victims of the Germans find themselves now in the unenviable position of competing against each other for the scarce attention of the world, and past suffering is a weak currency against current suffering. Hence the importance of at least securing the recognition of one's own status as bona fide victim, whatever the meagre moral and political benefits that come with it, seventy years after the Second World War.

But just as they are unequal in suffering, Poles and Jews are even more unequal in perceptions of suffering. A mayor of Nagasaki reportedly said 'There is only one thing worse than being the first city to be A-bombed: it is being the second one.' Indeed, Hiroshima is recognized as the international symbol of the new, post-Shoah atomic nightmare; Nagasaki is an historian's afterthought. And in their attempt to gain for their narrative a status akin to the universal recognition of Jewish suffering, the Poles are locked in the same trap.

One obvious way to reduce the status difference between them would be to undermine the validity of the recognition granted to the other side. If Hiroshima is downplayed, Nagasaki's relative position improves. But even if the irredeemably obscene threat of Holocaust denial is growing world-wide, its presence in Polish discourse is very limited. The empirical evidence of the horror unleashed by the German war machine is still hugely visible all over the country, and Holocaust denial would fatally entail also the denial of the most traumatic event in Polish history. This venue, mercifully, is all but closed to Polish participation.

What remains, then, is the painstaking, ever-vigilant defence of the historical record, the way it is seen and remembered in Poland. Historical research, from Jan T. Gross's **Neighbors** onwards, is revealing even more details about the scale and atrocity of the participation of a segment of the population of occupied Poland in the German extermination of the Jews. It is thus becoming ever more difficult to deny not only that the Jews suffered more, but also, increasingly, that Poles have a part of responsibility for that suffering. This makes it even more important to recall that, even though many more Poles than the nation's historical memory cares to remember were perpetrators, they were also all potential victims, and three million did die, at the hands of both German and Soviet occupiers. Furthermore, as stressed earlier, Polish participation in the German murder of the Jews was on an individual, not on a national or state level – unlike in all other occupied nations of Europe. Hence the importance of the bitter polemic over the term 'Polish death camps'.

The term appears not infrequently in journalistic reports on the German death machine, and usually means nothing more than a geographical reference, shorthand for the cumbersome 'German death camps set up on occupied Polish territory'. Yet on the face of it, it can also be read to mean 'death camps set up by Poles', or 'run by Poles', or even 'run by Poland'. With knowledge of the history of the Second World War getting dimmer with each passing decade, such a reading could well emerge, to the obvious detriment of both the historical record and of the Polish national interest. It is hardly surprising that Polish public opinion reacts violently to such a threat, and that Polish diplomatic missions abroad have standing instructions to protest forcefully each time the expression appears in the media.

The historical record is absolutely clear: there was no Polish participation in the German death camp enterprise, and the camps themselves were set up on occupied Polish territory simply because it was where most of the Jews to be murdered were living. Given that fact and given the immensity of the unintended slur, correcting the terminology should have been a simple thing. Yet only recently did major media organizations, such as the New York Times, the Wall Street Journal and Associated Press, modify their style-books to preclude the use of the incriminating expression. And still it keeps reappearing, though less frequently than a decade or two ago. Many in Poland genuinely suspect a sinister reason for its obstinate reappearance: it is an attempt to create the image that the Poles were the perpetrators of the Shoah alongside the Germans (and in the extreme formulation, instead of the Germans). Conspiracy theories abound that the driving force behind the alleged campaign is the Germans (to be able to deny their historical guilt) or the Jews (motivated by an alleged hatred of Poland). The idea that the injurious expression is used because it is shorter, and in most cases writers using it have no appreciation of its importance in Polish eyes, is extremely difficult to convey to even an open-minded Polish public.

Matters came to a head when, in May 2012, US President Barack Obama used the fatal expression in his presentation of a posthumous Presidential Medal of Freedom to Jan Karski, a Polish Second World War hero (among his many exploits as a member of the resistance, he had clandestinely entered a German camp in occupied Poland and was then smuggled out to personally brief Allied leaders; his testimony was widely disbelieved and marginalized). The enormity of the gaffe was not immediately obvious to the President, but after furious reactions from Poland (Obama had 'offended all Poles', Prime Minister Donald Tusk said), and also from American Jewish organizations such as the American Jewish Committee, he had no doubts. 'I regret the error' he stated in a letter sent to his Polish counterpart, Bronisław Komorowski. 'There simply were no "Polish death camps"'. This should have set the record straight – yet the entire incident was barely noted in media outside of Poland. The issue will probably still linger.

Besides, there remains the more complex case of accusations mainly seen as unfair by Poles, but often supported by the testimony of Jewish survivors. 'The "illegal" Jews, i.e. those hiding on the "Aryan side", much more feared the local population than the Germans' wrote survivor Ryszard Kujalnik in a letter in *Gazeta Lubelska*, a newspaper published in liberated Polish territory, as early as November 1944[19]. In ninety per cent of the cases, he assessed, arrests of Jews who were in hiding came about as a result of denunciation. Most survivors would tend to agree with his assessment, and so does much of post-war non-Polish historiography – and also, increasingly, contemporary Polish historiography[20]. Assessments of the nefarious role played by the Polish population might, if anything, be revised in an even more critical direction. 'All that we know about this subject, i.e. the fate of Polish Jews under German occupation – *through the very fact that it has been told* – is not a representative sample of the Jewish fate. These are all stories (seen) through rose-

19   As quoted in Feliks Tych, op. cit.

20   Cf. e.g. Jan Grabowski, 2004, *„Ja tego Żyda znam!" Szantażowanie Żydów w Warszawie 1939-1943*, Warszawa, Wydawnictwo IFiS PAN.

tinted glasses, with happy endings, by those who survived. ... We know nothing about rock bottom, about the ultimate betrayal which they had fallen prey to, about the Calvary of ninety per cent of pre-war Polish Jewry. This is why we should take at face value the shreds of information which are at our disposal, while being aware that the truth about the destruction of the Jewish community may only be (even) more tragic than our representation of it based on the accounts of those who survived', writes Jan Gross in the conclusions of his ground-breaking book, **Neighbors**[21]. This methodological requirement is to an extent well-founded and necessary. Yet it also opens the possibility of new interpretations that go in a different direction.

The vision of Polish society as uniformly hostile to Jews trying to survive, with the exception of the rare few who risked their lives to save them, as expressed in Kujalnik's letter (in which he also gives due recognition to the rare heroes), is consistent, as noted, with the memories of survivors. Using Gross's methodological requirement, we would have to say that reality, if anything, was even worse. Yet it also has to be noted that this vision is not necessarily consistent with the social reality of the time, but only with how it was remembered by people who were not – to say the least – dispassionate observers of the events concerned. The view that, with the exception of a few heroes, everybody else was the enemy had a high survival value. People tending to have a more positive vision of Polish society would have tended to trust other people more, and therefore to run a higher risk of placing their trust also in untrustworthy people. In consequence, they ran a higher risk of being denounced and subsequently murdered – and their stories, and the image of Polish society that would come with them, have not survived. At first glance, this might seem a spurious argument – for did not the fate of such hypothetical more trusting people prove that the harsher view was amply justified? Not necessarily. It only proves that there were more scoundrels than the trusting people believed – but not that it was right, from an analytical point of view, to believe that most people were scoundrels, even if that belief was useful from the point of view of survival.

This is not nit-picking. Gross is right that we need to take survivors' testimony at face value – unless there are reasons to treat it otherwise. Yet Rotem, for instance, was clearly wrong in his belief that the 'Aryan side' of Warsaw was part of the 'normal world'. This in no way invalidates his testimony. It just shows that it needs to be put in context – from not only an historical, but also a psychological point of view; from his perspective, that of an inmate of the ghetto, Warsaw on the other side of the wall

---

21   Jan Tomasz Gross, 2000, *Sąsiedzi: Historia zagłady żydowskiego miasteczka*, Sejny, Pogranicze.

could not fail to be seen as 'normal'. The case of Hulewicz is more complicated. Her testimony, too – or rather the lack of it – also needs to be treated at face value, even if Gross's requirement was in all probability to be applied to the testimony of Jewish survivors, and not Poles. It is unthinkable to assume she was not aware of the ghetto, all the more so because she had by accident ventured into it – and even though in 1941, two years before Rotem's escape through the sewers, the situation there was somewhat less dire than in 1943. Still, the fate of the Jews, walled in and subject to horrible conditions and unbridled violence, was markedly and visibly worse than that of the residents of the 'Aryan side' of the city. Yet is seems to have made no impression on her, to the extent that she did not feel the need to remark on the subject, even in a book published almost half a century later, when it was common knowledge what happened behind the wall. Barring the implausible assumption of the author's moral insanity, we need to conclude she did not refer to the ghetto because it lay outside her mental universe: whatever happened there was happening to 'them' and not to 'us'. In other words, and expressing cognitive rather than moral reproach, it was not her concern.

The eminent Polish Jewish historian Feliks Tych, in a magnificent essay on the representation of the Shoah in Polish wartime memoirs[22], makes exactly this point. Having sampled more than 400 works, both published and unpublished, he concludes that 'the authors of most of the analysed texts either failed to take any notice of the phenomenon of the Shoah, or failed to recognize its exceptional character in terms of civilization.' The reasons for that were varied, ranging from lack of identification with the murdered Jews perceived as alien, to covert – or overt – satisfaction that 'Poland's enemies' were being eliminated in a way which was, to be sure, criminal and supposedly never would have been used by the Poles themselves, but that nonetheless could produce a desirable outcome: a Poland free of the Jews. In some cases, when the memoirists are urban dwellers, the events themselves escape their attention because they take place behind the walls, where outsiders need not look, unless they badly want to. In rural Poland the murder took place in the open and could not be concealed – but in these regions there were fewer witnesses with a proclivity to putting what they saw in writing. The foundations of the Polish memory of the Shoah were laid in the cities, where it was easier not to see. In a nutshell: the event was too huge to be recognized and noted. It escaped perception, as it were, and therefore did not gain the place it should have occupied in post-war Polish memory.

---

22   Feliks Tych, op. cit.

This is not to suggest there was no moral reaction, but simply that there was not enough of it. Jewish suffering was not adequately recognized by these authors – and subsequently by Polish memory – because it had been too huge. Polish suffering – as exemplified in Rotem's statements – was not recognized by Jewish memory because it had not been huge enough. Two opposite cognitive strategies brought about similar results.

This cognitive parallelism obviously does not imply a moral one as well. It was the Jews who had depended on the Poles for help, not the other way round – and Polish reaction, or rather the lack of it, to the immensity of the Shoah had been a contributing factor to making that help largely unavailable. Though this moral failure was usually not explicitly noted in Polish writings about the Second World War, it remained a nagging moral issue Poles were aware of, but did not know how to deal with. Hence the highly defensive Polish reactions each time the issue was addressed, usually by outside critics. And hence also the Polish obsession with looking for analogous moral failures within the Jewish perspective.

It is true the lack of recognition of Polish suffering, common in Jewish public opinion even today, bears no moral credit. Yet it would be ludicrous to equate this with Polish non-recognition of the nature and immensity of the Shoah in wartime, and the consequences it entailed. The indifference to Polish suffering among many Jews is certainly proof of a certain moral callousness – yet nobody lost their life as a result. It is also true – as many Polish historians are quick to point out – that the Jewish police in the ghettoes had played an abominable role in assisting the extermination of their compatriots, and that the moral implications of this criminal failure have yet to be fully internalized. Yet the fact that some Jews were persecuting other Jews can certainly not serve as an excuse for some Poles to persecute Jews as well, or even provide a moral counterbalance. The Jewish police were acting under horrendous constraint, and in concentration camp-like circumstances. The Polish denunciators and blackmailers acted out of their own free will, and under circumstances that were incomparably freer. But another accusation often made by Poles in response to Jewish condemnations of Polish inaction – or, worse still, action – towards Jews in occupied Poland deserves more serious consideration. The occupation referred to, however, was not German but Soviet.

It is a fact of historical record that the Soviet invasion of Eastern Poland on 17 September 1939 was greeted with visible enthusiasm by certain Jewish groups all over the invaded territory. Hastily erected welcome gates and cheering groups of youngsters met Soviet tanks as they entered Polish towns. For the Polish neighbours of these young Jewish enthusiasts there was only one possible reaction to that behaviour: the Jews were committing treason. The Soviet Union, after all, was but the latest avatar of a perennially hostile Russia, which had attempted to invade Poland barely nineteen years earlier, and had occupied most of the country for over a century before that. It was unthinkable to express joy at the coming of those troops, which eventually took half of interwar Poland's territory, while their German allies took the other half. The belief in the 'Jewish treason of 1939' was one of the sources of wartime Polish antisemitism, and it continues to fuel it even today.

Historians – including Jan Gross, whose seminal works on the Soviet occupation helped to elucidate these issues – have largely come to a consensus on the events of September 1939 in Eastern Poland. They have shown that the Jewish enthusiasts represented a relatively small section of the larger Jewish community, and their reasons for welcoming the invading Red Army were variegated. They included relief that this was not the Wehrmacht, and some kind of state order was being re-established (pogroms were already breaking out as the Polish state crumbled); the genuine belief in the promises of Communism, as attested for example by the fact the invaders' officers corps included many Jews, something rather unthinkable in the Polish army at that time; and also a real Schadenfreude at the downfall of a Polish state that had made it very clear, in the previous years, it desired to be rid of its Jewish citizens. All this, however, makes the shock and outrage felt by Polish neighbours regarding those Jews no less legitimate and understandable. Jewish historiography has yet to internalize the conclusion that Poles might also have had some reasonable cause for considering the Jews as hostile – with all the concomitant consequences.

The examples provided and analysed above do not pretend to paint a complete picture of the issues in the memory of the Shoah on which Polish and Jewish perspectives sharply differ. The intention is rather to indicate such issues do exist; but these discrepancies are not necessarily caused by ill will, or attempts to deny responsibility alone. Rather, they are almost unavoidable consequences of the different and incompatible historical circumstances in which the two groups found themselves during the Second World War. While such discrepancies should therefore be considered legitimate, their very existence is a major stumbling block in attempts at dialogue between the two nations.

When discrepancies surrounding the historical record arise, the obvious solution is to examine that record and identify who is right and who is wrong. Yet such an attempt cannot be expected to succeed when the record itself changes depending on who is telling the story, and when the interlocutors have not only an intellectual interest in the matter, but tend to invest it with fundamental importance for their collective identities. Such is the case with divergent Polish and Jewish perceptions of events surrounding the Shoah. It is obvious the matter is central to the Jews. Yet it is also central to the Poles, for the Second World War was the fundamental historical event shaping the nation's self-perception and subsequent fate, and the Shoah is the central element of that event. Therefore, it is hardly plausible to expect that the parties can give up on the elements of their own representations of history, which they consider to be historically accurate, despite challenges to the contrary. Nor can outsiders with no personal or collective investment of their own in the issue hope to convince one side or the other to adopt their findings, whatever they might be. On the contrary – the influence of outside historians over the historical perceptions cherished by either group seems to be in direct proportion to their willingness to accept that group's basic historical tenets; witness for example the popularity of the works of British historian Norman Davies in Poland.

The only reasonable expectation, therefore, is that both groups, without giving up on what they believe to be true and what the other side is eager to question, will at least accept a basic premise: the other group's narrative, from that group's point of view, is just as legitimate as 'our' narrative is to 'us'. In other words, we are facing together a situation in which reasonable people can honestly and truthfully believe to be true, things that other equally reasonable people can just as honestly and truthfully believe to be false. We must recognize this disagreement as a difference in perceptions grounded in experience, not a confrontation of truth and falsehood. Only under such circumstances can debate be conducted without the hostility it usually generates. And once, in the course of that debate, the other side's reasons become clearer, there can indeed be hope that a conjoint – if not necessarily shared – vision of contested history might eventually emerge.

Entangled memories: Holocaust education in contemporary France

Sophie Ernst

Translated from French

Firmly established, plagued by conflicts

In some twenty to thirty years, the transmission to younger generations of what the genocide of European Jews entailed has become firmly established in France.

This transmission has significantly affected the entire French population, taking a paradoxical form of consensus, one that is perhaps superficial and definitely ambiguous, but nonetheless very real and now indispensable, to the extent of providing the paradigm of good and evil in politics. Not without misuse and not without controversy, the memory of the Holocaust provides the catalogue of images and concepts that allow the current historical experience to be visualized and gauged, and positions to be taken on the choices made. The paradigm shift is particularly profound for older people, who have known other times when, for example, among other paradigms developed in primary school history education, the figures and events of the French Revolution provided a framework for popular memory. Is this an enviable status? Probably not, but it is an envied status in any event and one that prompts many mimetic claims, more or less well-founded assertions from people who feel persecuted, and rage against the intimidating moral 'power' of the 'Victim'. But this conflict only strengthens the place of the Holocaust in the contemporary imagination. It requires only the additional task of having to deal with the abuse of memory by continual readjustments.

While elsewhere it is called 'Holocaust education', in France there is a preference for other terms, since the word 'holocaust', which has the historical meaning of 'sacrificial offering to God', has been vigorously rejected. This does not mean a stable agreement on an alternative choice of terminology has been reached: in France the term 'Shoah remembrance' is used, with or without capital letters, and the education authorities weighed each word carefully before deciding on 'education on the history of the systematic extermination of European Jews'. Does the 'straw of terms' really matter if we agree on the 'grain of things'? The incessant arguing over the terms we use does make sense, however, in a domain where the issues are serious, though difficult to grasp outside the spheres of certain specialists. The risk of controversy over a clumsy sentence, perceived as a threat at the very least, accompanies everything connected to Holocaust remembrance, and yet, at the same time, there is an extraordinarily strong consensus on the importance of its transmission.

Holocaust education has a universal dimension but it inevitably takes on a national form linked to the historical, political and social characteristics of the country that implements it, not to mention how schools are organized and prevailing educational principles. Hence in this section of the book I will link educational matters to the national issues that give them meaning. I would tend to use the category of 'the imaginary' – in the sense of the term used by Cornelius Castoriadis in *The Imaginary Institution of Society* – almost more willingly than 'memory' or 'history'. This should by no means be seen as a denial of history or a way of playing down representations of the genocide in a pejorative way, but rather as the need to clarify the historical phenomena by which a society develops its meanings, or the value categories by which it establishes itself as a political society. Education, from this point of view, is not so much the place for transmission, where something that already exists is repeated, as the place where we can imagine a way of building the present and projecting into the future, in which an 'imaginary institution of society' is actually developed, carrying an ideal and promise, caution and improvement, prohibition and significance.

From this point of view, however, in a quite obvious way in the early 2000s and more subtly today, Holocaust remembrance occupies a special, unique place in transmission, which is neither sacred nor trivialized but firmly entrenched in the school education system. It is respected while being constantly plagued by conflict that, rather than threatening teachers and students, at the end of the day helps to stimulate reflection.

Such a general assessment does not mean, of course, that everything will be fine and that we can make do with routinization of the current reality. It simply means that, at a time when the pursuit of aims requires that we pay attention to conflicting opinions and criticisms, without dangerous illusions or inappropriate complacency, it is essential to assess the progress made. Those involved in the transmission deserve recognition for the quality of their mobilization, which has managed to take a variety of forms and remain as close to the field as possible. No other education is supported to this extent by such a range of institutions and teachers, resulting in students taking a real interest.

Questions and doubts are nonetheless raised quite frequently in the press, with a considerable echo in Jewish communities that remain uneasy: when the press exposes difficulties arising here and there, such as hostile behaviour from students of Arab descent, are these rare or common phenomena? As pointed out earlier – and this is one of the least of reasons for disputes – the mere fact of naming or refusing to name the event 'Shoah', 'genocide' or 'extermination' has on occasion triggered a disproportionate controversy over the motives, presumed too shameful to mention, for preferring the use of one term over another. We may find these quarrels superficial and unreasonable and the accusations unjust, but often they have also made it possible to examine real difficulties in depth.

Other sources of conflict take their anger and fear from the various ways of assessing the current situation of Jews in France, in connection with the tragic and intractable problem of the Israeli-Palestinian conflict, or when particularly violent or sordid anti-Jewish aggression creates panic in the community. In fact, several partial truths are juxtaposed. On the one hand, and certainly owing to the appalled awareness after the Second World War of the horror of Auschwitz, a powerful dynamic supported by a large majority has brought about a historical and continuous decline in antisemitism, in the historical and well-defined meaning of the term, which has become rare and socially stigmatized. This has come to light in political sociology surveys carried out in particular by Nonna Mayer through the Centre de recherches politiques de Sciences Po (CEVIPOF), research centre of the Institut d'études politiques (IEP) public research and higher education institution in Paris, using rigorous empirical methods that can follow underlying trends in long series of statistics. People from older generations have no doubts about it: the xenophobia and antisemitism of the 1930s and 1940s were open and virulent in France, incommensurate with the current situation; the extreme right was vociferous and unrestrained, and antisemitic prejudice was commonplace in the population. It is no longer commonplace today.

Despite this major historical trend in the entire population, there are, nonetheless, shifts in the opposite direction, reflecting disturbing developments. On the one hand, although only residually so, traditional antisemitism is still nurtured by far-right nationalists. The different extreme right-wing movements have nevertheless tended – what with the stigma attached to antisemitic discourse and following the war of decolonization in Algeria – to transfer their original antisemitism to anti-Arab racism, which, on the other hand has grown continuously, whether in open or insidious forms, extending far beyond the scope of these extreme factions.

On the other hand, from a background of Arab hostility towards Jews and Israel, new forms of anti-Jewish hatred have evolved among marginalized populations exposed to social exclusion and harbouring violent resentment, tinged with religious, 'anti-Western', 'anti-Zionist', 'anti-white' ideology. Some far-left movements have thus supplanted the far right, spreading one of the most characteristic forms of antisemitism and putting over attitudes to justify resentment.

This situation has poisoned the lives of the most identifiable Jewish communities, undermined by insecurity, as well as those of Arab people, constantly singled out as Muslims, branded as Islamists and suspected of terrorism and antisemitism, in incessant amalgams. While most Arab people do nothing to foster this state of mind, they can end up yielding, out of bitterness and in self-defence, to the temptation that some Jews have succumbed to, of a more or less sectarian withdrawal into their own community. Almost all accusations draw their strength from the very legitimate fears that weigh on the security of minorities because of the deteriorated social, economic and political climate, when the distress of some – for fear of exclusion – leads to the hatred of others, expressed in acts of violence.

The rise of racism and antisemitism, at the same moment as the very commemoration that should prohibit it for ever, perturbed teachers, but did not cause them to give up what they now regarded as 'normal'. It spurred them to enhance their skills and taught them how to avoid traps and address the questions that challenged them. From this point of view, the training was effective.

To be 'firmly established' in a modern democracy, in a time like ours – which has been convincingly described by the sociologist Zygmunt Bauman as 'liquid modernity' – does not necessarily imply the absence of conflict, a stable and intangible installation in the tranquillity of consensus, or a single framework in which each element fits nicely into the unity of a common vision. France is not, or is no longer, the 'Cartesian' and centralized country that we might imagine it to be, where every institution applies a programme imposed from on high by the republican political will. There is admittedly a degree of uniformity and centralization prescribed in the school education system, which lends weight to the decisions of the political powers. From this viewpoint, we can track the improvement in the transmission as a series of governmental directives – following up political recognition with official discourse – have given it an important place in the curriculum, examinations, and teachers' initial and continuing education. What was only prescribed by the authorities, however, could very well have remained a dead letter as often happens in France, even for key lessons in the curriculum when they fail to generate the motivation of all sections of the population. But in fact this dictate has long corresponded in France to a strong social dynamic that has taken hold of it and lent it its full potential.

Disputes and controversies are undoubtedly perceived as painful by those involved in the transmission, such as teachers, educational mediators and the staff of memorial sites who, doing their best with a sincere dedication that often borders on abnegation, do not always grasp the reasons, whether valid or not, of such calling into question. Some, indeed, are justified, but others are pointless, offensive or absurd – such is the price of free debate.

But are these disputes and controversies not also a medium for elaboration? We could further argue that they are not futile. The necessary social conditions exist to ensure the debate will not be harmful and it will really represent progress in forming reasonable (or slightly more reasonable) opinions: it requires an interested and sufficiently informed public, gifted journalists and laws governing freedom of expression that ban incitement to racial hatred. The basic laws on press freedom include articles on the limits of such freedom and we must enforce them. This is one of the lessons learned from the experience of the 1930s. However, and this is one of the reasons for the current agitation, the emergence of new conditions for the debate with the advent of the internet has upset habits. Nobody controls the effects of the dramatic rise in this freedom of expression and people are certainly ambivalent about it, not knowing how to manage this innovation. Personally, and without pretending to know for sure, it seems to me the very open discussion we have had over all these years is less daunting than the lack of debate. In fact, this debate is strongly framed by the deep conviction that everything cannot be said and this ban, both legal and moral, permits a relatively reasonable regulation. It serves to work out meaning, as diverse communities, each with their own priorities and sympathies, take hold of an issue that they eventually make their own. Sometimes the process is long.

Minorities in France

The population and history of France have characteristics that expose the country to many and recurring causes for discord, including acute sensitivity. It is the only European country that retains, far behind the United States and Israel, a sizeable Jewish population, more or less organized in religious or cultural communities, falsely unified and truly divided, except regarding the transmission of Holocaust remembrance and the fight against antisemitism.

The two issues are experienced as inseparable in a problematic but hard to challenge equivalence. The 'memory against antisemitism' has come to serve as the identity cementing groups that are otherwise very different in many ways: the Ashkenazi Jews, who are highly assimilated and not very religious, are descendants of Eastern European immigrants directly connected to the past genocide and may therefore look on themselves as 'survivors', carrying the memory of a lost world and *Yiddishkeit* (or 'Jewishness' in Yiddish); and the Sephardi Jews from North Africa, who did not really experience the destruction of the European world, but strongly identify with the memory, which mingles with their own memory of dispossession and traumatic expulsion from North Africa where they had been firmly rooted since time immemorial.

French Jews are affected by this memory at many levels of their complex individual and collective identity. It should be borne in mind that French Jews are first and foremost completely French and, with rare exceptions, fully share the French 'imaginary' and the same obsessions, dreams and concerns as their fellow citizens, making them place the same expectations and the same concerns as everyone else on the transmission of memory: schools must transmit the memory of the Holocaust to prevent its ever happening again. Obviously, a special relationship is also added to the transmission, which they monitor closely, as direct descendants of survivors from the lost world and the last representatives of ways of life engulfed in a disaster, for some; as Jews who recognize themselves in the history of persecution and derive a part of their identity from it; as Jews currently exposed to the possibility of resurgent antisemitism who would like to use the commemorations to remove this threat; as Jews showing their solidarity with Israel; or even as imaginary Israelis, though they live in France, who would like to use the memory of the Holocaust to defend Israel's legitimacy and, a step above this, in a way that is far from being accepted by all Jews and causes severe clashes, to use the memory of the Holocaust to provide unconditional support to Israel, regardless of its politics. These are many reasons to be actively involved in the policy of transmitting history to young people, more or less lucidly. The conflict is permanent, however, and fratricide between those who believe that we must transmit this history so 'nobody will ever again lay a finger on a Jew', or – for those who opt for a humanist message of a universal nature – so 'no state will ever again commit a crime against humanity'. Fortunately, most French people adhere to both assertions without exclusion.

It is nevertheless a sensitive point for all those who have taken the Middle East conflict to heart, on whichever side. France supported the creation of the State of Israel and, regarding itself as a friend of the Jewish national homeland, also aspires to be a key partner of the Arab countries. A very widespread view held among the public at large in France, and quite often reflected in school textbooks, justifies the creation of the State of Israel as a direct consequence of genocide, reparation for harms suffered, and the 'solution' to the existence of refugees and survivors in the aftermath of war. This depiction of history is debatable in many respects but it does have the effect of closely linking Holocaust remembrance to the concerns of today. France also has the largest Arab community in Europe, as a result of longstanding immigration. With its debatable and controversial policy, Israel occupies a disproportionate place in foreign policy considerations and media news, a fact that greatly affects the generally tense and sometimes stormy relations between Jews and Arabs, and between official representatives of the Jewish community and French society at large.

In addition, there is the contentious resurgence of memories connected to the black communities that emerged from the first and second waves of colonization (slavery and colonialism) and the memories of the different protagonists of the wars of decolonization and the repatriation of French people from Algeria. For roughly a decade, between 2000 and 2010, the memories of crimes committed against national minorities were a constant subject of public debate, fiercely challenging what was taught in school history lessons. The public exposure brought these crimes to the fore and allowed their remembrance to be reconstituted according to the latest paradigms. It might not come as much of surprise that memories, in France, are perceived above all as grounds for insurmountable rifts and conflicts, with various denominations that have become clichés: 'memory wars' and 'victim competition' between 'communities' that the media find convenient to present as homogenous, united and aligned behind so-called 'representatives' with aggressive demands.

In this stormy context in which reciprocated grudges can become irrational obsessions and lead to actual physical assault, in an injurious climate of hatred and fear, it is, paradoxically, memory again that is considered the key to solving the conflicts it has engendered, so long as it is expressed in commemorations that can be shared by all and in genuine knowledge of the history of the past. Nothing better illustrates the eminent, founding function of memory in our societies than this renewed confidence, when in other societies and in earlier times it was considered absolutely necessary to consign these troubles to silence and oblivion and to erase all traces.

This confidence in rationalism and the power of knowledge is a tribute to the Republic's school tradition, although the doubts constantly expressed and the censure of dysfunction do reveal concern about how effective transmission really is. Teaching the history linked to these troubled commemorations is expected to promote peace yet at the same time it is constantly cited as a model of the impossible cohabitation of minorities. The media, and in particular the internet that has exploded in the century's first decade, seem to reflect a deeply worrying reality.

Nonetheless, other than in localized trouble spots where problems are concentrated, as in all the world's major cities, the situation on the ground seems to be fairly peaceful, according to teachers and to the few statistically significant empirical surveys.

There is a strong contrast between the denunciations appearing in the main national media, which maintain and support a persistent suspicion in Jewish community media, and the far more measured findings of those who teach and interpret memories. This is partly due to the somewhat delayed perception of media intellectuals, who tend to be out of touch with the situation on the ground. In fact, in the face of various situations of unrest, there has been very energetic yet subtle action, using innovative teaching methods, to avoid the pitfalls of transmission, the excesses and clumsiness of the earlier period that inevitably sparked protest. This is worth emphasizing: there is no sociological inevitability here, which would impose an inescapable scenario according to communities' ethnic and religious allegiance. Transmission policy must take into account prejudice and resistance; it is capable of working on them and eliminating them, but this does not happen spontaneously.

Positioning and mobilization of a national public system and pluralism of support organizations

In the school system and in society, however, not only has the situation calmed down significantly, but there is also a harmonious integration of these memories, far from the agitation of the 'memory wars' on which opinion leaders thrive. The French case makes it possible to identify a number of different factors and conditions that fostered this positive development and act complementarily and in synergy: on the one hand, a public statement of principle is required, a firm political commitment that clearly sets the limits of what is and what is not acceptable, of what is *common sense* in the society – major commemorations have this meaning. In the same vein, of what makes sense for everyone and helps reach young people, it is good for popular culture to take on problems of memory and allow them to be approached in numerous guises as individual characters in fictional films. French public television has played a big part by producing many films of varying quality, some of which are outstanding and have met with genuine popular success. Lastly, and this is what is less visible to the public but perhaps the most important aspect, it is well worth having the teachers who are responsible for the front line of transmission and exposed to related problems strongly supported by a dense network of local trainers and experienced, passionate and dedicated specialists. These have enabled teachers to better 'sense' their pupils, and better manage, with flexibility and in depth, the contrasting emotions expressed, to explain better and in suitable words the basic features of the genocide, to address calmly the reasonable objections concerning Israel, without making concessions to antisemitism. In terms of history, they have also meant that education can constantly renew itself by expanding its scope and refining the issues instead of staying stuck in a cycle of repetition about a handful of stereotypical aspects of memory. This is essential to steer pupils clear of boredom and a feeling of saturation caused by a monotonous message.

It is hard to say what the state's responsibility was, and what has been made possible by non-governmental organizations, what came from education and what is to be credited to museums or television. In fact, all sorts of initiatives have combined over the long history of the establishment of memory, and they have ended up creating an interactive and functional equilibrium between the robustness of a state policy and the reactive flexibility of small private structures working on projects. The cumbersome, hierarchical, sclerotic, stripped-down, impoverished state apparatus of the public education system could not alone have conducted such an energetic and creative policy. The work of a foundation involved in private initiative projects, and a Memorial created by the Jewish community, could never have created a dynamic able to spread throughout the population of France. The success to which we are paying tribute was the outcome of an unintentional but effective equilibrium between the state and civil society, between public and private institutions, between centralized national-scale and local policies, between formal education and popular culture conveyed by the main mass media, between sophisticated new works, pioneering research and high-quality popularization, between systematic learning in a school setting and mass culture involving adult society, and between the centre and the fringes. What I have called elsewhere a 'remembrance apparatus' permits a joint system, one foot in the state education establishment and one foot outside, with the result that remembrance of the Holocaust is possibly transmitted better in France than many other traditional subjects whose poor results are of concern to the public and the authorities.

In reports on transmission, two practices are always highlighted: trips to Auschwitz, and the personal testimony of former deportees. Just as I have not discussed the interesting, specifically French practice of teaching in primary schools, which retains an experimental, individualized aspect, so I will not refer to these practices that warrant separate consideration in painstaking detail. However, regardless of the very particular interest of these forms of transmission, there can be no certainty that these are majority practices or the most decisive. I think we overlook the impact of the more ordinary methods, such as regular teaching in secondary school curricula, fairly frequent school outings in the local area, and feature films and documentaries. From this angle, the existence of a network of professional mediators with very solid skills and ever aware of the latest developments, in terms of history and teaching practice, makes all the difference. The network performs the function of what is known as 'guidance', in a fairly vague way, but one that has real meaning in a time of mass consumption because it distinguishes between transmission that is fine-tuned and well-crafted and standardized work of mediocre quality.

We shall list these kinds of mediation in detail, at the risk of seeming tiresome. Transmission has taken all sorts of forms and vehicles; it is based on the rigour of the strongly centralized school establishment, and on the great expertise produced by memorial museums, whose work is essentially decentralized, rooted in local territories and associations, and focused on outreach. The transmission passes through a very large number of educational mediations, in the mass media, with the production of many highly varied and popular fictional films and documentaries; in culture, with effective support for high-quality arts productions – film, theatre, young people's literature; and in a wide variety of civil society organizations and associations. It is fully backed by state institutions with support from at least four ministries (defence, education, higher education, and culture) as well as from independent non-governmental organizations, which give it an enviable independence and flexibility, in skilfully constructed complementarity and cooperation. It receives material support and has its own well-funded institutions, advantages available to no other transmission.

In these times of austerity which have, over some twenty years, undermined education services and led to constant teacher-training cost-cutting, to the point of creating serious difficulties in all regular school transmission activities, it can safely be said that the crucial differential variable that partially explains this effectiveness is the scale of the material resources to hand. The state was able to use the large sums that were part of Jewish property expropriated during the Second World War to create a foundation to fund and facilitate all sorts of remembrance and cultural projects: the Foundation for the Memory of the Shoah (FMS). While the funding made the enterprise far easier, or more robust, it alone does not account for the quality and quantity of activities, or for their variety, intelligence and constantly renewed creativity.

This transmission in highly varied forms faces up honestly to the complexity of the matter, going much further than the initial exhortation of the 'duty of memory', which primarily expressed a feeling of profound trauma. It can do so because the resources allocated to transmission have helped create a sizeable group of specialist professional intermediaries, highly competent, stable and with a good reputation, which makes for experience and improved qualifications. Often trained by the state and the Ministry of Education, they nevertheless work in structures that are less rigid than the school system, in particular museums and memorials, and are professional and committed. One has only to compare this with the disastrous situation prevailing in other regular subjects of transmission, where the educational framework has been shrinking inexorably, in order to realize the extent to which the presence of these professional cultural mediators, greatly devoted to their mission, makes the difference between failed mass consumption and the spread of quality.

Are there any grey areas? Of course there are. However, time has shown the dynamic in place to be strong enough to withstand the shock of criticism, and to regroup to understand and resolve problems. The existence of specialized structures throughout France, with competent staff, for designing exhibitions, educational frameworks, research and tools, etc. enables informed reflection on specialist intellectual debates while remaining as close as possible to the situation on the ground with teachers and young adolescents, constantly on the lookout, and swift to integrate the slightest changes of circumstances.

Here we are addressing an essential criterion for quality in terms of education policy. The imposing edifice of the national education system, hierarchical and unbending, does not at present facilitate the free flow of ideas between top and bottom, does not take criticism easily and does not know how to learn from the experience of practitioners. And yet we cannot do without it. The existence of the public debate, however, and above all the dialogue maintained with and by non-state and non-educational organizations has made it possible to bypass the inertia and train teachers. On what we call the fringes of the education system, criticism has found outlets for expression and it is constructively reinvested. In comparison with all other sectors of education, the situation is far better. This very open reflection, almost in real time, with the dissemination of debates at the international level, is a condition of the dynamic that prevents the fossilization of transmission.

A French history

Wherever it is possible, if not easy, to teach, knowledge can be transmitted and the Holocaust commemorated without triggering an outcry and while sparking keen interest among pupils, as borne out by the numerous baccalaureate research topics chosen on the subject (selected by pupils themselves for in-depth study).

This does not mean it is simple, for substantive reasons unrelated or partly due to the plurality of identities in contemporary France.

The history of the deportation and extermination of French Jews, under the authority of and involving the French State apparatus, obliges teachers to explain to their pupils France's age-old deep-seated political divisions that still inform current identities. Long-standing rifts have given rise to the country's foundational division between the right and the left, felt so keenly as a powerful factor of national identity. The current period is distinguished from previous times in France, however, by great uncertainty and confusion in the benchmarking imagery of politics.

Since the French Revolution and throughout the nineteenth century and the lengthy, difficult and much opposed establishment of democracy, the French experienced their divisions with each camp harbouring the conviction it embodied the 'real France'. During the Second World War, the cards of that enduring conflict were reshuffled by the Occupation, producing the opposing figures of Collaboration and Resistance, both claiming to represent a lofty idea of the Nation, albeit associated with very different meanings. These capitalized entities in reality represented commitments entered into by a very small minority, but they established benchmarks and a set of words to denote 'good' and 'bad' in politics throughout the post-war period and thereafter. The passage of time, succeeding generations, new developments and all doctrines to which political scientists attach the prefix 'post' (post-communism, post-nationalism and post-colonialism) have blurred and confused the situation, making it very hard to elucidate. The great divisive stories that had previously determined the structure of identities and commitments gave way once people awoke to the mass crimes perpetrated in the twentieth century. None of the major ideologies based on emancipation through Progress has remained untouched; those that nonetheless survive in relatively new guises do so in a typically post-modern interplay of rhetorical recycling of inconsistent and shallow figures and motifs. The recent development of a form of political communication that skilfully twists references, cynically and openly playing with them, has to an even greater extent blurred references to 'the darkest hours of our history' and the legitimacies that emerged from them. It creates, in any event, great confusion that increases the country's uneasiness, apprehensions, stumbling blocks, fear of the future, and lack of understanding of the present.

History education in the school system, too, has been affected by the loss of benchmarks and struggles to find clarifying story lines, but it is generally agreed in French culture that the transmission of history is the main means of remedying such confusion, thus lending it strong legitimacy and vibrancy.

The anti-totalitarian paradigm did not provide a lasting substitute framework and is hardly useful for conflict management in a democracy. It can even prove counterproductive among young pupils who tend to understand 'totalitarianism' in the conventional sense of oppressive authoritarian dictatorship, tyrannical in speech – the 'Oriental Despotism' portrayed in classical texts by Montesquieu – and who are not wary of alluring and demagogic forms of deprivation of freedom and remain blind to the technical aspects of bureaucratic dictatorship.

As the spotlight turned afresh on Jewish deportee victims in France in the late 1970s, the infamous deeds of the Vichy government had to be appraised, leading to a shift in imagery and thus the identification of a new, and probably more elementary and more foundational, basis of legitimacy. This feat of imagery is as evident in public debate on topical issues as in the choices made about transmission. The issue of good and evil thence became less a matter of patriotic fidelity than a question of attitude to the mass crime that dared to sever a vulnerable minority group from the body politic. That is why the image of the Righteous people, who hid Jews and actively rejected the exclusion and elimination of their neighbours and contemporaries, has become so important in people's minds and become a mandatory element in school curricula. Certainly the mythology that has developed deserves some criticism from the standpoint of historical truth, even though it fulfils a genuinely felt symbolic need and plays the fundamental role of imparting legitimacy, as did the numerous versions of the Social Compact that marked the rise of liberalism in the eighteenth century. Emphasis on the Righteous person represents a kind of basic political requirement. It can be used to set a point for guidance in the hierarchy of values in politics, at two levels: firstly, it points specifically towards an ideal of ethical conduct valid for the individual; and, secondly, it lays down a founding principle as the boundary between what is acceptable in a democracy and what is not, regardless of all disagreements about the organization of life in community and about the distribution of power and wealth. The first principle in politics is that it is not acceptable to permit the slaughter of one's neighbours or of any other segment of humanity.

It is in this national context that one of the outstanding characteristics of Holocaust education in France, and clearly a force to be reckoned with, is taking root. The goal is to place the genocide in a historical context and to examine all explanations that can be gleaned from history, not limiting transmission to educational content consisting only of moral and civic considerations; correlatively, this historical knowledge is to be understood as deeply imbued with civic and critical significance. Ideally, all teenagers, at the end of secondary education to the baccalaureate level, must possess in-depth knowledge of the genocide's distant roots, the social and political configurations and triggering events that caused it, and the methods used. Study of memory of the event has been added recently, with the idea that memory is intrinsically historical and has important effects. This is an ambitious curriculum. It has become more or less a reality for those pupils best adapted to the elitism of the school system, while remaining mere fiction for many others. Yet the challenge it represents is widely accepted, and moreover, advocated and championed successfully. It is taught by a relatively united, qualified and dedicated corps of history teachers convinced of the importance of their role.

Memory and basic ethics

It is difficult to understand the great importance ascribed in the 1990s to memory of the genocide in the educational world without appraising the symbolic void filled by memory at that time, when all kinds of modernist ideologies of progress had waned or collapsed.

It filled the void left by genuinely educational, moral and civic transmission, on the one hand, and, on the other, by the great founding story of Progress through the Republic or by the other moribund 'great narrative' of Progress through Revolution. French education is meant to be an integral part of the Republic and has been set the solid and explicit institutional goal of producing free, active and independent citizens; but since the end of the 1960s, it has had the utmost difficulty in drawing up a curriculum for moral and civics education acceptable to the people, teachers and pupils alike. Ultimately, 'to educate' seemed to run counter to the ideal of critical judgement. Moral education as provided in the past lay in tatters, age-old civics education was discredited and the horrendous pictures of the camps aroused universal indignation and disgust. The unspeakable simply could not be discussed, thus constituting a rallying point. 'Never again!' was the only historical rallying cry for morality and politics thrown into disarray by the post-modern collapse of the great narratives of yesteryear.

Holocaust remembrance then emerged as this traumatic shock that is indivisibly educational and critical, as seeing photographs of the horror of the camps causes minimal trauma and is thus akin to vaccination to prevent all murderous racist excesses. Everyone considered that rational and objective transmission of historical truth about the genocide and about the deviancy, errors and lack of vision that led to such actions could play a pre-eminent role as an institution standing for shared values and, at the very least, rejection of the worst. As obviously nobody can or dares any more define what constitutes virtue, progress and freedom, evincing the blind faith that led the masses in the heyday of triumphant modernity, nothing but the rite of negative commemoration can be planned for the future. 'Never again' has become an absolute requirement, a categorical, terribly peremptory order that is fairly effective with teenagers. But, as a watchword, it is completely indeterminate in its practical and actual implications for education and preparation for life and its inevitable challenges.

Transmission of Holocaust remembrance fits all the more into content transmitted by schools because it fills a void. It is one of the last possible alternatives to the void in the crisis of meaning that undermines the country and, perhaps more broadly, the West. In an education system increasingly mired in a meaningless venture, reduced to the slogan 'all pupils must pass', in which success entails making pupils fit for fierce competition, few lessons are strong enough to be taught as values in their own right, as bearers of non-utilitarian values. Hence the strange fascination with the duty of remembrance in an education system that tends otherwise to give pride of place to the transmission of content to the detriment of all other educational dimensions, in which teachers are meant above all to transmit academic knowledge, far removed from any interpersonal issues.

Educators must nevertheless ponder the philosophical and practical question of whether commemoration that elicits people's emotion and capacity for empathy can be the sole basis of moral and civics education. Even if it is backed up by sound knowledge of the past and an accurate analysis of the historical developments and processes giving rise to the Nazi regime, memory of the Holocaust cannot be the sole foundation on which moral and civics education rests. How can it be linked to other entirely different components to create a blueprint able to lend fresh impetus to humanistic education and to post-disaster humanism?

Can we really encourage young people to take up citizenship responsibilities and prepare for the future with only the credo that the horrors of the past must be avoided? Can the only point of reference for policy formulation and community life be the anxiety-provoking idea of preventing disaster and combating everything liable to produce a rerun of the 1930s? Can people live in the present without looking to the future, otherwise than by dreading the past? The time has come to raise once more the question of moral and civics education designed for our time – negative commemorations will obviously play a decisive role in Holocaust remembrance, but a new balance must generally be struck by taking different dimensions into account, by developing a secular conception of morality and by promoting a higher idea of politics. 'Only for the sake of the hopeless are we given hope.' This quote from Walter Benjamin could be associated with the transmission of memory of the Holocaust, as part of a broader and more positive project, in which it would have its rightful place.

Conclusion: sound and flexible supporting mechanisms

The problem in transmission experienced during the period under consideration was not one associated with an *introduction* and all the problems raised by claims, concealments, half-truths, genuine falsehoods, legitimacy, resistance, ground-breaking activism and educational innovation. France had gone through all of those aspects in the earlier period, in which all kinds of powerful forms of transmission were tested by teachers who were particularly committed and thus generally very well armed for the job, in terms of both the knowledge and the meaning to be conveyed. We have moved to a very different stage, marked by the provision of mass education, which must perhaps be understood structurally rather than only quantitatively, or rather by considering all structural changes entailed by the shift to large numbers. The provision of mass education inevitably raises problems of organization, management, failures, standardized training, tools and evaluation. The issue of educational approach is considered macroscopically rather than microscopically and is more concerned with rules and standards than with scoring exceptional successes that cannot be replicated. This educational approach is concerned with 'best practices', but must pay sustained attention to bad and improper ones, too, if they are likely to spread, and it must never lose sight of intermediate practices and standardization. It must resist the utopic delusion of trying to make the exceptional the rule, and though haunted by the idea of identifying primarily what can be widely propagated, it must nonetheless retain a sense of the 'achievable best' and be receptive to genuine, creative and required innovation. It must establish frameworks for research and training, give thought to partnerships, consider acceptance and impact, find tools for evaluation, create resources, design course material and provide resources. It must fit into the various educational structures, timetables, distinctions drawn between subjects and examinations; these must be made operational in their repetitiveness, without neglecting to bring about changes to meet genuine criteria. It must learn to manage standardization that is likely to lead to trivialization and set 'content' to which demotivated teachers and bored pupils glumly submit. In a word, it must tackle all bureaucracy-related risks and ills, wherever the initial impetus was experienced as an extraordinary, overwhelming and decisive revelation.

Mass education has fortunately retained some of its initial impetus, while fully meeting the organizational requirement arising from mass enrolment. It opens up an opportunity and constitutes a privilege.

Paradoxically, the history of the Holocaust is transmitted properly to pupils because memory is alive and active in society. Holocaust remembrance should make it possible to raise a major present-day moral and political issue, namely the status of religious, cultural and ethnic minorities in a body politic. Foreign, immigrant Jews in precarious circumstances had been the first to be deported from France and were treated more harshly. As a result, in the post-war period and until recently, the bearers of that particular memory considered it to denote a common cause with all minorities, all population groups different from the majority and thus likely to be marginalized and persecuted.

Such transmission is suffused with the energy generated by conflicting interpretations of basic issues. If teachers are generally and effectively mobilized for Holocaust education, demonstrating enviable dynamism and capacity for renewal, it is because the numerous reasons for vigorous involvement in this urgent struggle for the present and for the future have given rise to a wide variety of approaches, media, institutions and forms, all constituting, in a word, a substantial mechanism in support of education. As noted above, transmission is solidly established in France, owing to a tight-knit network of large and small organizations, private initiatives and public policies. Its 'establishment' intrinsically reflects dynamics in which conflict and disquiet trigger debate, reflection and continual adjustments.

Democracy is a reality only at this cost and it leaves us no respite. The same goes for Holocaust education, which has become a cornerstone of citizenship education, at the critical point where politics is attached securely to ethics.

2

1903 • Rohan ATLAN 1915 • Jean ASZERMAN 1898 • Gisèle ATL
1914 • Estelle ATTAS 1921 • Lucien ATLANI 1911 • Germaine ATTA
ATTYASSE 1898 • Guy AUBER 1925 • Irmgard AUBRY 1909 • Pessia AUFLEGER 18
914 • Léon AUSCHER 1900 • Eda Henriette AUSIEFF 1931 • Geneviève AUSIEFF
USTERER 1907 • Maurice AUSTERLITZ 1887 • Rebecca AUTOFAGE 1893 • Claire AVID
AVIDOR 1929 • David AVIGDOR 1880 • Lydia AVIGDOR 1887 • Nissim AVIMELEK
AVISSAY 1925 • Donna AVLAGON 1871 • Estelle AVLAGON 1907 • Nissim AVLAG
AM 1927 • Léon AVRAM 1905 • Mireille AVRAM 1924 • Nissim AVRAM 1904 • Pierre AV
le AVRUTIK 1939 • Esther AVSIPOFF 1876 • Moïse AVSIPOFF 1877 • Berthe AXELRAD
rges AYACHE 1911 • Jules AYACHE 1902 • Léonie AYACHE 1870 • Reine AYACHE 190
eph AZARIA 1900 • Fanny AZENSTARCK 1921 • Dora AZIZA 1911 • Charles AZOULAY
uliette AZOULAY 1897 • Moïse AZOULAY 1916 • Simone AZOULAY 1899 • Victorine
Michel BAACH 1942 • René BAACH 1941 • Sally BAACH 1901 • Perez BABAN
houl BABANI 1920 • Moyem BABIC 1896
Corona BACHNER

The pedagogy of Holocaust education

The use of the expression 'Holocaust education' suggests that teaching and learning about the Holocaust has become an institutionalized field of education. This is certainly true if one considers the number of institutions dedicated to transmitting the legacy of the Holocaust that have emerged in recent years, and the fact that engaging with the subject in education, or in pedagogical research, requires a high degree of specialized expertise. For instance, although Holocaust education may provide a context to deal with human rights, it is obvious that all specialists of human rights education cannot deal with the Holocaust, and the contrary is also true. Indeed, the fact that Holocaust education has emerged as a field does not imply that teaching and learning about the Holocaust has become or should become a standardized set of practices. What it covers and what it aims at are still very much subject to discussion, although certain good practices and guidelines have surfaced.

Educating about the Holocaust focuses first and foremost on the study of history: of the Second World War, of Nazism, of the Jewish people, and in a broader approach, of crimes against humanity and genocide. It also has a strong relation to the *devoir de mémoire* (duty of remembrance) and is therefore equally a tool for the commemoration of victims. In that sense, it also provides an avenue to deal with the memory of history, as well as with how history is researched and understood over time. Therefore Holocaust education is as much about analysing facts as it is about how knowledge is constructed and about how cultures of remembrance evolve through the manifestation of different historical narratives. Beyond these purposes, Holocaust education should help students make connections with their life and the societies they live in, and to reflect upon their own role as active citizens.

Research in Holocaust education: Emerging themes and directions

Doyle Stevick and Zehavit Gross

Research in the field of Holocaust education is blossoming. The practice of Holocaust education around the world is rich, complex, diverse, culturally rooted, challenging, and often problematic as well. The subject's power and potential seem to support its proliferation, in good ways and bad; its growing pervasiveness may undercut its potency, and quantity does not ensure quality. The emerging awareness of the Holocaust in places far from Europe testify to its globalization and universalization as a moral touchstone, a shared point of reference if not a measuring stick, for human rights abuses around the world.

Not unlike a vaccination, it is hoped that exposure to the Holocaust, the world's greatest self-inflicted disease, will inoculate future generations against its replication or imitation, in Europe and beyond. Naturally, awareness, sensitivity to discrimination, support of human rights, and active engagement as citizens are critically important elements in preventing human rights abuses of any kind, but they may be far from sufficient. Our noblest hopes and ambitions for Holocaust education must still fit within realistic models of the factors and forces that lead to human rights abuses in the first place. We must be cautious about hopes that a single vaccination can hope to quell so pervasive a disease as human rights atrocities throughout history.

The purpose of this chapter is to map out some of the recent developments in Holocaust education research around the world, and to consider how this work is beginning to coalesce into a coherent field. We hope and expect that this growth in the field, which is in our view one of the most dynamic, innovative and exciting in all of education, will ultimately contribute to strong theoretical development, a canon of key works, sustainable networks of scholars, policy makers and practitioners, and other attributes of fully mature fields of study.

The Purposes of research in Holocaust education

It is important to take a moment to consider the purposes of research. At an initial level, we have to discern exactly what is happening in Holocaust education around the world. Descriptive studies help us to establish this baseline of understanding.

Although we are beginning to develop a fuller picture of Holocaust education, a great deal more work needs to be done on this seemingly basic task. Taking a specific case helps to illustrate this need. In the countries of Central and Eastern Europe, for example, we have less information about what is happening than in more extensively studied countries such as Israel, Germany, and the United States. Often, just one scholar will be publishing about Holocaust education for a particular country. That scholar's work must, by necessity, be focused and limited.

For any given country, we would at the very least be interested in the policies that are in place, the curriculum that is offered, the fidelity of the curriculum in its implementation in the classroom, the quality of textbook treatments, the knowledge and comfort level of teachers with the material, the prior knowledge, attitudes, and responses of students to the history, and the ways in which prominent minority groups in the societies, such as Russian-speakers or Roma, relate to the subject. Israel, and some Western European and English-speaking countries, approach this maximal level of coverage, but in other cases, we may have little more than a single survey of textbooks or a set of interviews with teachers. The picture is akin to a badly eroded mosaic: some compelling tesserae remain in place, and we can attempt to sketch in the missing lines, making inferences from what we've learned in similar cases, but much more remains unknown than what has thus far been documented.

What the mosaic metaphor assumes, though, is a snapshot, a fixed point in time, while Holocaust education is changing rapidly all over the world. Our need for ongoing, high-quality descriptive studies is persistent and will not abate. Only with continuing research can we gain a longitudinal perspective that captures the nature and degree of change occurring in the field. It is important to note that the research in question requires a degree of familiarity with the local languages of the countries involved, in many of which such research is not popular and may even be risky to an insider scholar's career. The problematic and contentious politics of research must be taken into consideration. Courageous scholars and practitioners do continue to do this work, and they often benefit from outside partnerships or support.

Descriptive research can serve a number of purposes, and Habermas's characterization of knowledge into three human interests can help us to think further about the nature and purposes of research, particularly in relation to Holocaust education. The first category involves what Habermas calls a technical interest. Knowledge that serves a technical interest helps to solve problems; it is instrumental in nature. It is concerned with effectiveness, and what works. In Holocaust education, it could involve basic questions of how to achieve certain basic knowledge acquisition goals most efficiently and effectively. Research in this tradition is rooted in the natural sciences and positivist research paradigms. It helps us to understand knowledge levels, trends, methods, outcomes, and measurement. Instrumental knowledge for the technical interest aligns with theory building, broad generalizations and experimentation.

Habermas distinguishes this technical, problem-solving approach from a practical concern with communication and understanding. A primary concern of research in this tradition is with meaning. We know that the Holocaust is deeply meaningful in diverse societies, and often in profoundly different ways. If we considered the paradigmatic categories of victim, perpetrator, bystander and helper, for example, and applied them (imperfectly, to be sure) at the national level, we could ask 'How is the Holocaust meaningful in Israel, Germany, Switzerland and the United States?' The answers in each society are quite different. As Schweber writes: 'On even a cursory comparison of Holocaust education debates in the US, Germany, and Israel, what surfaces is the importance of national contexts in framing curricular issues' (p. 463). Further, we do not mean to suggest that there are homogenous responses across each of these countries. Rather, events take on meaning in relation to local histories and from within different cultural frameworks. The purpose of research in this tradition is to understand. Understanding the historical experiences and perspectives of Estonians, Latvians and Lithuanians can help us, for example, appreciate why people from these nations often display increased scepticism of the evidence of Holocaust atrocities that was produced by the Soviet regime (Stevick, 2013). While notorious for political persecutions and show trials, the Soviets also liberated many concentration camps and thus documented the crimes that occurred there. The fundamental corruption and illegitimacy of the Soviet state for those who were formerly under its hegemony generates an added layer of suspicion of anything produced under Soviet authority, an understandable but challenging dilemma that we must respect as we try to grapple with the legacy of the overlaid traumas of Nazi and Soviet dominion in those lands. Such understanding may function as a precondition for dialogue, engagement, and potentially transformation as well. That transformation, though, may be not just of others – my technical use of instrumental knowledge to attempt to change others' views – but of ourselves as well. This self-transformation is the third type of human interest Habermas articulates.

Habermas's emancipatory interest is concerned with self-transformation. This introspective approach initially seems of somewhat peripheral interest here. However, research and advocacy are very closely linked in Holocaust education. Deeply-rooted values and commitments often drive engagement in both areas.

These commitments are often manifest both in a set of normative principles that guide research and advocacy, but also in our implicit theories of how things work. Martin Carnoy (1992) revealed how implicit conceptions about government undergird many political conflicts within countries, and notes how those underlying beliefs seldom crack the surface. His insight applies well here. Habermas encourages us to reflect upon how 'the way one's history and biography has expressed itself in the way one sees' (MacIsaac, 2006).

This tradition has tremendous value in our field. First, it allows us to distinguish clearly between the normative and empirical bases for our advocacy. We often support practices or positions in the field both because we feel they are right and because we suspect they work most effectively. These distinct foundations of our views require different treatment. We may feel it is morally right to have tenth graders spend two weeks on the Holocaust. We may find, however, that for long-term retention and understanding, students benefit more from spending a week on the Holocaust and a week on Rwanda, with an emphasis on comparisons and contrasts. The former is a moral question, the latter an empirical question. Achieving clarity about the normative and empirical bases for our work can help us to discern whether we are asking the right moral questions. In this case, we may be using Holocaust education as a means to certain ends, such as understanding human rights or genocide prevention. We may want to reframe our moral discussions around the ends we hope to achieve, and rely on empirical research on the comparative effectiveness of different means to those ends.

The second benefit of Habermas's emphasis on reflection and self-knowledge in the emancipatory interest comes in unearthing our implicit and often unconscious theories of how things do work. When we are able to identify and to articulate our working assumptions, we can subject them to scrutiny and critical examination, treating them as hypotheses to be tested empirically. In a field once racked by denial, which persists in a number of contexts, we feel a moral imperative to follow the evidence, even if it leads us to uncomfortable conclusions. When we encounter sceptics, whether of educational research or proponents of conspiracy theories about the Holocaust itself, we hope to foster a reference to evidence. 'Well, how would we know? Where is the evidence supporting this perspective? Here is the evidence on which we rely, here is how we obtained it, and here is how we interpret it.'

The case of Holocaust remembrance is notable in this regard. We support remembrance out of deep moral conviction. We also believe – or perhaps hope? – it can contribute to cultivating a global culture of peace and understanding, respect for human rights, and potentially even the prevention of genocide and other atrocities (Annan, 2010). Underlying this advocacy is a set of beliefs, assumptions or theories about how it could actually do so. Fracapane (forthcoming) has articulated a relationship between remembrance, education and behaviour that merits investigation. However, as Schweber notes: 'commemorative activities...are rarely studied in terms of reception' (p. 471). According to the discussion above, we might ask a cascading set of questions. At the descriptive level, what is actually being done in remembrance activities in different societies? At the technical level of instrumental knowledge, we could ask whether events of commemoration increase students' interest in the Holocaust, nurture empathy for persecuted people, or engage them more actively in the community. For the practical interest in communication and understanding, we want to know what the Holocaust means to the students. How do they make sense of it? How do they relate it to their personal histories and local circumstances, if at all? When we return to the emancipatory interest, we explore where our assumptions proved incorrect, and seek not only to correct them, but to understand the underlying roots of our errors, whether normative or theoretical, that might lead us astray again the future. By suggesting that we research remembrance activities at a variety of levels, we are not asserting that they should not occur if they are not 'effective'. We are not suggesting that such questions should be resolved by evidence, or by evidence alone. Rather, we are advocating a reference to evidence, and an effort to continue research, to inform our discussions and to anchor our normative decision-making.

We believe that the Holocaust is probably the most extensively and carefully documented event in human history. We marvel at the ongoing discoveries and new perspectives that continue to emerge about the Holocaust. But any encounter with the Holocaust reminds us of how much we still don't know, and never will. Despite the massive, long-term international effort to document, interpret and understand the Holocaust, we have much to learn and many questions to resolve, and many more to raise. There are ongoing debates and competing theories about, for example, how we can explain widespread German participation and local collaboration in mass killings. In this one aspect, like the Holocaust itself, there is much we don't know about Holocaust education. Let us start, though, with some of the things we are learning.

Surveys of research in Holocaust education

We would note two distinct strengths of the field of Holocaust education before beginning a discussion of contemporary research in the field. First, it is a field of remarkable innovation. Holocaust education was a pioneer in the use of first-person testimonies in classrooms (Hondius, forthcoming). Concentration camps, death camps, and other significant historical sites have been used for education and commemoration for decades. These sites have been quite innovative in developing new approaches to engage and inform students and others. While 'book learning' is profoundly abstract, these uses of people and places have been quite powerful, and have influenced other fields as well. As teachers grapple with the enormity of the Holocaust, they have sought many creative approaches to convey what is so difficult to understand; these efforts may be problematic as often as they succeed (for a discussion of simulations, see Fallace, 2007). The successes, however, can be profound and transformative, and can often be reproduced by other Holocaust educators and be applied in other fields as well.

We feel the innovation in Holocaust education itself is matched by the diversity of approaches to the field. Methodologically and theoretically, a wide variety of scholarly tools have been brought to bear on Holocaust education. Such diversity poses its own challenges as well. It is much simpler to conduct a meta-analysis of research when there is a consensus around constructs, methods, populations, and so forth. In Holocaust education, for which a common theoretical basis has yet to emerge, the whole may not yet be more than the sum of its parts, but the parts are nevertheless rich indeed.

This richness has implications for our approach to this survey. Rather than attempt a critical analysis to unite the entire field, or to survey it around a few key questions, we take a discursive approach in the hope of further cultivating its existing richness and pointing to productive directions for future research. To do this, we will discuss highlights from two recent and important reviews of literature about Holocaust education. Then, we will discuss the most important empirical research we have had the privilege to be involved with over the last four years for UNESCO and special issues of journals for *Prospects*, *European Education*, and *Intercultural Education*.

Two valuable surveys of Holocaust education have appeared in recent years (Schweber, 2011; and Davis and Rubinstein-Avila, 2013). Schweber emphasizes divisions in the uniqueness/universal camps, and between traditional and post-modern research paradigms. However, as she notes: 'The list of ways to section the field is dauntingly long given its short history' (p. 466). Her work continues to consider pressing questions of practical application, including 'what is known about where the Holocaust is taught, in what kinds of venues, how, by whom, and with what effects' (p. 466). She notes in particular the curricular creep that brings the Holocaust to younger and younger students, generating nightmares for some while maintaining a 'general lack of comprehension' (p. 467) among others. Jennings' (2010) ethnographic study of a bilingual class's preparations for and reactions to a Holocaust unit is one of the finest qualitative studies in the field. In addition, she draws attention to the educational approaches to the Holocaust in a range of religious communities. Her helpful review closes with an exploration of the diverse educational settings in which education about the Holocaust takes place, and a consideration of the contents of curricula that have been studied.

Davis and Rubinstein-Avila (2013) focus on three major issues in the Holocaust education literature: the emergence of Holocaust education in the national curriculum of schools around the world, including the challenges to implementation; the relationship between memorialization and education; and how Holocaust education can be related to critical contemporary concerns such as racism and human rights. They single out six issues in particular that influence the particular direction of individual countries' approaches to Holocaust education, namely: the direct connection of that country to the Holocaust itself; the type of government the country experienced after the war; the attractiveness of forgetting and the desire for normalcy; the historical prevalence of antisemitism in that society; issues surrounding the purpose for teaching about the Holocaust in the first place; and the contemporary politics around the Holocaust, not least each country's stance towards Israel.

Davis and Rubinstein-Avila note several key dynamics in the field, including the problematic origins of the term and the preference for Shoah, as well as the diverse definitions of the Holocaust itself. Even major organizations have different boundaries and emphases for their definitions. Should the parameters include the entire Nazi period, including the persecutions of Jews, or just the mass killing itself? It could be our terminology has not yet sufficiently captured the realities of the interrelated yet distinct genocide of the Jews on the one hand and the totality of Nazi crimes on the other. Should it consider Jews exclusively, or note the experiences of other persecuted groups, including Roma and the disabled?

Foster's (2013) major survey of more than 2,000 teachers in England offered seven possible definitions (p. 146), plus the opportunity to add their own; these definitions provide a great resource for discussing what is meant by Holocaust education. Foster found that two-thirds of teachers preferred definitions that did not emphasize the distinctively antisemitic focus of the Nazis, lumping the Jews together with all other targeted groups, and thus were not in alignment with major international organizations such as the International Holocaust Remembrance Alliance (IHRA, formerly known as the Task Force), Yad Vashem, the United States Holocaust Memorial Museum or the Imperial War Museum. It is possible that the question, by forcing educators to select just one response, prompted them to select the answer that best reflected the full contents of what they taught rather than the most focused definition of the Holocaust itself. For example, a teacher might well emphasize the antisemitic character of the Holocaust, yet teach that it was an inclusive hate that claimed many additional victims; the same teacher might thus choose the definition that most fully matched the content of their teaching rather than the most precise analytic definition of the Holocaust itself. Regardless of the precise numbers at work, Foster has identified a key issue that requires additional research in England and beyond.

Additional key points discussed by Davis and Rubinstein-Avila include the role of the media and the efforts of international organizations and non-profits (see also Fracapane, forthcoming). Another is the risk of failure of Holocaust education, a real possibility for an event that was 'massive in scale, hugely complex, extreme and unprecedented in its horrors, and verged on incomprehensibility in the evil of its totality and of its countless constituent events' (Gross and Stevick, 2010, p. 18). Short (2013) discusses the risks of failure in general and Meseth and Proske (2010) document a teacher who struggles to reconcile his students' conduct with the moral lessons he feels are intrinsic to the material, while Stevick (2013) reflects on the alleged role of Holocaust education in the tragic actions of a former student and white supremacist. Memorialization is also a key topic of interest.

Memorial sites, often sites of atrocities, strive to serve a dual function of education and memorialization. The relationship between the two has not yet been well researched, and thus not well theorized either. In line with the emphasis on failure, David and Rubinstein-Avila (2013) note that Andrews (2010) asks a difficult and provocative question about whether such visits to genocide sites elicit a 'purely emotional response while visits to familiar and still relevant locations allow students to "create deeper layers of meaning than visiting Birkenau" (Andrews, 49)' (p. 159). Andrews's point is difficult but worthy of empirical research. Certainly, we believe memorialization and education can at times be complementary forces, particularly in specific settings. We also acknowledge that at times there may be tensions between the two.

However, Andrews's comment seems to invoke a false dichotomy between emotional and cognitive functions. Rather, we would suggest the key point is which emotional reactions are potentially constructive or destructive. It is a given we are more apt to learn about things that engage us and that we care about. Learning can also be an emotionally difficult process that challenges core beliefs and assumptions (for a perspective on an adult's experiences and reflections on this process, see Stevick, 2013). Indeed, if we hope to transform xenophobic attitudes, which can have connections to family beliefs, cultural practices, and even religious views, then understanding the emotional, affective and dispositional dimensions of transformational learning is imperative. This subject marks an additional area in which inter-disciplinary research will be critical. Affective learning (see, for example, Anderson, 2000) can enhance cognitive learning, and may indeed be a worthy objective of learning itself. A more nuanced integration of affective and cognitive learning, and of commemoration and education, can only enrich our approaches to museums, memorials, and other historic sites.

Recent empirical studies of Holocaust education

Elie Wiesel (2010), after reading the two volumes of articles on Holocaust education that were published in the UNESCO International Bureau of Education (IBE) journal *Prospects*, beautifully articulated our shared purpose as Holocaust educators and researchers: 'identify the evil, unmask it, deprive it of its poisonous power–which is hatred–and then try to understand and to make people understand its incomprehensible nature and extent' (p. 5).

We will briefly introduce these and more recent contributions to the field, taking care to point out key themes or issues that may be relevant to other contexts and invite research. In providing a framework for the larger project, Gross and Stevick (2010) take up the issue of research in Holocaust education, and in particular, the relationship of Holocaust education practice to ongoing Holocaust education. Remarkable discoveries continue to be made in our evolving understanding of this tremendously broad and complex phenomenon, and our support for Holocaust educators should occur on a continuing basis, rather than allowing our understanding and our teaching to become stuck at a certain stage when our overall understanding is constantly evolving. In particular, we considered the passing of the generations that perpetrated, witnessed and experienced the Holocaust. This loss constitutes a break in the continuity of memory that must be addressed through various means, which can include training of children of survivors to speak to classrooms, studies in inter-generational and societal memory, and deliberate forms of remembrance that take this ongoing loss into account. In addition, this piece takes up the issue of the meanings of the Holocaust, and in particular, the differences that emerge between long-free societies and those that were under the Soviet bloc.

Research, however, is conducted under certain assumptions about epistemology, or what is knowable and how it can be known. This fact holds no less for Holocaust education. In fact, since it is impossible to provide a comprehensive account of the Holocaust in any given national curriculum, choices must be made about what to include, and crucially, what to exclude. Here, we enter the politics of knowledge:

'Knowledge is not neutral, and the distribution of knowledge is not a neutral process. The value of a fact, a piece of knowledge, is not absolute and its meaning, derived from a socially dominant or marginal ideology, is reconstructed in the dynamic interaction of people within the school.' (Stevick and Gross, 2010, p. 190)

Indeed, it is possible to use a set of facts, all of them true, to create a portrait that is incomplete or misleading. For example, it may be more comfortable for Holocaust educators to focus exclusively on the Jewish victims, because antisemitism feels like more of an historical problem, than the treatment of the Roma, which is pressing and immediate. In this specific context, focusing on the fundamentally Jewish character of the Holocaust can be a means of avoiding ongoing issues of discrimination in society. Indeed, Bărbulescua, Degeratua and Guşu (2013), who work at the Elie Wiesel National Institute for the Study of the Holocaust in Romania, documented six distinct phases through which Romanian textbooks evolved, ranging from complete silence and representing their fascist leader Antonescu as a saviour of Jews through to a comprehensive account that includes the Roma as well as the Jews as victims.

The issue of the Roma has particular resonance today given the rise of hard right political parties in countries such as Greece and Hungary, the latter of which is discussed in detail in connection to Holocaust education by van Iterson and Nenadović (2013). Continuing with the focus upon Romania, Kelso discusses her work in training teachers about the Romani genocide in Romania. She explores the many 'cognitive barriers' that make it difficult for teachers to assimilate the new information and to reconcile their understandings of the past with the parts of history that have been deliberately rendered invisible for generations. In this area, as Kelso notes, American and European groups have put emphasis, hoping to strengthen minority rights and democracy. Fracapane (forthcoming) and Polak (2013) also note the critical place of international efforts in relation to the Holocaust, with Polak focused on how these efforts relate to Romani peoples. Polak draws attention to two important websites that have recently been developed. We have known for a long time that the web was a haven for white supremacist and other racist organizations, but in Holocaust education we have not begun to take full advantage of the medium as an educational tool; in particular, we would benefit from research specifically on this subject. In addition, we have little or no documentation of education about the Porjamos in Romani communities.

Holocaust education in Israel

The situation in Israel is quite different (Gross, 2010b). Israelis grapple with the Holocaust from a very young age, and its presence and importance to national identity is not to be underestimated. It has not always been thus, however, as Gross (2010a) documents. The period of 1943 to 1961 was marked by public denial. The Jewish community in Palestine, and later the Israeli public, initially ignored the Holocaust, either by suppressing or repressing its memory. Two modes of denial, suppression and repression, occurred: 1) actual silence, in which suppression stems from an inability of the survivors as well as the public to discuss the issue, and 2) a selective attitude, or repression, that referred only to the heroic aspects of the Holocaust when the Jews resisted Nazi tyranny, such as the Warsaw Ghetto Uprising of April 1943. In the general public discourse during this period, European Jewry was portrayed as 'sheep going to the slaughter', and this was seen as a sign of shame. Therefore, survivors quickly learned not to speak about their Holocaust experiences.

Public recognition followed in the period between 1961 and 1980. Public acknowledgment and recognition that the Holocaust had actually happened and had a tragic and humiliating facet began during the Eichmann trial in 1961. When the first testimonies were heard, people began to acknowledge the information and a new trend emerged: people wanted to hear the testimonies of the survivors. The Eichmann trial of 1961 was the first in a series of events that raised the need to include the study of the Holocaust in high school history books in Israel.

The next phase covers 1980 to 2000. In 1980, the Knesset (Israeli Parliament) amended the State Education Law to include as one of its goals 'awareness of the memory of the Holocaust and the heroes'. In addition, the Ministry of Education decided that the high school matriculation examination in history would include the topic of the Holocaust (Segev, 2000). In the two decades after 1980, Holocaust education became a separate, compulsory subject. In the 1990s, in what is known as post-Zionist criticism, some scholars began to condemn what they saw as the cynical political use of the Holocaust by the Zionist movement, which viewed the

Holocaust as justifying the expulsion of the Arabs from Palestine (Segev, 2000; Zertal, 2002). They also argued that the pre-state Jewish community had not done enough to rescue the Jews from the concentration camps.

The period from 2000 to the present can be termed Deconstruction. Following the public criticism and enhancement of the post-Zionist discourse, a new history textbook published in 1999, which belittled the place of the Holocaust, Zionism and the state of Israel, aroused a huge public debate and was the subject of a discussion in the Knesset. The textbook was rejected 'because it didn't draw the appropriate historical lessons from the Holocaust' (Porat, 2004, p. 619). The public criticism also led to the development of 'alternative' memorial ceremonies that related to other persecuted minorities in the Holocaust (e.g. Roma) and other genocides, raised criticism of a civic nature about the discrimination against minorities in Israel, and concentrated on lessons one should draw from the Holocaust. These scholars criticized the institutional commemoration ceremonies that emphasized the symbols of the Holocaust and its historical context (the Nazi and Fascist regimes), instead of concentrating on the meaning of atrocity and hatred, and what such movements might lead to.

Just as we must be careful not to present a homogenized image of a single, unitary Jewish identity of victims during the Holocaust, we should not assume such homogeneity within Israel today. Indeed, in relation to the Holocaust, different views are not uncommon. As Davis and Rubinstein-Avila (2013) point out, Ze'ev argued for differences between the left in Israel and its Orthodox Jews and traditional Zionists: 'by controlling Holocaust memory, "its production, interpretation and distribution" (p. 374), Zionist historiographers and educators have effectively constructed the contours of collective memory in Israel, utilizing this history for the purpose of nation building, and forming some of the central features of its collective identity' (p. 155).

Such internal differences and tensions can lead to new resolutions and approaches, potentially cutting short this period, and launching new ones whose characteristics are yet to be seen (Gross, 2013). The relatively well-documented history of Holocaust education in Israel enables us to develop hypotheses about other cases (Gross, 2012). It also allows us to begin to make distinctions between international (or universal?) experiences and ones that are particular to a specific context and culture. In this way, we can begin to develop a theory of stages through which societies may pass when grappling with the Holocaust (or potentially with genocides in general). While some of the events in question were particular to Israel, the Eichmann trial had an international impact, and Hannah Arendt's dispatches from the courtroom are influential to this day.

Holocaust education in the former Soviet Bloc

Gross's periodization of Israel's history of Holocaust education can be contrasted with the successor state of the lead perpetrators, first West Germany and then united Germany. It seems likely that no country has approached Germany's effort to take responsibility for its history and the atrocities it instigated and committed. Meseth's (2012) treatment of the stages through which Germany developed in its relationship to the Holocaust is quite powerful, and particularly its analysis of how the former West and East Germanys had to integrate their disparate relationships to and interpretations of the Holocaust. East Germany's anti-fascist interpretation of the Holocaust had allowed its citizens to distance themselves from the atrocities in ways that West Germans did not. Meseth (2012) argues that 'the universalist ethical orientation in German memory discourse must be seen as embedded in the context of an emergent transnational memory of the Holocaust' (p. 15). Indeed, by linking periodizations such as Gross's and Meseth's, we are able to begin to unlock the transnational dynamics of Holocaust education, both in international efforts to advance Holocaust education and as part of broader movements of globalization (on which, see MacGilchrist and Christophe, 2011) and universalization. The universalization of the Holocaust has both promise and peril: even as it becomes a common moral reference point and even a template for regarding atrocities, it can create opportunities for countries that collaborated with Nazis or sheltered Nazis to bypass the local or national moral dilemmas in favour of an abstract, transnational lens.

If Israel was overwhelmingly a home to Holocaust survivors and Germany predominantly the country of perpetrators, the countries of Central and Eastern Europe in which the Holocaust was predominantly carried out are a complex mixture of bystanders, victims and perpetrators. This fact, compounded by a half-century of propaganda, the suppression of free historical research and the inability of survivors to publish their experiences, not to mention the extensive suffering under Soviet military force and occupation or hegemony, has resulted in, at best, a complex relationship throughout the region with the Holocaust. It remains to be seen whether the East German experience in united Germany will provide a rough template for the paths of Central and East European countries that have been accepted into full European Union membership, but their structural similarities are suggestive.

In addition to the longitudinal analysis of Romanian textbooks mentioned above, Michaels's (2013) account of the evolution of textbooks in Slovakia also provides an historical perspective that can be mapped against the experience of Israel and Germany to develop a sense of universals, international dynamics, and national/local particulars in societies' ongoing relationship to the Holocaust. As Michaels (2013) notes, early international advocacy of Holocaust education in Central and Eastern Europe in the 1990s took place against the backdrop of the conflict in the Balkans, and the perception that resurgent nationalism both contributed to the conflict and to the ethnic cleansing, and was reminiscent of the kinds of intolerance that contributed to genocide. Michaels also notes the sensitivity of a country's autonomy and self-determination in the midst of apparent sacrifices to enter the European Union and NATO so soon after emerging from the Soviet bloc. Within this context, countries felt compelled to legitimize their independence anew. For this purpose, earlier periods of independence were often celebrated, even if their records were less than heroic, fascist, or even complicit in Holocaust atrocities. In addition, historic diversity was often de-emphasized in favour of explicitly ethnic conceptions of citizenship, rather than political ones.

The cascading independence of former Soviet bloc countries between 1989 and 1991 left a different periodization for the region in its grappling with the Holocaust, and for Germany as well, since integration soon followed. The dissolution of the Soviet Union surely had an important, if indirect, impact on Israel as well, since approximately a million post-Soviet citizens immigrated to Israel, at the time nearly twenty per cent of the total population, though we have not yet seen much research on its influence in this specific arena. This is another area ripe for research, particularly given the overwhelmingly Eastern European character of the Holocaust (roughly five of the six million Jewish victims of the Holocaust were from Central and Eastern Europe, and the largest national groups of victims in descending order were pre-war Polish and Soviet citizens, then Romanian, Hungarian, and Czechoslovak Jews (Snyder 2009)).

Conclusion

Much additional high quality Holocaust education research is appearing beyond the studies mentioned above. We can make only brief mention of them, though any individual piece may spark the reader's interest, and the whole may provide a sense of the contours of the growing field. Many studies are helpfully moving beyond the framework of a single country, though Cowan (2013), for example, shows both how much is happening in a single place like Scotland, and how countries with less direct links to the Holocaust are forging meaningful connections. Bromley and Russell (2010) have documented the expanding use of the term Holocaust in textbooks all over the world. Chyrikins and Vieyra (2010) consider the powerful impact of the Anne Frank House's work across Latin America, while Clyde (2010) explores the civic leadership of a group from a wide range of countries who visit Holocaust sites together. MacGilchrist and Christophe (2011) consider globalization and the Holocaust, even while introducing the helpful if difficult concept of subjectivation. Stevick and Michaels (2012) attempt to elaborate on this concept and two others, appropriation and common sense, as part of a larger effort to understand different perspectives on the Holocaust, particularly in Central and Eastern Europe. In that same issue, Dietsch (2012) documents how historians in the Ukrainian diaspora promoted a version of history that problematically related the Holodomor to the Holocaust. Stevick (2010) explores the politics of the Holocaust in Central and Eastern Europe at the turn of the century by documenting how one small country dealt with unwelcome international pressure to adopt a Holocaust commemoration day while not undermining their prospects for joining NATO and the European Union.

Like many societies, the passing of generations poses a challenge that is complicated in diverse communities. Proske (2012) takes up these challenges in a German classroom, as a teacher from one generation tries to navigate the question of guilt and the concomitant moral expectations with a diverse classroom. Rutland's (2010) study of Australian Jewish teachers working with Muslim students documents some of the challenges teachers can face, while Short (2013) emphasizes that most Muslim students behave in an engaged and respectful manner when the topic arises. While these brief citations can hardly do justice to the rich contents of these empirical studies, they are indicative of the robust, diverse and creative approaches to research in a critically important area.

The beginning of this overview suggested that different research orientations make distinct contributions to our work. We need to know what is effective, and research in the natural sciences tradition focused on causality is needed. What are the outcomes of different approaches? This focus on instrumental knowledge aligns with Habermas's emphasis on technical interests. However, for us, the Holocaust is more than anything a profoundly meaningful event. The most urgent questions for us concern its evolving meaning in different places, how diverse children make sense of it, and the broader network of cultural beliefs, values and assumptions that shape its reception and interpretation. This emphasis on meaning reflects Habermas's emphasis on practical knowledge for understanding, understanding that can enhance communication. In this sense, the challenges of engaging with different responses to the Holocaust, for example, across Central Europe and Western Europe, creates an opportunity for broader understanding, better communication, and a way to move beyond the unproductive politics of memory surrounding the Second World War that too often divide us when common ground can, and must, be found. Habermas's third interest in emancipation invites us to humility, to a recognition there is still much we can learn and many ways in which we can improve our understanding by recognizing the limitations on our own thinking derived from our personal experiences and cultural perspectives. By embracing this openness to revising our own views and perspectives, particularly in the light of evidence, we model a stance we hope others will adopt as well, paving the way for more constructive dialogues about our pasts, their meanings and our futures.

References

Anderson, L.W. and S.F. Bourke. 2000. *Assessing affective characteristics in the schools*. Mahwah, NJ, Lawrence Erlbaum.

Andrews, K. 2010. Finding a place for the victim. *Teaching History*, No.141,pp 42–49.

Annan, K. 2010. The Myth of Never Again. *The New York Times*, June 17. http://www.nytimes.com/2010/06/18/opinion/18iht-edannan.html.

Bărbulescu, A., Degeratu, L. and Guşu, C. 2013. The Holocaust as reflected in communist and post-communist Romanian textbooks. *Intercultural Education*, Vol. 2, No.1-2, pp 41-60.

Bromley, P. and Russell, S. G. 2010. The Holocaust as history and human rights: a cross-national analysis of Holocaust education in social science textbooks, 1970–2008. *Prospects*, Vol. 40, pp 153–173.

Carnoy, M.1992. Education and the state: From Adam Smith to Perestroika. R.F. Arnove, P. G. Altbach and G. P. Kelly (eds.), *Emergent issues in education: Comparative perspectives*. Albany. State University of New York Press, pp 143-159.

Chyrikins, M., and Vieyra, M. 2010. Making the past relevant to future generations. The work of the Anne Frank House in Latin America. *Intercultural Education*, Vol. 21 (S1), pp7–15.

Clyde, C. 2010. Developing civic leaders through an experiential learning programme for Holocaust education. *Prospects*, Vol. 40, pp 289–306.

Cowan, P. 2013. Reconceptualising the Holocaust and Holocaust education in countries that escaped Nazi occupation: a Scottish perspective. *Intercultural Education*, Vol. 24(1–2), pp 167–179.

Davis, B. L. and Rubinstein-Avila, E. 2013. Holocaust education: global forces shaping curricula integration and implementation. *Intercultural Education*, Vol. 24(1–2), pp 149–166.

Fallace, T. 2007. Playing Holocaust: the origins of the Gestapo simulation game. *Teachers College Record*, Vol. 109, pp 2642–2665.

Foster, S. 2013. Teaching about the Holocaust in English schools: challenges and possibilities. *Intercultural Education*, Vol. 24 (1–02), pp 133–148.

Fracapane, K. (forthcoming). International organizations in the globalization of Holocaust education. In Z. Gross and E.D. Stevick, *Holocaust Education in the 21st Century: Teaching the Shoah in Practice, Policy and Curriculum*.

Gross, Z. 2010a. Holocaust education in Jewish schools in Israel: Goals, dilemmas, challenges. *Prospects* Vol.40(1), pp. 93–113.

Gross, Z. 2010b. The Secret of the Success of Holocaust Education in Israel. *Education & Society*, Vol. 28 (2) pp 29–44

Gross, Z. 2012. Globalization and Holocaust Education. *Education and Society* Vol.30(3), pp 79–93.

Gross, Z. 2013. Teaching about the Holocaust: major educational predicaments, proposals for reform and change – an international perspective. *International Journal of Educational Reform* Vol. 22(2), pp 135–149.

Gross, Z. and Stevick, E. D. 2010. Holocaust education—international perspectives: challenges, opportunities and research. *Prospects*, Vol. 40, pp 17–33.

Hondius, D. (forthcoming). Education by eyewitness: examining the history and future of direct encounters with Holocaust survivors and resistance fighters. Z. Gross and E.D. Stevick (eds), *Holocaust Education in the 21st Century: Teaching the Shoah in Practice, Policy and Curriculum*.

Jennings, L. B. 2010. Challenges and possibilities of Holocaust education and critical citizenship: an ethnographic study of a fifth-grade bilingual class revisited. *Prospects*, Vol. 40, pp 35–56.

Kelso, M. 2013. 'And Roma were victims, too.' The Romani genocide and Holocaust education in Romania. *Intercultural Education*, Vol. 24*(1–2)*, pp 61–78.

Macgilchrist, F. and Christophe, B. 2011. Translating globalization theories into educational research: thoughts on recents shifts in Holocaust Education. *Discourse: Studies in the Cultural politics of Education* Vol 32 (1), pp 145–158.

MacIsaac, D. 1996. *The critical theory of Jurgen Habermas*. Retrieved from: http:// physicsed. buffalostate.edu/danowner/habcritthy.html

Michaels, D. L. 2013. Holocaust education in the 'black hole of Europe': Slovakia's identity politics and history textbooks pre- and post-1989. *Intercultural Education*, Vol. 24(1–2), pp 19–40.

Polak, K. 2013. Teaching about the genocide of the Roma and Sinti during the Holocaust: chances and challenges in Europe today. *Intercultural Education*, Vol. 24 (1–02), pp 79–92.

Proske, M. 2012. 'Why do we always have to Say we're sorry?' *European Education*, Vol. 44(3), pp 39–66.

Rutland, S. D. 2010. Creating effective Holocaust education programmes for government schools with large Muslim populations in Sydney. *Prospects*, Vol. 40, pp 75–91.

Schweber, S. 2011. Holocaust education. H. Miller et al. (eds.), *International Handbook of Jewish Education*, pp. 461–478.

Short, G. 2013. Reluctant learners? Muslim youth confront the Holocaust. *Intercultural Education*, Vol. 24(*1–2*), pp 121–132.

Snyder, T. 2009. The Holocaust: The ignored reality. New York Review of Books, Vol. 56(12).

Stevick, E. D. 2007. The Politics of the Holocaust in Estonia: historical memory and social divisions in Estonian education, pp. 217–244. Stevick, E. D. and B. A. U. Levinson (eds), *Reimagining Civic Education: How Diverse Societies Form Democratic Citizens*, Rowman and Littlefield.

Stevick, E. D. 2008. Foreign influence and economic insecurity in international partnerships for civic education: the case of Estonia. E.D. Stevick & B.A.U. Levinson (eds), *Advancing Democracy through Education? U.S. Influence Abroad and Domestic Practices,* Information Age, 2008, pp 101-132.

Stevick, E. D. 2009. Overlapping democracies, Europe's democratic deficit and national education policy: Estonia's school leaders as heirs to a Soviet legacy or as agents of democracy? *European Education*, Vol. 41(3), pp 42–59.

Stevick, E. D. 2010. Education policy as normative discourse and negotiated meanings: engaging the holocaust. *Prospects*, Vol. 40, pp 239–256.

Stevick, E. D. 2011. Finessing foreign pressure in education policy through deliberate policy failure: Soviet legacy, foreign prescriptions, and democratic accountability in Estonia. W. J. Jacob, J. and J. Hawkins (eds), *Policy debates in comparative, international and development education,*. New York, Palgrave, pp175-197

Stevick, E.D. 2013. Dialogue and transformation in Holocaust education? Reweaving the tapestry of experience, research and practice. *Tertium Comparationis Journal für International und Interkulturell Vergleichende Erziehungswissenschaft, Vol. 19, No. 1, pp. 10-20.*

Stevick, E. D. and Gross, Z. 2010. Epistemology and Holocaust education: history, memory and the politics of knowledge. *Prospects*, Vol. 40, pp 189–200.

Stevick, E.D. and Michaels, D. 2012. The continuing struggle over the meanings of the Shoah in Europe: culture, agency, and the appropriation of Holocaust education. *European Education*, Vol.44(3), pp 3–12.

Stevick, E. D. and Michaels, D. L. 2013. Empirical and normative foundations of Holocaust education: bringing research and advocacy into dialogue. *Intercultural Education*, Vol. 24(*1–2*), pp 1–18.

van Iterson, S. and Nenadović, M. 2013. The danger of not facing history: exploring the link between education about the past and present-day antisemitism and racism in Hungary. *Intercultural Education*, Vol. 24(1–2), pp 93–102.

The Holocaust in textbooks: from a European to a global event

Falk Pingel

The classroom is a meeting point of various societal interests that strive to influence content and methodology of the teaching process. Three main spheres of influence can be differentiated: educational policy, research and pedagogy:

Educational policy is determined by the political authorities whose agendas are represented through state-commissioned curricula. These curricula, in turn, decide why something should be taught and, in the case of history, be remembered. The political framework of an education system is strongly shaped by national traditions. The curriculum reflects the extent of control exerted by the educational authorities of a society (open/closed, prescriptive/discursive curriculum).

Subject-oriented research provides the realm of knowledge, theoretical models and explanatory sets that developers of curricula and authors of textbook have to take into account. Content and methodology should be in accordance with research findings. However, research findings are often controversial. Furthermore, they do not offer clear criteria for the selection of specific content that should be taught. Although research is based on international standards, research approaches can be biased, in particular when sensitive issues related to collective identity patterns are at stake. Research can be misused to justify political aims; in this case, research often neglects international comparative aspects, particularly in history and civics.

Pedagogy sets limits as to what can be taught to pupils of a certain age group in a limited period of time. It defines what is comprehensible to students in terms of their intellectual capacity and what is digestible for them. This takes into account that their value system and ability to form moral judgments is still developing. The pedagogical framework of a classroom is strongly shaped by national or even regional conditions and often depends on various factors (i.e. number of students per classroom, frontal teaching versus student-centred teaching, fact-oriented memorization versus development of critical thinking, chronological versus thematic approach).

The dominance of a nation-centred approach

Up until now, in most countries of the world, history is essentially taught as history of nations rather than as 'history of humankind'.[23] As a rule, national history forms the core of the curriculum and makes up the largest part of schoolbook contents. Relevance to one's own national history primarily guides international content.

Therefore, negotiating the position of teaching the Holocaust in a history or civics curriculum has always to take into account how the topic is related to sensitive issues of national pride and official politics of remembrance, and how the topic can be embedded into particular national traditions or streams of historiography and pedagogy.[24] During the post-war decades, the Holocaust was regarded as but one aspect of the crimes and events during the Second World War; there was hardly any reason for examining the specific didactic challenges the teaching of the topic poses. They only become obvious when the topic is no longer regarded as an annex to the war but taught 'in its own right'.

Until the turn of the century, the position of the Holocaust in the curriculum was heavily dependent on the particular national political and pedagogical traditions of teaching history. This context-dependency has resulted in different teaching objectives and different forms of teaching and learning about the Holocaust.

In most countries of the perpetrators and victims, the Holocaust has been part of the still prevailing chronological approach to history which ranges from ancient times to the present.

Regarding Germany as the country of the perpetrators, one crucial interpretative issue has been if and how the Holocaust can be integrated into the continuity of German history. The remembrance of crimes committed by one's own nation or state poses a severe challenge: how can the reference to a 'negative past' be incorporated into a 'positive' historical consciousness? Or is this an impossible task altogether?

---

23 I draw on the following in F. Pingel (2001) Teaching the Holocaust in its own right – a reassessment of current pedagogical orientations,: *Beiträge zur historischen Sozialkunde, Special Issue 2001: Teaching the Holocaust and National Socialism*, pp. 3-10 (German ed. in: *Holocaust und Nationalsozialismus*, E. Fuchs, F. Pingel andV. Radkau (eds), Wien: Studienverlag, 2002, pp. 11-23) and F. Pingel (2006) From evasion to a crucial tool of moral and political education: teaching national socialism and the Holocaust in Germany, *What Shall We Tell the Children? International Perspectives on School History Textbooks*, S. J. Foster andK. A. Crawford (eds), Greenwich, Conn. Information Age Publishing, pp. 131 153.

24 Bertrand Lécureur (2012) *Enseigner le nazisme et la Shoah. Une étude comparée des manuels scolaires en Europe*, Göttingen, V&R Unipress.

Does the remembrance of disgraceful collective deeds of such an enormous scale as the attempted annihilation of a whole people leave us with desperation and helplessness, unable to construct a consistent view of what is apparently 'our' past?[25] The questions of why and how the Nazi dictatorship developed into a genocidal system is still a pressing issue for young Germans. It would not be appropriate to disassociate the Holocaust from the chronological view on German history and treat it under a separate systematic topic such as 'violation of human rights'. A recent analysis of textbooks found that, consequently, human rights issues are not mentioned explicitly in German textbooks when addressing the Holocaust.[26] However, this analysis does not consider the fact that the whole Nazi system is presented as a continuous process of depriving people of their democratic and basic rights. In the past, German textbook authors strove to show to the students the step-by-step conversion of the German state institutions from an already shaken democracy to a violent dictatorial system in order to explain how the Holocaust and other mass crimes could happen. One could say that understanding the unfolding of the dictatorship was regarded as more important than confrontation and empathy with its victims.

Also in countries that were occupied by Germany, the Holocaust was addressed within the context of national history for a long time. However, since the Jews represented only a minority of the population, and they did not belong to the nucleus of the nation, their persecution was excluded from a national remembrance that focused on heroism, resistance and the suffering of the majority population.

Trends to demythologize national history, which had arisen since the 1970s and gained further ground after the collapse of the Soviet system, opened up debates on the interactions between the majority population and minorities during Nazi occupation. These debates questioned the dominance of the paradigm of resistance, and placed more emphasis on collaboration, indifference and apathy, and suffering. Through questioning the traditional national paradigm, a more humane narrative evolved, dealing with the moral challenges a dictatorial system poses to its people.

---

25 The current director of the Buchenwald concentration camp memorial, Volkhard Knigge (2001), has coined the term 'negative past'. Memorization of a negative past refers to the 'reflection on committed crimes ... as opposed to the comprehension of suffered crimes.' See also R. Koselleck, 2002, Formen und Traditionen des negativen Gedächtnisses, *Verbrechen erinnern. Die Auseinandersetzung mit Holocaust und Völkermord*. V. Knigge and N. Frei (eds), München, C. H. Beck, pp. 21–32.

26 P. Bromley andS. Garnett Russell, 2010, The Holocaust as history and human rights: a cross-national analysis of Holocaust education in social science textbooks, 1970-2008, *Prospects* Vol 40, , pp. 153-173.

These developments made the curricula more responsive to allotting more space to and placing more emphasis on the persecution and suffering of the Jews as one of the most significant events of the Second World War. The image of the war itself changed as well. The presentation of military events has become less important, while the impact of the war on the people – soldiers as well as civilians – has become a focus using biographical accounts, illustrations, etc.

However, with the breakdown of the Soviet system, competing memories emerged, putting mass crimes committed by communist states on a par with the Holocaust. These developments have led to contradictory results. On the one hand, they contribute to forming an overarching concept of state-committed mass crimes against humanity that shaped the twentieth century. On the other hand, they tend to stir debates about the significance of these crimes for the respective national narratives and by that obscuring the human dimension and stressing political aspects instead. In some Eastern European countries, textbooks have almost neglected the topic of the Holocaust well into the twenty-first century, because the fate of the Jews did not become a focal point of public historical debates that centred on competing memories within the majority population instead. The debates on the place of the Holocaust in one's own national narrative are not over yet. In almost all countries that were directly affected by the Holocaust, a more politically driven narrative competes with a human rights-oriented representation. At best, both approaches complement each other; in the worst case, the one tends to de-legitimize the other.

Conceptualizing the Holocaust as a universal paradigm: achievements and pitfalls

International trials, increasing thematic research, and the implementation of transitional justice in post-conflict areas after the Holocaust have further developed the understanding of 'crimes against humanity' and 'genocide' using the Holocaust as the prime example. This almost world-wide development also had an impact on the educational sector of countries that were not affected by the Holocaust. Many of these countries have integrated the Holocaust in their curricula and textbooks over the last twenty years. Here, persecution and annihilation of the Jews under National Socialism are dealt with because they represent a monstrous event of universal significance. From this perspective two potentially conflicting interpretations arise:

> The Holocaust represents a singular, incomparable event in world history that ought to be treated precisely for its unique dimension;

> An understanding of the Holocaust is possible solely by way of comparison with other examples of genocide. It is perhaps the most atrocious, yet only one amongst several examples of the fact that even in the modern world inhumanity can take the upper hand.

In both cases, the Holocaust is a paradigmatic event. The paradigmatic approach has far-reaching didactical implications; not all of them are without risk for the teaching process.

An international or even global approach to history shows more clearly than a nation-centred narrative that certain historical events have different meanings in different national contexts, whereas others seem to have a global significance beyond particular national narratives. Reflecting on the competition between as well as the sharing of memories, authors of history textbooks in Western Europe pay increasing attention to commemoration procedures and politics of remembrance to enable students to understand the processes of shifting memories, which are not fixed through the historic events but influenced by interests people have in history. The German-French history textbook documents this in an exemplary way; it presents pictures of Holocaust memorial sites in different parts of the world, posing the question to students why, on the one hand, the Holocaust is being remembered at all these places, and why, on the other hand, the size, the design and the function of the memorial places differ.[27]

In general, a presentation of the Holocaust which de-contextualizes it from its concrete historical background omits/elides a detailed description of the Nazis' rise to power and the establishment of their system of domination and suppression.[28] The connection of the Holocaust to German history remains somewhat ambiguous in this approach. Taking into account the limited teaching time designated for addressing the murder and persecution of Jews under National Socialist rule, curricula tend to concentrate on the worst phases of this history and have little opportunity to deal with the various steps from discrimination and exclusion to extermination. Explanations remain on a more general level, such as the influence of racism and antisemitism. These streams of thought are simply identified with German history, or they represent more general European trends. But nevertheless the relation of

---

27 *Histoire/Geschichte. L'Europe et le monde depuis 1945/Europa und die Welt seit 1945* (2006). G. le Quintrec and P. Geiss (eds), Paris, Nathan, Stuttgart, Klett, pp. 36-37.

28 Dan Diner,2007, *Gegenläufige Gedächtnisse*. Über Geltung und Wirkung des Holocaust. Göttingen, Vandenhoeck & Ruprecht. Critical comment on the separation of the Holocaust from the Second War context in public commemoration.

the Holocaust to German national history becomes almost accidental. Astonishingly, as time passes since the Second World War and Europe becomes increasingly integrated, the Holocaust stands also in some English textbooks as an example for the possibility of genocide in the whole modern world, rather than a specific part of German history. This is in stark contrast to the traditional representation of the Holocaust in the countries of perpetrators and victims, where the interrelatedness of the Holocaust and the respective national narrative has often posed the most crucial issue.

A shortcoming of de-contextualization of the Holocaust is that it excludes the wide range of (Nazi) racist persecution that was directed, amongst others, also against the Sinti and Roma and people with disabilities. Although textbook authors take the Holocaust as *pars pro toto*, it often remains the only case of genocide that is taught in detail, so that the totality and diversity of the racist threat is never really addressed. An analysis of US textbooks has found that some of the textbooks mention only Jews as victims of Nazi racism.[29]

Although it seems at first glance that no direct relation may exist between the national narrative of history and the Holocaust narrative, the integration of the latter into the curriculum can nevertheless serve as justification for one's own national perspective. In their research project, Patricia Bromley and Susan Garnett-Russell state that Tunisian textbooks use the Holocaust to denounce the low moral standards of Western European countries that collaborated with the Nazis. They question the value of Western human rights education in the light of the Holocaust and colonialism. Reference to the Holocaust is meant to weaken the centrality of Western concepts of morality and to strengthen the legacy of Western colonialism.

In a more subtle way, some groups in South Africa, where Holocaust education has been adopted into the national curriculum, welcome this education as a justification for the fight against the racist apartheid system. On the one hand, it puts the South African case into a wider international or even global context; on the other hand, it may hinder a thorough, critical and painful inquiry of crimes committed in the fight against apartheid. Some countries still reject the inclusion of the Holocaust into their curricula; in this case, politically endorsed strategies of active denial are often at

---

29   David Lindquist, 2009, The Coverage of the Holocaust in high school history textbooks, *Social Education*, Vol. 73(6), pp. 298-304

work (like in some countries of the Middle East).[30] However, sometimes it is also felt that the Holocaust is alien to one's own history and takes students' minds off one's own traumatization in recent history. The dissemination of Holocaust education is interpreted as a new kind of cultural hegemony of Western experience.

In contrast to this, we find in some Croatian, Serbian and Bosnian textbooks an almost inflationary use of the term genocide, which is applied also to state-committed killings by the enemy that occurred in early modern history or the Middle Ages. In this way, it is insinuated that the enemy has shown a genocidal behaviour over centuries.[31]

Comparative approaches if not carefully performed tend to simplify matters. Some Chinese textbooks show pictures of the Holocaust when dealing with the massacre of Nanjing committed by Japanese troops during the Second World War. The message is clear: the acts of the Japanese troops represent a 'Holocaust' or 'genocide'. In contrast, Japanese textbooks make a clear distinction between the European war on one hand where genocide, mass deportation and slave labour were carried out and became a symbol for inhuman warfare, and, on the other hand, individual brutal acts of the Japanese army necessitated by the enemy's behaviour , which do not fit into the Holocaust paradigm.[32] In these cases, the Holocaust – or the term 'genocide' – is seen as an acknowledged universal symbol that is used in order to present one's own history more convincingly. Here, the history curriculum provides us with examples of the 'container function'[33] the globalization of the Holocaust may produce.

Despite the pitfalls and shortcomings a universal concept of the Holocaust may generate, the globalization process apparently stimulates a tendency to de-nationalize methodology and content of school curricula.

30 G. Achcar , 2010, *The Arabs and the Holocaust: the Arab-Israeli war of narratives*, Trans. G. M. Goshgarian, London,Saqi; G. Nordbruch,2002, *Narrating Palestinian Nationalism. A study of the new Palestinian textbooks*, Washington, The Middle East Media Research Institute (MEMRI).

31 F. Pingel, 2004 „*Sicher ist, dass...der Völkermord nicht mit Hitler begann und leider auch nicht mit ihm endet.' Das Thema „Völkermord' als Gegenstand von Unterricht und Schulbuch*, Genozide und staatliche Gewaltverbrechen im 20. Jahrhundert. V. Radkau,E. Fuchs andT. Lutz (eds), Wien, Studienverlag

32 J-B. Shin, 2012, *The Second World War in World History Textbooks of Korea, China and Japan. In History Education and Reconciliation – comparative perspectives on East Asia*. U-S. Han, Takahiro K.,Biao Y.,and F. Pingel (eds), Frankfurt/M: Peter Lang, pp. 119-134.

33 D. Levy andN. Sznaider, 2005, *The Holocaust and Memory in the Global Age*. Transl. A. Oksiloff, Philadelphia, Temple University Press

Towards a human rights-based teaching approach?

In the past, teaching programmes and textbooks reflected a country's set of values, serving as a fixed corpus of knowledge and a range of officially recognized behavioural attitudes that were to be inculcated in pupils' minds. Recent research has proved that the process of globalization has intensified long-term trends of harmonizing methodological requirements, of defining common basic knowledge and propagating general values. John Meyer and his research team see the national education systems embedded in a world society that challenges narrow national concepts of what should be known and transmitted from one generation to the next.[34]

According to Meyer, this global trend leads to a growing need to reorganize the conception of national societies and states around notions of being part of a global collective. This world-wide process undermines isolated national educational structures. John Meyer adds to this: 'In the emergent world curriculum older models of closed and conflicting national states, the primordial national identities and the subordination of individuals to these states are all greatly weakened....The individual human person...[has to be] seen as a member of human society as a whole rather than principally as the citizen of a nation-state.'[35]

The textbook analysis by Bromley and Russell seems to corroborate this trend regarding the presentation of the Holocaust in textbooks. According to their findings, 'the nature of the discussion' shifts 'from a historical event to a violation of human rights or crimes against humanity'. Textbooks of countries 'more connected to world society' and emphasizing 'human rights issue, diversity in society and a depiction of international, rather than national, society are more likely to discuss the Holocaust.' The aim is to learn about global trends and to sensitize students to injustice, the violation of human rights, etc. Bromley and Russell connect their findings expressly with neo-institutional theories supporting the view 'that the social and cultural realms of the contemporary world are increasingly globalized and the notions of human rights are a central feature of world society.'[36]

---

34 A. Benavot andC. Braslavsky (eds.), 2006, *School Knowledge in Comparative and Historical Perspective. Changing Curricula in Primary and Secondary Education*. Hong Kong: Comparative Education Research Center/The University of Hong Kong, Springer.

35 J. Meyer, 2006, *World Models, National Curricula, and the Centrality of the Individual*, Benavot andBraslavsky (eds), p. 271.

36 Bromley andRussell, p. 153.

As we have already seen, events with a global significance are running the risk of becoming a mere vehicle for a variety of teaching objectives, and of losing the specific meaning they had for the actual people who were affected by them. In other words: Globalization has to be localized and personalized in order to transmit a didactical message that makes the global significance of the event applicable to students' views and experiences. The diary of Anne Frank has become such an individual document with a global message that can be found in history textbooks world-wide. It is so persuasive because it encapsulates both the desperate plight of the persecuted with no escape from death in the end, and the search for alternative options to keep hope and social, human behaviour alive as long as possible.

To deepen students' understanding of the real situation confronting perpetrators as well as victims, a variety of teaching programmes have been developed that strive to confront students with the problem of choice under constraints. Teaching materials with a general human rights approach that addresses issues of behavioural attitudes and moral choices demand the students' personal moral and emotional involvement. Such teaching requires a classroom situation that allows for an open debate and needs teachers who are able to handle emotional statements. Teachers often use role play and simulation – pedagogical tools that are not easily applicable in the normal classroom situation. All the more so, it is important that the teaching material offers approaches/sources that allow individualizing victims as well as perpetrators. Often, the teaching focuses on the victims in order to arouse empathy and understanding. As important as this may be, it has little value if the reasons and motivations of the perpetrators are not addressed also. Furthermore, the dichotomy of victim and perpetrator should be dissolved as this dichotomy transmits too simple a model of dictatorship in modern mass society. Research offers more sophisticated models that can easily be understood by students; Raul Hilberg's triad of perpetrators, victims, and bystanders can be differentiated further.[37] The social and ideological background of perpetrators has triggered a controversial academic debate. The explanatory models range from the concept of 'ordinary men' to 'willing executioners'.[38] Because antisemitism is mentioned in most studies as one of the driving forces that led to the Holocaust, it is important to discuss the role of ideology and propaganda in preparing people for participating actively in or simply tolerating acts of genocide. In spite of

37   R. Hilberg,1993, *Perpetrators, Victims, Bystanders. The Jewish Catastrophe 1933-1945*, New York, Harper Perennial.

38   C. Browning,1992, *Ordinary Men: Reserve Police Battalion 101 and the Final Solution in Poland*, New York, HarperCollins; D. Goldhagen,1996, *Hitler's Willing Executioners: Ordinary Germans and The Holocaust*, New York, Alfred A. Knopf

the many sources available which deal with stories of perpetrators, the teaching material still tends to transmit a simplified image of perpetrators concentrating on leading figures like Hitler and Himmler or members of the SS.

Concentrating on persecution and suffering always bears the danger of 'victimization', i.e. viewing the Jews solely as victims of persecution. This can be particularly the case when the Holocaust is the only Jewish topic in history classes. Precisely because Jewish history rarely occupies a central spot in national traditions and is limited to the history of discrimination and persecution, the impression young people get about 'the Jews' remains deficient.

Since the human rights approach takes the Holocaust as a paradigm for genocide, it is open for comparison with other instances of genocide. To deal first with a more remote example (in time and space) may help educators and students to address mass crimes committed in one's own country. However, it is important not to simplify matters and equate different cases. A comparative approach should enable students to make distinctions and identify similarities as well as differences. This is easily said; it is, however, more difficult to make comparisons in the classroom. Often, students are so captured by the tremendous horror of the Holocaust and have so many questions in order to understand why it could happen that they are not able to treat another example with the same attention, engagement and accuracy. The transfer of knowledge remains one of the most ambitious learning objectives of a universal approach to the teaching of the Holocaust.

At the same time, we must also take into account that pupils in ethnically mixed societies may refer to different examples of historic trauma that are closer to them than the Holocaust. Teachers should not dismiss such contributions as unwelcome interference and refer to the singularity of the Holocaust. Students are scarcely interested in academic debates about the 'singularity' of the Holocaust. They conceive history very much from a perspective that is shaped by the present. This perspective may lead them to diverse reactions concerning an historical event such as the Holocaust. They may reject it or disassociate themselves from it because it represents mere 'history'. Or, just the opposite, they feel so much attached to it they are not able to distance themselves from it and to analyse it rationally as a historical event that differs from their life.

Summing up

If we deal with the increasing global significance of the Holocaust in the development of history curricula and history teaching, it is important to reflect first on the close relationship between the history of the Holocaust and the national master narratives of different societies, which are often loaded with conflicts. Secondly, we have to consider the pitfalls or even misuse of the Holocaust as a global symbol apart from the concrete historic context in which it happened. Thirdly, and in contrast to these problematic points, research has shown that the prevailing paradigm of national history is increasingly questioned by an emerging global, human rights-oriented model. This development supports trends to teach the history of the Holocaust as a paradigmatic event on a global level. Finally, we have to take into account didactical challenges that the global model poses.

In short, applying the global model in any concrete case (1) requires a careful examination of the closeness of the Holocaust to individual national narratives, (2) should offer tools for the individualization of perpetrators, bystanders and victims, (3) should open perspectives for making comparisons without trivializing or equating historical events and present experiences, and (4) requires an open classroom situation that is not focused on frontal teaching.

Historic Sites as a framework for education

Matthias Heyl

Sites of former atrocities, mass crimes or human-induced disasters – however you call what happened there – can serve as an important source in education. It is different to learn about the Holocaust in a classroom than to stand in front of the crematoria of Auschwitz. It is necessary to teach about the Holocaust in the classroom, but it seems to be a different experience to be confronted with the place where the events happened, where history took place.

What information can a historic site give? Usually, it does not speak for itself. Especially years after the events, with all the changes that have happened since, the remnants of the past – buildings, walls, fences, paths – have lost their former functions, and need to be explained. These traces can be used as sources with a kind of 'forensic' approach. We need narratives and narrators to be able to read them and to tell the stories, and we need other means of information, to make the invisible visible, to be able to read the place and understand it as a source and resource for interpretation.

But there are limits, as Jorge Semprun, survivor of the Buchenwald concentration camp, learned already on 13 April 1945, only two days after American troops had liberated the camp. Semprun tried to guide a group of women around the camp who were absolutely not prepared for what they would be confronted with, as Semprun was not prepared to tell them. [39] The women, laughing and giggling in the beginning, were expecting something horrific and horrifying, an emotional sensation, somehow, without really having in mind what this would mean to them, and to their guide, a survivor himself. Semprun tried to impress the women with his knowledge as a former inmate of the camp, but already two days after the liberation, the place had changed: 'The big square where they had the roll call was deserted beneath the spring sun, and I stopped, my heart beating. I had never seen it empty before, I must admit; I hadn't ever really seen it. I hadn't really seen it before, not what you call seeing.'[40] He found that the place was not perceivable as the place it had been until two days before. When one of the women stated that it does not look too bad, Jorge Semprun decided to show them a few things. 'I take the girls into the crematorium, by the small door, the one leading directly to the cellar. They've just realized it's not a kitchen, and they suddenly fall silent. I show them the hooks from which the men were hung, for the crematorium cellar also served as a torture chamber. I show them the blackjacks and the clubs, which are still there. I explain to them what they were used for. I show them the lifts which used to take the corpses to the second story, to directly in front of the ovens. We go up to the second floor and I show them the ovens. The poor girls are speechless. They follow me, and I show them the row of electric ovens and the half-charred corpses which are still inside. I hardly speak to them, merely saying: "Here you are, look there." It is essential for them to see, to try to imagine. They say nothing, perhaps they are imagining.' [41] In front of a four-metre high mountain of corpses, he felt it was 'nonsense', trying to explain it that way. His audience had already left, except for one woman. ' "Why did you do that?" she says.

---

39   J. Semprun,1990, *The long voyage*, New York, p. 70ff.

40   Ibid, p. 70.

41   Ibid, p. 74.

"It was stupid," I admit. "But why?" "You wanted to visit the place," I reply. "I'd like to see more."' [42]

To the survivors, the sites are places that bring back their own memories of what happened there. To all other visitors, they are places that evoke stories, ideas and fantasies, but they come from narratives, books, films and other media, not from their own experience. Sometimes, their expectations are even misleading. Usually, when people are entering a memorial site of a former German concentration camp, they have images in mind, like those of masses of corpses, barracks, the ovens from the crematoria or a gas chamber, and they are expecting to see some pieces of evidence of what happened there. They are longing to see the iconic images on the spot itself. At Ravensbrück Memorial, the historic site of the central German women's concentration camp, I learned over the last ten years I have been working there how powerful these images are that people bring with them.

We developed a programme for students, in which they start their visit to Ravensbrück as sort of 'explorers'. We invite them to walk along the grounds of the memorial site for one hour, and they can go wherever they want, as long they respect the limiting signs, walls, fences, barriers and boundaries. Afterward, we get together again and ask them to show us the places they are most interested in. With this approach we change the setting of a guided tour: they are guiding us to the places they want to know more about, and we encourage them to ask their questions, instead of answering questions we are never asked. With this methodological approach we usually manage to get to all places we find relevant in our 'ordinary' guided tours. The students start asking ('What was this building?') and we answer ('The disinfection.'), which raises new questions ('What does "disinfection" mean?'), and then we are in the midst of the story, but they have asked for the information themselves.

With a second programme, derived from this active method, the students are asked to take photos of the places they are interested in. They can use their own cameras, or the ones we provide for them. The cameras need to be compatible with our computer, so that we can transfer the photos to our projector. In a classroom, we let the students see their photos and ask their questions. We learned a lot in this programme about the stereotypes in perceiving the place. Usually, the photos are quite similar to those of other groups and individuals. You can easily see the iconic view of a former concentration camp: the photos show walls with remnants of the electric barbed wire, buildings like the prison with its cells, the crematorium with its

---

42   Ibid, p. 76.

ovens and chimney, or artefacts and art representing the terror, suffering or solidarity among the prisoners. Sometimes you can clearly see some sort of 'attraction' for evil, or attempts to present a picture of the inner emotional sensations people have been looking for. Sometimes, we show a group the photos of a different group, so they start to think and ask why the photos are so similar.

This little detour into pedagogy shows clearly what we educators in Ravensbrück learned through these new methods: people are entering the historic sites already with a variety of powerful images and expectations in mind. We have to deal with these pre-existing images; for example, during a guided tour, passing by a building with a chimney that was not the crematorium, we need to address this simple fact. The visitors often project their expectations on the site, which can be misleading enough.

Using the site as a source requires us to be as concrete as possible. Let me lay out another example from Ravensbrück. While walking on the street that led from the train station to the concentration camp, we talk about the transports, about the connection between the town and the camp, and we derive a solid perspective of the relations of victims, perpetrators and **bystanders**, from what the visitors can see today: a street made from small cobblestones. At the same point, we need to tell that this street was a result of slave labour, and we can speak about the working conditions of the inmates of the camp. We can add narratives like that of a butcher's son, who delivered meat to the concentration camp from time to time, as a 16-, 17-year-old boy. The meat was not for the prisoners, but for the SS men. Strangely enough, despite the fact that most of the SS men were not allowed to enter the inner part of the camp (here, inside, it was female guards who took over the rule over the prisoners, following the orders of the male SS administrators), their canteen was inside, close to the gate. In the 1990s, the butcher's son told the story that whenever he was delivering the meat to the camp, he felt confirmed in his perception of the camp: this was a camp for 'criminals', 'anti-socials', 'enemies of the Reich', 'sub-humans' – people 'unworthy to live'. When he looked at the prisoners, he felt a great distance from them, and even a kind of disgust. They looked different from 'ordinary women'. The shape of their body was different, some of them with shaved heads, all of them with weakened bodies (under conditions of hard slave labour and permanent malnutrition), often smelling awful (because of the hygienic situation in the camp and all kinds of diseases). Thus, he felt confirmed with what he had heard before, often enough, from his parents, peers and teachers: Ravensbrück was a concentration camp where all these dangerous people were treated the way they deserved to be treated. But once, when he entered the camp, he saw something that caused an emotional sensation in him, and this contradicted his perception completely. A new transport had arrived in the camp, shortly before he entered it. The women were already registered, without their belongings, and they waited to be sent into the shower building. Thus they were undressed, but they still had their hair. In my interpretation, it may have been a sexual sensation as well for the 16- or 17-year old boy, but what he said about it in the 1990s was at this very moment he felt the place was a place of crime – the women waiting for the shower, standing there, naked, looked like 'ordinary women', the way women looked in 'normal' life. Somehow, he said, he felt the camp changed ordinary women within hours and days into human beings fitting into the national-socialist stereotype of 'sub-humans'. This story, in an educational setting, can lead into a discussion on Nazi ideology and its impact on 'ordinary Germans', who, in their majority, supported and shared it. Not everybody was aware that the SS had established this ideology in such a radical way in real life, by using their total power to define who was to live and who was to die. And they did not only decide, they also killed according to their own rules and definitions.

The street from the train station to the camp leads directly through the former SS housing area, to the camp gate. On the right side, you can see the former houses of the female guards. On the left, there are the former *Führerhäuser*, family houses for the high-ranking SS officers. Visitors often feel quite puzzled when they learn that the SS officers lived in these houses together with their families, wives and children. This offers another educational opportunity to address the perpetrators' perception of what they were doing, and to contextualize it in the framework of widespread Nazi *Volksgemeinschafts* ideology: They did not perceive their actions as crimes, but as fulfilling a difficult and important 'task' for *Führer, Volk und Vaterland* (the leader, the people and the country). In their perspective, their actions were not immoral, but an expression of a so-called 'higher moral', from which by definition parts of humankind had to be excluded.

These examples show how the focus on specific places can be used to derive questions and issues about the historic site in general. To achieve these educational goals, it is essential to work with knowledgeable and educationally skilled professionals. They need to know the place and its stories, and they should be able to tell them. To tell the story on the spot itself, where 'it' happened is different from all classroom activities. This does not mean that we could replace classroom activities with a visit to a site of former mass crimes. The classroom should be the space for a good preparation of a field trip. The students should be able to see a place like Ravensbrück in its context. The more they know before visiting such a place, the more they are able to connect their knowledge of the context with the specific questions the place raises. And the classroom offers the necessary space for follow-up activities, which should enable the students to make connections between the historical event and current issues. For the crimes of the past raise some very urgent current questions. Of course, places of human suffering are very much connected with the desire to show respect for and empathy with the victims. But we need also to find out what made the perpetrators tick. How could ordinary human beings become perpetrators? And why and how did a large number of bystanders become perpetrators? These are urgent and current questions not only for a retrospective view, but also for the present and for the future: whenever we say 'Never again!' we should be aware of the risk of repetition in the future by bystanders and perpetrators.

A very challenging part of the educational work at historic sites of mass crimes is confronting the history of memorialization and commemoration after the liberation. In a place like Ravensbrück, large parts of the former camp area were used by the Soviet Army as a military camp, from the liberation in 1945 to the early 1990s. Thus a huge part of the former camp was not accessible to visitors, since the memorial's opening in 1959. Even today, some sections are still not accessible to the public because of still-dangerous leftovers from the 'Soviet' period. And the memorial itself, situated in former East Germany, had its own problem with lack of knowledge, because its main function in East Germany was to give support to the founding myth of the state, by portraying Ravensbrück as a place of heroic resistance under the leadership of the communists. Therefore, the memorial was not too interested in the stories of the vast majority of non-communist women and men who were imprisoned in Ravensbrück. Only since the 1990s has broader and deeper research been done on Ravensbrück's complex story. In April 2013, the first exhibition based on this research opened to the public. This is probably one of the reasons why using the site as a source for information has become so extraordinarily important here. It has helped us to distinguish between telling the story in a deductive way, starting with the actual site in front of visitors' eyes, and telling it in an inductive way, in which you project the story on the site, as museum exhibitions usually do. What we try to achieve is a balanced way of telling the story, so that the visitors start thinking and raising questions themselves. And real places, instead of safe surroundings far from where history happened, help to raise different questions.

Shedding light on the invisible: towards a gender-sensitive education at memorial sites

Angelika Meyer

Translated from German

'We tell ourselves stories in order to live. And these stories keep changing'[43]

In a symposium on the subject of 'Post-war German literature and the Holocaust' in 1997, the literary scholar Ruth Klüger spoke in her lecture on Alfred Andersch about her own experience in the Auschwitz extermination camp. In it, she referred to what was for her the specifically female experience of imprisonment. These remarks aroused criticism from one participant who had also been a prisoner in Auschwitz, to the effect that the criminals did not distinguish between male or female victims. The aim was to exterminate the Jews, irrespective of their sex, origin or social standing. But according to Kluger, victims were indeed separated and differentiated. This situation exemplifies a new debate which began in the 1990s. Since then, more and more publications have appeared, essentially in the sphere of feminist research, offering interpretations of so-called female identity in relation to the Holocaust which are specifically theoretical and methodological in their approach. These include publications by Dalia Ofer and Lenore L. Weitzman, *Women in the Holocaust,*[44] Carol Rittner and John Roth , *Different Voices: Women and the Holocaust*[45] and Myrna Goldenberg. *Memoirs of Auschwitz Survivors. The Burden of Gender.*[46] In the historiography of women in National Socialism and the Holocaust, there have been more and more gender-based approaches over the years, in which

---

43 Quote from J. Didion, 2012, *Annika Reich: 34 Meter über dem Meer*, Munich, p.5.

44 D. Ofer and L. L. Weitzman, 1998, *Women in the Holocaust*, New Haven.

45 C. Rittner and J. Roth, 1998, *Different Voices: Women and the Holocaust,* Minnesota.

46 M. Goldenberg. Memoirs of Auschwitz survivors. The burden of gender, 1998, D. Ofer and L. L. Weitzman (eds) *Women in the Holocaust*, New Haven. For an overview of the development of feminist Holocaust research, see J. Liebman Jacobs, 2004, Women, genocide, and memory. The ethics of feminist ethnography in Holocaust research, in *Gender & Society*, Vol. 18 No. 2, pp. 223-238.

women are no longer defined as a homogeneous and identifiable group. The role of female perpetrators, forms of gender-based remembrance[47] and, for example, the roles played by the body, race and sexuality in National Socialism[48] were key issues. Gender normativity and thus the accompanying power structures were frequently scrutinized.

In historical and civic education at the sites of National Socialist crimes, gender-based approaches are becoming increasingly incorporated, but the results are still rarely published and can only partly be found in teaching methods. There is plenty of research on the meaning and purpose of education at memorial sites, but so far there have been hardly any empirically valid results about the recipients, or the visitors to the memorial sites.[49] The category of gender has long since maintained its place in the methodology of the historiography, yet the relationship between teaching about the past and gender has only dimly appeared in practice in historical and civic education.[50]

Gender in historical and civic education at memorial sites

Gender plays a powerful role as a category in human life. The category of sex, which distinguishes male and female, acts as a means of social regulation and the establishment of power structures. The term 'gender' serves as a sociological term applying to all perceptions, standards and ideological aspects of sex and its institutional, political and social forms.[51] In relation to work at memorial sites, the

---

47 See I. Eschebach, S. Jacobeit and S. Wenk , 2002, *Gedächtnis und Geschlecht*, Frankfurt/New York.

48 See E. Fritsch und C. Herkommers, 2009, *Sammelband Nationalsozialismus und Geschlecht. Zur politisierung und Ästheisierung von Körper, „Rasse"'und Sexualität im, ' Dritten Reich'und nach 1945*, Bielefeld.

49 See T. Lutz, Von der Bürgerinitiative zur Stiftung, 1998, Der Bildungsgehalt der öffentlichen Debatten um den Umgang mit dem Prinz-Albrecht-Gelände in Berlin, H. Behrens-Cobet, *Bilden und Gedenken: Erwachsenenbildung in Gedenkstätten und Gedächtnisorten*, p. 85.

50 As literature, the following publications are referred to here: H. Zumpe,2004, Gedenkstätten und Gender – (k)ein Missverständnis?, *Zeitschrift für Geschichtsdidaktik* Vol. 3, , p. 165-170. L. Moldenhauer, A. Freundt, and K. Baumann (eds), *Oldenburger Beiträge zur Geschlechterforschung. Frauen in Konzentrationslagern: Konzeption eines Führungstages unter geschlechtsspezifischem Aspekt in der Gedenkstätte Bergen-Belsen, Schriftenreihe, Oldenburger Beiträge zur Geschlechterforschung*, Vol.5, 2004.

51 Plößer, Melanie, 2005, *Dekonstruktion – Feminismus - Pädagogik. Vermittlungsansätze zwischen Theorie und Praxis*. Königstein andTaununs (eds), p. 186.

term 'gender' helps to make the structure of sexuality visible in a historical context. At the same time, it provokes insights into one's personal concept of sex.[52] Recipients and teachers are not only part of a discourse of remembrance but also a discourse about sex, which reflects boundaries, legitimization processes[53] and power structures. Gender as an analytical category is relevant in many ways at memorials to National Socialist crimes, with regard to the historical events, the pedagogical interaction, the presentation of the place, and the representation of stories in exhibitions. Gender-sensitive education means seeing that gender stereotypes are not merely images, which we obtain from gender roles, but the result of social relationships that have become entrenched over time. The commemorative acquisition of history should be seen as educational processes, which are governed by social relations. In each education process, social identities are reactivated, and function as effective sexual identities in a sexually structured society.[54]

The works and theories of Pia Frohwein and Leonie Wagner on the relevance of the category of gender in education at memorial sites attracted attention in Germany. They proposed the thesis that memorials are being increasingly feminized, whereby learning processes and methods are aimed primarily at girls and women. Methodological approaches such as talks by witnesses of the time, empathy with victims and self-examination would appeal primarily to girls' sensitivities; boys and men were more interested in power structures and violence, which in an educational setting are morally condemned and abandoned, and therefore cannot be addressed.[55] They suggested a gender-sensitive education, which is based on the following premises: (1) showing that history is constructed as 'female' and 'male', (2) recognizing that thematic interests are encouraged or discouraged by the determination of gender roles, and (3) understanding that learning behaviour is influenced by the speaker's and recipient's perception of gender.

52 M. Franke, O. Kistenmacher, A. Prochnau, K. Steen,: Geschlechterreflektierende Gedenkstättenpädagogik. Männlichkeit als Konstrukt sichtbar machen, T. Hilmar 2010, *Ort, Subjekt, Verbrechen. Koordinaten historisch-politischer Bildungsarbeit zum Nationalsozialismus.* Vienna, pp 139-159.

53 A. Messerschmidt, 2003, *Bildung als Kritik der Erinnerung*, Frankfurt a. Main , p.252.

54 Messerschmit (2003), p. 47.

55 P. Frohwein and L. Wagner, 2004, *Geschlechterspezifische Aspekte in der Gedenkstättenpädagogik*, Gedenkstättenrundbrief, No. 120, Berlin, pp. 14-21.

'Doing Gender' – the example of the Ravensbrück memorial site

Even though gender studies exist in universities and the category of gender increasingly attracts attention, educational practice (primarily in lower schools) remains largely unaffected. Establishing gender as a category in civic education requires a gender-sensitive understanding of perceived proven knowledge ('doing gender'), in order to combat the entrenchment of gender roles and interpret history in new ways.

The Ravensbrück women's concentration camp is often addressed in discussions regarding the role of gender in crimes in concentration camps. Gender is associated with the biological sex, not with the social construct, and thus the answer to the question of gender seems to lie in the history of women's suffering.

While the Ravensbrück memorial education department is concerned with gender approaches in historical and civic education at the memorial site, there is a need to apply these analytical categories to all sites of National Socialist crimes. According to Matthias Heyl, Director of the Ravensbrück Memorial Education Department, a thorough education at a memorial site requires a situational narrative, which is locationally and biographically specific. It is about explaining the site and seeing its traces of history. Such an education needs a guide with the narrative, analytical, and methodological skills to render the history and its actors accessible and vivid to visitors.[56] This requires a multifaceted presentation, with an emphasis on empathy, and a forensic attitude to the site.[57] Care must be taken in this educational context to ensure that, first of all, the presentation resonates with the different interests and motivations of the students, and secondly, that it involves them in the personal stories of victims, perpetrators and bystanders. Finally, this subject-approach demands a sense of gender consciousness to raise awareness of the social and cultural effect of standardization of the sexes.

Based on three case studies, I would like to characterize the relevance of gender in the everyday setting of historical/civic learning at the Ravensbrück memorial site.

---

56 M. Heyl, 2009, Gedenkstättenpädagogik als historisch-politische Bildung im 21. Jahrhundert. *Mauthausen Memorial neu gestalten*, Conference Report to the 1st Dialogue Forum, Mauthausen, . Ministry of Internal Affairs, Department IV/7, Vienna, p. 44.

57 M. Heyl, 2011, Erziehung nach Auschwitz – Bildung nach Ravensbrück. Historisch-politische Bildung zur Geschichte des Nationalsozialismus und seiner Verbrechen. K. Ahlheim; M. Heyl, 2011, *Adorno revisited. Erziehung nach Auschwitz und Erziehung zur Mündigkeit heute*. Kritische Beiträge zur Bildungswissenschaft; Vol. 3. Hannover, p.118.

These are pragmatic observations of education practice that address the question of gender-based attributes, self-awareness and the historical perception of gender in the educational process.

Personal interests versus sexual differentiation: dominance of the binary code

Education should be seen as inseparable from the teachers, and their own educational and social background. A visit by a class of schoolchildren to the Ravensbrück memorial site in 2011 showed the heteronormative treatment of the recipients. The teachers said the group had already visited the Sachsenhausen memorial site (on the same day), where the boys learned the stories of male prisoners. But here where the prisoners were women, it was now the girls who were asked to pay attention. The students were differentiated by the gender binary, which shaped the way the teachers reflected the supposed interest of boys and girls in their educational content. In other words, the logic was that the recipients would necessarily be especially interested in certain aspects of history based on differentiation by biological sex. The history was thus constructed in two parts, as their own particular story and the story of 'others'. And the story of the 'others' was deemed irrelevant. This approach is in total contradiction to the subject-oriented education, which fosters a connection for each individual visitor. Instead, the concept of a dual biological sexuality was unthinkingly reproduced and entrenched, and the notion of traditional gender roles formed the basis of the students' learning.

This heteronormative approach is often used to address the subject of pregnancy and birth, which is bound up with the biological female body. From September 1944 to April 1945 alone, 522 births were recorded in the Ravensbrück concentration camp and 260 children were recorded as having died the same day of their birth.[58] The inhumane treatment of pregnant women, the murder of new-born babies and enforced abortions are testimony to the crimes of Nazi nurses and doctors and a shocking chapter of the Ravensbrück story. However, it is not only women who are interested in the subject. As part of a scholarly project at the Ravensbrück memorial site, a working paper on the subject of 'Children in Ravensbrück' was prepared as a contribution to the thematization of these crimes. Frequently, when teachers prepare their students for memorial site trips, they often assign these topics to girls, who, in the context of social desirability, do not articulate they may not be interested in

---

58   B. Strebel, 2003, *Das KZ Ravensbrück. Geschichte eines Lagerkomplexes*, Paderborn, p.266.

this subject. There are groups of themes such as care, maternity, female solidarity, mother-child relationships or child welfare that are again and again ascribed as female. For example, the writer Barbara Degen expresses this in her publication **Das Herz schlägt in Ravensbrück. Die Gedenkkultur der Frauen**, when she speaks of a system of mutual support as a female genealogy of survival and female knowledge of birth, life and death.[59] If we regard the world only in terms of the standardized gender roles assigned to us, there is a danger that teachers and multipliers imbue femaleness with an aura of mystery. This obscures the various ways to view gender, Holocaust remembrance, and the debate over the National Socialist crimes. Both for girls, who are forced to take an interest, as well as for boys from whom the subject is withheld because it could not be of interest to them, learning about this topic is thus based on rigid, standardized gender stereotypes.

Holocaust – Gender – Homophobia

The correlation between the construction of gender, heteronormativity and antisemitism can be seen in the treatment of Jewish prisoners in Ravensbrück. When Jews were deprived of their rights by the Nuremberg Laws of 1935, Jewish women were accused of defiling the race, hunted down and sent to the Ravensbrück women's concentration camp.[60] In November 1941, the doctor and psychiatrist Dr Friedrich Mennecke was assigned to Ravensbrück for 'Action 14f13[61] (the murder of prisoners in the concentration camp who were sick, old or no longer able to work in a programme of murder by euthanasia). Sixty-three photos of the assessment documents remain today. Thirty-seven of these show Jewish women, nineteen of whom are described as prostitutes[62], including Mary Pünjer, a Jewish woman from Hamburg. Mennecke writes about her in his assessment: '... married full Jewess. Very active ("saucy") lesbian. Constantly haunts "lesbian bars" and engages in sexual activities.'[63] Mennecke selected Jewish prisoners on the basis of the files of investigating authorities, and then made his assessment. Again and again,

---

59   B. Degen, *Das Herz schlägt in Ravensbrück. Die Gedenkkultur der Frauen, Schriften aus dem Haus der Frauengeschichte*, Opladen & Farmington Hills, Vol. 5, p.106.

60   See L. Apel, 2003, *Jüdischen Frauen im Konzentrationslager Ravensbrück 1939-1945*, Berlin, p.75 ff.

61   See L. Apel, 2003, *Euthanasiemorde in den Konzentrationslagern*, p.296.

62   Apel, 2003, p. 300.

63   C. Schoppmann, E. Conrad, M. Rosenberg, M. Pünjer, H. Schermann (eds), 2012,, Vier Porträts, in I. Eschebach , *Homophobie und Devianz. Weibliche und männliche Homosexualität im Nationalsozialismus*, Berlin , p.106.
     See: http://www.stolpersteine-hamburg.de/index.php?MAIN_ID=7&BIO_ID=903.

descriptions and formulations can be read such as 'Jewess suffering from venereal disease', 'antisocial full Jewess', 'sexually obsessed Jewess' or 'whore'. Half of the 1,600 women selected were Jewish. They were deported to the Bernburg Sanatorium and Mental Hospital and there they were murdered. Sexual relations between women were not directly punishable, but loving relations between women did not match the National Socialist ideal of good child-bearing mothers and thus did not uphold the idea of the *Volksgemeinschaft* (the German 'ethnic' community).

The story of Mary Pünjer is sexually coded. From a gender-sensitive educational theoretical perspective, the perpetrators' image of the 'obsessive Jewish lesbian' expresses complex relations between cultural normativity and sexual stereotyping in terms of power relationships and a policy of exclusion. In order to understand this, the National Socialist standardization of the body needs to be decoded. The image of Jewish women as obsessive, lecherous and sexually uncontrollable needs to be explained, as part of the National Socialist antisemitic hegemony: a contrast between the presentation of a 'German woman' as sexually pure, whose body connotes the people, and the 'Jewish woman' as lecherous and abnormal, whose sexuality is geared only to personal appetites, including in the choice of a female sexual partner. The interplay of antisemitic hostility, contempt for women and homophobia is a huge challenge for the historical and civic education of young people who, as they grow up, find themselves torn between uncertainty and assurance about their own sexuality and their body.

Female perpetrators – the existence of 'mannish' women

Most guided tours of the Ravensbrück memorial site for classes of schoolchildren start in the area of the former female guards' houses. The students generally recognize them as guards' houses. But as they discuss the guards, they characterize them chiefly as male. When asked whether they might have been men or women, many schoolchildren say that the guards must have been men. This provides the opportunity to discuss the perception of relations between the sexes. Some students wonder whether the guards could possibly have been women, as it was ultimately a women's concentration camp. But it was often countered that the guards must have been men, as ultimately men were the ones who invented concentration camps. Guarding means the exercise of dominance and control, and this aspect is ascribed to the male sex. When the students learn that the housing blocks provided accommodation for the former guards, they probe the topic of gender even further.

'If they really were women, then they must have been MANNISH WOMEN.' When asked what a mannish woman is, they explain that such people are big and sporty with broad, unfeminine shoulders and they are 'tough customers'. The situation is intensified in some students by the thought: 'SHE is a man.' 'Why woman as a man?' 'Because she is violent and brutal.' In this situation, a young man who feels implicated grows indignant: He is not inherently brutal and violent as a man. Thus questions circulate about the perception of femaleness and maleness, and at the same time the students talk about their own sexuality. The simple exercise of tracing the legacy of houses can thus illuminate the question of who is described as violent at a particular moment and his or her sexual attributes, as well as increase understanding of one's role in identifying these characteristics as male or female. It is here that the female guards' acts are described more precisely, victims' stories are told, the guards are characterized as responsible for hunger, humiliation, injury and murder, and the circumstances of their historical and actual autonomy are made clear. In the gender-based education process, therefore, there is a chance to dismantle the stereotype of the perpetrators as abnormal women. The question of violence and crime can then be settled by tracking the exercise of power. Notwithstanding the fact there was a male level of command, women can also be recognized as sources of violence and death. Their behaviour, its causes and effects in relation to perceptions of gender, are open to debate.

Shedding light on the invisible

The question remains as to whether we are able to view the world only in terms of allotted role identities. What do we really see? How is this perceived reality constructed? What remains invisible? At what point in time do we start to typify the opposite gender and for what reason? And what effect does this have on our learning and recognition process? 'We invariably communicate from our little boxes – with open or (mostly) closed doors.'[64] Our emancipating goal is to step out of our boxes.

It is not possible to draw any general conclusions regarding gender-sensitive education at memorial sites from the above examples, and more experience must be gathered and discussed. But certainly, the category of gender must be employed as an educational tool at memorial sites. Only then can we develop gender-sensitive

---

64 R. Arnold, 2007, *Ich lerne also bin ich. Eine systemisch-konstruktivistische Didaktik*, Heidelberg, p.182.

methods. These serve to challenge the gender order and its role in the process of telling the story of Ravensbrück, shed light on gender relations and thus, in the future, explain their influence on its history. This applies not only to the Ravensbrück 'women's' memorial site in particular, but can be applied at every memorial site in telling the story of the crimes of National Socialism.

For a gender-sensitive decoding of history, we need to investigate which constructions of gender are revealed. Are there perceived constructions of maleness and femaleness? Are there marginalized and secondary constructions of maleness and femaleness? There is still hope that the education process can be changed through gender-sensitive examination. The perception of gender thus helps us to reflect critically on the attribution of gender-conditioned patterns of behaviour, challenging the absolute characterization of history as male, and supports a growing realization that there are many different concepts of maleness and femaleness in society.

Comparing genocide in the classroom: Challenges and opportunities

Paul Salmons and Matthias Haß

Comparative approaches to historic events can be useful in educational settings to demonstrate the significance of events and to clarify their developments. Due to its magnitude, the Holocaust is often used as a comparison to other mass crimes in history or in the present. In the following, we will start out with a rationale for relating the Holocaust to other genocides; highlight a number of educational opportunities in such comparisons; and then consider some of the challenges and obstacles that lie in comparative studies of the Holocaust in educational settings.

This article is based on a presentation by Paul Salmons (University of London) at the UNESCO seminar on 'Holocaust Education in a Global Context' (27 April 2012). It also includes recommendations of the Task Force for International Cooperation on Holocaust Education, Remembrance, and Research (now, International Holocaust Remembrance Alliance, IHRA).

Rationale – why study the Holocaust and why relate it to other genocides?

According to archaeological evidence, mass violence has been a feature of human societies since at least Neolithic times. These atrocities, however, have rarely been incorporated into the stories we tell ourselves about ourselves. For centuries, communities have written out of history their deliberate destruction of other human groups. The story of genocide has been a history of forgetting. Only very recently has mass violence been the subject of intensive academic research.

That study really began with attempts to understand and explain the destruction of European Jewry by the Nazis and their collaborators during the Second World War. It is not because what today we call 'the Holocaust' was any more horrific or brutal than previous cases of mass violence, but it has entered the collective imagination to an extent not seen before. Unusually in the history of genocide – which always is carried out by a group with an overwhelming monopoly of power against a largely defenceless population – this time the perpetrators were defeated in a wider conflict, and so their crimes were exposed and examined to an unprecedented degree. The circulation by modern mass media of film and photographs of atrocities taken as Allied forces entered the camps gave the lie to the Enlightenment ideal of the 'progress of western civilization' and raised challenging questions about how this could have happened in the modern world, in the heart of 'civilized' Europe.

The capture of millions of pages of Nazi documents and the analysis of that material evidence in the Nuremberg and later war crimes trials provided an archival basis for scholarly research into those searching questions. In subsequent decades, the discovery of documents hidden by the victims, such as the Ringelblum archive buried beneath the Warsaw ghetto, allowed historians to move beyond a perpetrator-oriented narrative. Attention also turned to the collaboration and complicity of non-Germans throughout Europe, and on the knowledge and response of the Allied powers; and following the end of the Cold War, the opening to western historians of archives in the former Soviet Union led to an explosion of new research, including a huge number of micro histories examining a wide range of countries, government departments, industries, agencies and individuals involved in the Holocaust.

All of this has led to the intensification of historical study, the development of new methodological approaches to examining the evidence, sophisticated conceptual and categorical ways of thinking about this traumatic past, and the emergence of detailed, nuanced and complex ways of understanding. The result is that the Holocaust is undoubtedly the most extensively documented, most intensively studied, and best understood example of mass violence in human history.

Emerging out of the study of the Holocaust has been the broader field of genocide studies, which has followed many of the methodological approaches, categories and conceptual frameworks. Scholars have examined why and how societies descend into mass violence; the causes of genocide and its warning signs; the motivation of the perpetrators and their collaborators; the response of victims, bystanders and rescuers; the reactions and responsibility of the international community – all questions that were brought into sharp focus by the study of the murder of European Jewry, and which have been further developed and advanced through the study of other genocides. As such, the Holocaust may be said to be the foundational case of genocide research; but the study of other genocides has allowed for more powerful ways of thinking about mass violence than would be possible if scholars focused exclusively on Nazi crimes.

Opportunities

The questions raised by the Holocaust and the study of other genocides can seem overwhelming, but it is precisely this challenge that affords a major educational opportunity – put simply, many young people recognize the importance and significance of this subject: they know that it matters. While deeply troubling, these questions are also intrinsically engaging – their view of the world disturbed, students want to understand how and why societies can degenerate into mass violence. So educators are in a potentially powerful position – students can be very highly motivated and prepared to engage more intensively than with many other subjects because they feel that learning about genocide is relevant and important.

When the human story is at the focus, many students are then deeply moved and their humanity and sense of justice engender a desire to learn more about possible prevention. The dilemmas, choices and decisions faced by people in such extreme circumstances reveal the full range of what human beings are capable of, not only the worst of human behaviour but also great courage, resilience and altruism. This human story is also extremely engaging.

While each case of mass violence has its own specific causes, follows its own course and can only be understood in the context of its own time, still it might be possible to analyse common patterns and processes of genocidal situations and of the developments toward genocide. If we are able to identify these patterns, we might be better able to identify warning signals and strengthen efforts towards the prevention of genocide. Taking a comparative approach to learning about the Holocaust and other genocides should enable students to clarify not only the similarities but also what was distinctive and different about each case of mass violence, and to understand the particular historical significance of each of these events in its own right. Relating the Holocaust to other genocides may then lead to a process of reciprocal learning, where deeper understanding about each event can lead to new insights about the genocidal process that are not possible through the study of a single case in isolation.

More research is needed into whether learning about past examples of mass violence helps to create more active citizens who will strengthen efforts at genocide prevention. But the least we can expect is that students will be alerted to the potential for mass violence in the contemporary world by gaining knowledge about the history of the Holocaust and other genocides. Furthermore, by examining the historical background of cases of mass violence, students are placed in a position to identify injustice and discrimination in forms prior to mass murder. Holocaust and genocide education therefore can be used in a productive way as a comparative framework for events of lower levels of violence.

Holocaust education may also include attempts to come to terms with this history after the fact. The concept of transitional justice (attempts to respond to demands for justice after pervasive human rights violations) has been developed over the last twenty-five years, although its roots can be found in the time after the Second World War and the attempts to establish a new system of international justice, especially with the Nuremberg Trials and the Genocide Convention. Elements of the concept can be transferred to the field of Holocaust and genocide education. How do we deal with the consequences of genocide in the contexts of justice, politics, culture, and society? The scale of the Holocaust and its unprecedented and paradigmatic character requires an analysis of how different European societies dealt with the consequences of the Holocaust. What were the challenges? Which paths taken proved to be successful, which failed? Learning about the reactions of families, communities and societies to the events of the Holocaust and about the attempts of the survivors to live with their experiences can help young people to consider similar issues for those responding to genocide today.

Study of the Holocaust might also be helpful in the learning process about one's own country's violent and traumatic past. Most societies have difficulty in addressing atrocities committed by their forebears, as this disturbs the self-image fostered by that society's foundational myths. When the history of that society's crimes, the behaviour of its perpetrators and bystanders, and the suffering of its victims are addressed, emotions and tensions can rise. Although the Holocaust is sometimes used as a kind of 'screen memory' – a way of displacing suppressed anxieties so that they can be examined more safely – it does not have to be the case that the Holocaust is a mechanism to avoid confrontation with one's own troubling past. It could be that it opens the possibility to move from the Holocaust to a deeper reflection on atrocities closer to home, perhaps even very recent crimes against humanity.

The opportunity, therefore, is for teachers to draw upon the vast and expanding body of knowledge and conceptual understandings that have emerged out of Holocaust and genocide studies and to allow young people to reflect on why and how societies collapse into mass violence; to examine a number of cases to see if there are commonalities and patterns that might be helpful in identifying warning signs; and to consider how efforts at prevention of genocide might be strengthened. To our thinking, study of the Holocaust and other genocides are essential to young people's educational literacy and all young people should have an entitlement to learn about and to reflect upon these mass crimes and their continuing significance in the modern world.

Challenges

There are a number of challenges that face teachers in relating the Holocaust to other genocides and crimes against humanity, so it makes sense to differentiate them into several categories. Educators and institutions working in this field can help support teachers in meeting these challenges, and so a number of recommendations are made below to help stimulate the development of this work.

Practical challenges

The potential to teach about the history of the Holocaust and other genocides using a comparative approach may be constrained by factors within a particular school system. This could depend, for example, on the dictates of a mandated curriculum, as well as the syllabi of public examinations. But the integration of a comparative approach in Holocaust and genocide studies also depends upon the degree of support from the head of the school, the attitude of school governors, the parent body, and others. In addition, there is often a lack of curriculum time, and a lack of effective, practical, age-appropriate classroom materials that have been developed for a comparative genocide approach.

These external factors have to be taken into consideration when thinking about the possibility of young people studying comparative genocide in school. Often they might be the limiting factors that inhibit the efforts of teachers to compare the Holocaust to other genocides, so thought must be given to how to overcome these potential obstacles.

Teachers need to be able to make the case for curriculum time that will allow the development of a comparative approach relating the Holocaust to other genocides. Therefore a clear rationale is essential to explain the educational value of this work. It is hoped the rationale offered previously in this short paper may help teachers in this regard. Furthermore, educational institutions working in this field may wish to devote time, resources and expertise to developing age-appropriate materials, classroom activities and schemes of work to support teachers in the classroom.

Challenges regarding aims

A comparative approach needs thorough preparation, thoughtful planning and a clear analytical framework. This raises challenging questions – how do we develop a genuinely comparative set of parameters? What are the criteria for such comparisons? The rationale and motivations for comparing the Holocaust to other genocides need to be openly stated. If the purpose is to better understand how and why societies collapse into mass violence, to seek to identify potential warning signs in order to improve efforts at prevention, then these aims will help to establish the criteria for comparative analysis and may help teachers to move beyond simply exploring a series of discrete cases of genocide.

But teachers and educational institutions also need to be alert to the danger that comparisons to the Holocaust are not always made for sound educational reasons. Each comparative approach to understanding genocide in an educational setting happens in a concrete societal context, with images and presumptions of the past and the present held by teachers and students, policy makers, and developers of curricula and textbooks. All have specific interests and motivations in comparing different genocides. There is a danger of drawing false comparisons, of comparing the Holocaust to other genocides in order to diminish the Holocaust or to conflate with other crimes in ways that avoid difficult issues within a country's own national history. One example: the concerns that equivalencies drawn between Nazi and Soviet crimes can allow national communities to present themselves as common victims, rather than also acknowledging their roles as perpetrators and collaborators.

Thus the aim to better understand the causes, patterns and warning signs of mass violence must be clearly differentiated from comparisons that seek to equate, diminish or trivialize the Holocaust or the genocides to which the Holocaust is compared, for political or social agendas or in the service of competing memories. It is therefore essential to recognize that differences between historical events are as important and significant as their similarities. It is important to be alert to the difference between comparing genocides, which is possible and legitimate, and comparing the suffering of individual victims or victim groups, which is not. Thought must be given to how to explore differences between genocides without creating hierarchies of suffering, and care must be taken to acknowledge different victim groups without either equating all cases or falling into the politics of competitive memory.

We must also avoid appropriating the Holocaust to further a particular position regarding current political events. This politicization – using the Holocaust as a political weapon, e.g. in the Arab-Israeli conflict, either by comparing leaders to Hitler, accusing Israel of being a Nazi state, arguing that another Holocaust of the Jewish people is an imminent danger, or using the Holocaust to justify actions does not do justice to either the historic event or the complexity of the current conflict.

Intellectual Challenges

A commonly cited rationale for studying the Holocaust is because it will help us to prevent similar atrocities in the future. But it would be a mistake to assume that study of the Holocaust in itself provides a straightforward explanatory framework for other examples of mass violence. While research into the Holocaust may provide important models and insights, clearly all historical periods and events have their own distinctive features, and different cases of mass violence will have different causes. So, to be able to discern patterns and warning signs, it is essential to look not only at the Holocaust but at a number of different cases. The value of a comparative approach may then be that certain patterns emerge allowing us to conceptualize and better understand genocidal processes, and this in turn may further efforts at prevention, helping to identify warning signs that alert communities to the need for intervention.

However, even then it remains difficult to move beyond the study of a series of discrete cases and to develop an overview of genocidal processes. Furthermore, a genuine comparison requires good substantive knowledge not just of one, but of two or more, of these cases of mass violence. Limitations of the curricula, time and resources may not allow the depth of analysis that each historical case of genocide demands. The danger then arises that, in attempting a comparative approach, neither are explored or understood in sufficient depth. As a result, both genocides may be presented and addressed in an oversimplified manner, leading to distortions of the past and rather weak generalizations and conclusions.

The subsequent demands on both teachers and students are clear. We are dealing with enormously complex historical moments, involving thousands of perpetrators, perhaps hundreds of thousands or even millions of victims, but also the complex problems of understanding how apparently functioning states and societies come to collapse into mass murder. To address these questions in the case of the Holocaust alone often goes beyond the limits of time, energy and comprehension and a comparative approach places even greater demands upon both teacher and learner.

This is a particular challenge given the lack of educational material that actually does compare/relate the Holocaust to other genocides. Educational institutions working in this field may be able to support teachers by offering professional development that updates their substantive historical knowledge of the Holocaust and other cases of mass violence, and explores how these together can inform our understandings of genocidal processes.

Pedagogical challenges

Broadly we can say that there are two distinct approaches to teaching about the past in our schools. One focuses on the transformative power of learning a *body of knowledge*, a narrative account, and emphasizes the 'lessons to be learned' from this narrative – the morals, values and dispositions it is said to develop in the student. The other stresses the importance of learning about history as a disciplinary *form of knowledge* – this explores how we know what we know and reveals to the student how historical narratives are constructed, on which historical sources they are based, and what different interpretations and accounts are possible, giving rise to different meanings.

This distinction is particularly important as the Holocaust is so often used as a vehicle for transmitting particular viewpoints, attitudes and dispositions, to promote a wide range of social, political and moral agendas. There is good reason to suspect that the narrative, 'lessons from the past' approach is not especially effective. Students understand how such 'education' works and can be good at giving the 'correct answer' – i.e. the one the teacher wants – in class, but this does not mean the intended moral lesson has necessarily been assimilated: we know from research and from learning theory that people are not so easily 'inducted'. Furthermore, we need to be aware that the shaping of the past to fit particular 'lessons' runs a risk of distorting and oversimplifying the past and militates against complex and nuanced understandings.

So, we would advocate an approach to teaching and learning about the Holocaust and other genocides that adopts a disciplinary approach to history and develops young people's critical thinking. Students risk manipulation by those who seek to use the Holocaust as a motif or a rhetorical device when speaking about other issues. Rather than using the Holocaust and other genocides to promote particular viewpoints in the classroom, we would argue students need to have the tools to critically examine comparisons between the Holocaust and other phenomena. This is less likely to come from a narrative 'body of knowledge' approach or one that stresses moral lessons, and more from a disciplinary way of thinking that can be fostered by teaching history as a form of knowledge, incorporating multiple narratives, examining different interpretations, understanding why accounts differ, and being able to test these different claims about the past on the basis of historical evidence and the rules of historical enquiry.

Clearly, a major challenge in this regard is that a disciplinary approach cannot simply be adopted for teaching and learning about the Holocaust and other genocides if it is not part of the broader culture of history teaching. In such contexts, educational institutions may need to give particular attention to teachers' professional development in teaching history as a disciplinary form of knowledge, rather than giving a narrative account intended to provide moral instruction.

Emotional Challenges

Exploring the histories of the Holocaust and other genocides brings a range of emotionally charged and challenging issues. As already noted, for centuries communities have erased their deliberate destruction of other human groups from the historical record. There may be deep emotional and social-psychological reasons for this – a selective forgetting about our past, because it raises extremely distressing and challenging issues we would rather not confront.

So it must be clear that by addressing the Holocaust or any other genocide in an educational setting, we are exposing our students to cases where entire societies collapse and where thousands of ordinary people become complicit in genocidal actions – cases in which we see the very worst of what human beings are capable. Educators, but also policy makers, school book developers and people who work at memorial sites and museums, have a duty of care to those young people who are exposed to this difficult knowledge. Therefore, they need to consider carefully:

How to support young people through such encounters, entailing tremendous violence and suffering?

How to engage young people emotionally without traumatizing them?

How to encourage intellectual curiosity and emotional empathy for the victims?

The temptation may be to provide a cathartic ending, a redemptive narrative where students will not be 'left in despair'. Yet while we do not want young people to give up on humankind, we would also warn against bringing resolution and closure, which may not be authentic to the histories being studied. Indeed, if we bring closure for our students then we allow them a 'way out' of struggling with the very issues we say we want them to confront – how and why do societies sometimes descend into mass violence? What can be done to recognize and act upon the warning signs of such crimes? These are not simple questions to be resolved with acts of commemoration or 'happy endings'. Rather, we should provide space and support for young people to become more involved in efforts towards genocide prevention.

Challenges due to the culture and tradition of the educational system

A strong and often positive feature of school education is to take complex ideas and make them accessible and understandable to young people. As a consequence, in a topic-led approach, there is a perceived need to close a subject, to end it and resolve the issues raised so the class can consolidate and move on to the next subject area.

But when dealing with such difficult events as the Holocaust or genocide, we ought not to allow these subjects to be rendered 'safe'; rather, we should expect our young people to wrestle with the deeply troubling issues that they raise and – having subjected them to this knowledge – we then have a responsibility to support our students in this endeavour.

Are teachers prepared to allow their students to continue to struggle with these issues? Can we resist our desire to bring resolution, to end with a redemptive, uplifting narrative? It is our belief we should not settle what ought to remain unsettling, because it is possible our students may come to better, deeper, more meaningful understandings than those we offer as catharsis.

It may be we need new and distinctive pedagogical approaches that refuse a redemptive narrative and resist closure, but which instead continue to support young people as they try to come to terms with a world in which mass violence is possible. Such an approach would be demanding of the teacher, of course, stretching beyond the formal ending of the 'topic' and perhaps beyond the classroom, but it may be a more authentic response to the challenges raised by our confronting the Holocaust, genocide and other crimes against humanity.

Holocaust research in a comparative perspective

Peter Longerich

Holocaust research can serve as an important resource to develop international programmes that address more general questions of genocide and mass violence, as well as strategies for prevention. Such international programmes, however, reach out to countries that are a great distance from where the murder of the Jews by the Nazi regime occurred, or that are dealing primarily with the consequences of mass violence in their own society. In these countries the Holocaust may seem rather irrelevant to their own history. The task before us, therefore, is to use our knowledge of the Holocaust to better understand other historic tragedies without presenting the Holocaust as a sort of internationally standardized 'meta-narrative', which would face the risk of competing with the memory of other historic cases of extreme violence.

Certain new developments in the field of Holocaust research affect the way that the Holocaust can be used to study other genocides. Since the opening of the East European archives about two decades ago, Holocaust research has undergone a momentous change. A great many studies have appeared since the mid-1990s, giving us a much more detailed picture of the murder of European Jews. This is certainly true of the local and regional history of the Holocaust: there are now hardly any blank spaces left on the historical map of the Holocaust.

But in addition in the last two decades, numerous works have appeared exposing every aspect of the way the killing machine functioned right across Europe, from policing and occupation policy to concentration camps and extermination camps. Authors have opened up new thematic approaches to the subject of the Holocaust: the history of systematic plunder as a precondition for mass murder; the practice of 'working to death' within the framework of the Nazi forced-labour programme; or the nexus of demographic planning for racial selection, settlement policies, mass deportations and mass murder.

Under the impact of such research in the last couple of decades, our picture of the Holocaust has evolved. The stereotype of the 'desk-bound murderer' is being steadily replaced by a more precise description of the perpetrators, operating at all levels of the hierarchy, full of conviction, and eager to facilitate the machinery of death. Historians' earlier conception of anonymous, industrialized killing in death factories is increasingly being augmented by another image of the murder of the Jews. About half of all victims were killed 'face to face': either in massacres proclaimed as executions; in the bloody 'cleansing' of ghettoes; or – often on the pretext of anti-partisan actions – by hunting down people taking refuge in forests or other hiding-places.

Where Holocaust studies previously foregrounded the genesis of the 'Final Solution' (as Christopher Browning called it), that is to say the question of the decision-making process that set the murder machine in motion, another complex of problems has emerged. Research is about to place Jewish persecution in individual countries within the larger context of German domination of the European continent, and meticulously bring out the individual factors that accelerated or restrained the persecution of the Jews in each case.

Moreover, the picture of the victims has changed. Interest has increasingly moved away from depicting the victims as an amorphous, preponderantly inert mass, and towards presenting their individual and collective sufferings, as well as their attempts to preserve some vestiges of autonomy in the midst of persecution. Not least, the focus has shifted towards various forms of resistance and the conditions under which it occurred.

We have also learned, especially in relation to the second half of the war, one essential fact: The reaction of the persecuted is not only significant as part of the history of the victims, but also more and more influential for the whole development of the Holocaust in Europe. Whether expressed in flight, in seeking refuge, or in various forms of resistance, this reaction in turn affected the attitudes of the persecutors.

At the beginning of the twenty-first century, Holocaust research has become a growing international research area, which has developed its own infrastructure with research centres, professorships at universities, conferences, journals and series of book publications. Not least, however, Holocaust studies have become increasingly interdisciplinary: an almost unimaginably vast research field has opened up, accommodating contributions from disciplines as diverse as literary studies, geography, media studies, musicology and art history. Holocaust studies have become a laboratory for different approaches and debates, and a significant resource for verified research results, for knowledge and methodological intelligence.

The Holocaust is by no means finally and terminally investigated. High quality research helps to develop new perspectives and questions on a higher intellectual level – and will attract more high quality research. If we compare results of Holocaust research with other historic case studies, or even transfer research results to other historic case studies, we realize the Holocaust is both: it is the most extreme case and the best researched case of genocide.

The second part of this claim indicates the Holocaust can be used as a resource base to research other comparable historic cases; the first part of the claim, however, may appear to suggest the opposite. It seems the Holocaust is such an extreme event we have to view it as incomparable, respect it as unique. The concept of the Holocaust as historically 'unique' is generally based on the following arguments: (1) the intent of total annihilation, which was (2) developed on the basis of a determinist racist ideology and (3) the systematic execution of this will to totally exterminate. Combined with each other, these criteria indeed constitute a fundamental difference from all other cases of mass atrocities. This fact often leads to the conclusion that an extreme, unique case like the Holocaust is inaccessible to historical explanation, standing outside history. This is a view shared by many intellectuals. Saul Friedländer, for instance, wrote in 1991:

'Paradoxically, the "Final Solution", as a result of its apparent historical exceptionality, could well be inaccessible to all attempts at a significant representation and interpretation. Thus, notwithstanding all efforts at the creation of meaning, it could remain fundamentally irrelevant for the history of humanity and the understanding of the "human condition". In Walter Benjamin's terms, we may possibly be facing an unredeemable past.'

However, this statement did not hinder Friedlander from writing a huge two-volume opus in which he found a way to present the Holocaust (based mainly on sources which were written by the victims) and to explain it with his concept of 'redemption', which the Nazi regime tried to achieve by killing the Jews. Indeed, the notion that the Holocaust is inexplicable is hardly tenable. If we give up in our attempts to explain this crime that marks the century, if we exclude it from history, we have to ask ourselves about our pretensions to engage in history in general.

A few years ago, historians started to talk about the unprecedented nature of the Holocaust in order to overcome the problem of its historical uniqueness. It was an unprecedented event at the time when it occurred, but since then we have the precedent and we can study it. We also have to take into consideration the possibility it can repeat itself in one form or another. If you approach the event in this manner, 'uniqueness' does not stay in the sphere of historical philosophical speculation; rather the historical specific and until then unique can be used for broader analysis of historic events.

If we can use the Holocaust as a resource base for other historic events, we need to clarify how we define such 'other' events. The concept of genocide was developed by legal experts and political scientists rather than by historians. I consider myself an outsider and I have the impression a lot of time and energy in this scholarly field was put into definitions and differentiations. Which historic cases are legitimately called genocide? Does political persecution also constitute a form of genocide or solely the extermination of a *genos*, a group in which membership is defined mainly through birth? Is genocide only a concept of the twentieth and twenty-first centuries? Are there aspects of modernity that differentiate genocide from other forms of mass killings? How do we differentiate between genocide and civil war, or bloody revolution if we know that most genocides occur in the context of war or internal political struggles for power?

It seems to me we can identify two cases only – in addition to the Holocaust, an extreme case itself – that are generally recognized as genocide: Armenia and Rwanda. The classification as genocide is more or less debated in all other cases. In view of these issues of definition, one could come to the conclusion to avoid the term genocide in scientific language and replace it with another term, for example 'extreme forms of mass violence'. The lively debate around the term genocide, on the other hand, shows the legitimate need to identify specific forms of mass violence as inordinately disastrous and therefore also mark them in terminology.

The question of defining the events leads us to the core issue of comparability of the phenomena in question. On the one hand it seems adequate to recognize categorical differences. The Holocaust is not only another link in a long chain of atrocities. It is defined through specific characteristics and it makes good sense to separate general forms of mass violence from scenarios that aim at the destruction of a people as a whole or in parts with verifiable intentions. We can therefore implement a hierarchy: at the top we have the unprecedented case of the Holocaust, followed by genocides, which nonetheless have to be defined separately, and finally we have to deal with other cases of mass violence. These again need to be differentiated from the phenomenon of violence induced by humankind. However, it would be fatal if the implementation of these hierarchies and categorical differences led to impermeable barriers for comparative studies or the transfer or knowledge.

The problem can be solved. If we strive to understand the phenomenon of the destruction of large groups of people, we should not begin with a complete comparative study in which all historical events in question must meet the criteria of a predetermined matrix – for example, the United Nations' definition of genocide. It is much more expedient to use an open model of comparison in which specific aspects of the Holocaust, of genocides and of other forms of mass violence can be analysed without limiting the comparative samples through a rigid system of classification.

I would like to specify how the transfer from different historical events might work with a few examples from Holocaust studies. I start with the question of decision-making.

In the past, historians of the Holocaust have devoted considerable time and effort to determine exactly a certain date, on which Hitler took the decision to murder European Jewry. With the unfolding of Holocaust research during recent years and growing awareness of the complex character of the Nazi policy of extermination, the concept of one central decision as a starting point for the mass murders has been replaced more and more by a new model. The emphasis here is to locate the decision for the final solution within a continuum of a decision-making process.

In this process, one can distinguish a number of points of escalation. They can be interpreted as reactions to the expansion and radicalization of the war, or, one should rather say, the Nazi perception of the radicalization of the war and its causes (i.e. their speculation about the decisive role of a worldwide Jewish conspiracy). However, decision-making about mass murder did not stop after the principal decision for a 'final solution' was taken. On the contrary, we must bear in mind that even after spring and early summer of 1942, when the systematic execution of Jews was extended to most parts of Nazi-occupied Europe, the fate of many millions of Jewish people hung upon further concrete life-and-death decisions. It took up to two more years until the mass murders were extended to countries like Denmark, Greece or Hungary. What has to be explained is the considerable energy that existed to keep the murderous machinery going and the extension of murder to new territories and groups of victims. In other words, putting more emphasis on a process of developing decision-making avoids presenting the mass murder of European Jews simply as the implementation of a decision taken at a particular moment, or as a kind of automatic process.

A couple of years ago, Donald Bloxham explicitly used this model of a complex decision-making process in order to re-examine the history of the Armenian genocide. Historians of the Armenian genocide struggle, like Holocaust historians, with the difficulty of precisely reconstructing the planning of this mass murder. One of the major obstacles is the fact that the responsible political body, the Young Turks' Committee for Unity and Progress, systematically and successfully concealed its deliberations – which is no surprise for a researcher in the field. Bloxham argues that the first arrests, massacres and deportations of Armenians since the beginning of 1915 should not be seen as a first step to implement an already existing plan for the complete annihilation of the Armenians. In his interpretation, the escalation of the killing can only be understood against the background of the intensification of the war during the first month of 1915 as perceived by the Ottoman regime and as reaction to the Armenian uprising in the city of Van. These factors can be seen as the catalyst force that caused the Young Turks to transform the ongoing regional massacres and actions of ethnic cleansing into a country-wide programme for the annihilation of the Armenian population. And, Bloxham explains, this fundamental escalation in the decision-making process is not sufficient to explain why the mass murders were continued until 1917. Again, this escalation can only be explained against a background of a long antecedent, i.e. the policy of the Young Turks to achieve national and ethnic homogeneity at the expense of the Armenians, who had to be removed in one way or the other.

That decision-making leading to genocide should be seen as a process is one of the main topics of Jacques Sémelin´s work. Sémelin has successfully shown how relevant research findings about the policy of extermination during the Nazi period can be successfully used to better understand the cases of Rwanda and Bosnia, and to explain them. Detailed research on the genocide in Rwanda, as done by Scott Strauss or Timothy Langman, for instance, has brought to light certain elements of a process of decision-making, preparation and execution of killings, and rejected the claim of a spontaneous uncontrolled wave of violence. In his work on Cambodia, Alexander Hinton, also emphasizes the procedural character of decision-making. In his view, a combination of factors were decisive: fundamental societal and economic changes that affected Cambodia in the 1970s; the policies of the Khmer Rouge to establish a social utopia on the ruins of the old order; and the imagination of an internal enemy based on newly developed criteria of social-economic and other differences.

In all of these cases, we can identify two important elements: The mass murders are part of far-reaching attempts to fundamentally transform existing societies, and the regimes had special units at their disposal that would carry out the mass murders in close cooperation with parts of the traditional apparatus of power.

This brings me to a second topic, upon which I will elaborate only briefly. Holocaust research has gained great insights about the perpetrators, their behaviour, their mentality and their motives. Both knowledge and methodology might be useful for other fields of research as well. For example, the discovery that the groups of mid- and high-ranking officials took the initiative to start and expand extreme forms of mass violence is critical. These groups had freedom to act and used this freedom for a variety of reasons to carry out what was in their interest. They were convinced of the correctness of their murderous 'work'.

In order to make these findings of Holocaust research fruitful for other case studies, it would be advisable to focus on certain key groups of middle and higher level perpetrators and to ask particularly how these people were formed in the period immediately before the crimes were committed.

One could easily identify, in addition to decision-making and perpetrator studies, a number of other examples to explain how findings in Holocaust research can be transferred to other areas. There is, for instance, the ambivalence of secrecy and openness that characterized the treatment of the Holocaust in the Nazi public sphere. It also has brought to light how many bystanders were in fact enriching themselves at the expense of the victims and became accomplices of the crime. This ambivalence created a grey zone of ostentatious ignorance, not wishing to know, speculations, rumours, but also shame among those who became willing or unwilling witnesses of the crime.

It is indeed possible to use the extensive knowledge we have gained about the Holocaust for other forms of extreme violence against social groups without questioning the historic significance of the Holocaust. It is also possible without the inappropriate attempt to implement an international standardized history of the Holocaust that would overshadow the different historic memory of these events in every country.

3

Global perspectives on Holocaust education: Case studies

The internationalization of Holocaust remembrance has not led to the emergence of a monolithic and homogenized memory of the genocide of the Jewish people. The Holocaust is indeed remembered against the historical background of the societies in which it is taught and the present challenges they face. Chinese, Americans, French, Rwandans or Argentinians will apprehend this history differently because they have different relations – if any – to the historical event, and because their own historical experience and national and local memories are different.

The Holocaust as a transnational subject, however, may serve as a prism through which to address local traumatic issues. Aleida Assman explains that 'the Holocaust has not become a single universally shared memory, but it has become a paradigm or template through which other genocides and historical traumas are very often perceived and presented. The Holocaust has not thereby replaced other traumatic memories around the globe but has provided a language for their articulation.' (GHI Bulletin No. 40, spring 2007, p. 14). Comparing and contrasting one's own history with that of other countries can provide learners with essential tools to explore new dimensions of their own national past and eventually draw lessons from it. They may come to understand that history is the result of multiple narratives and of a variety of experiences that can conflict with one another. The idea of understanding and reconciliation in a society goes hand in hand with accepting conflicting memories. Traumas cannot be abolished, nor can they be marginalized or minimized, but they can be negotiated through a mutual acknowledgement of the sufferings of different groups and their divergent perceptions of history.

The following case studies show that Holocaust education is a frame to deal with such dilemmas and ambiguities. Furthermore, it provides an opportunity for local traumas to be seen from the broader context of the common human experience. In this regard, Holocaust education, much more than providing a shared frame of reference, also serves as a guidepost and a warning that can inspire meaningful connections with an uncertain present, hence the development of approaches linking the history of the Holocaust with the promotion of human rights and democratic ideals. Through Holocaust education, one can come to realize that as much as it is a dreadful past, genocide also remains a risk of our times.

Holocaust Education in a Global Context

National memories in the prism of Holocaust history

Projections of Holocaust remembrance on the recent past of Argentina

Daniel Rafecas

During the 1930s and through the 1950s, Argentina played an unfortunate role internationally. The governments of these decades – the military dictatorships and the rule of the conservative party that remained in political power due to election fraud, joined by the most radical faction of the Catholic Church firmly controlled the destiny of the country during the era of the so-called Third Reich and other reactionary political movements in the Western world.

The Argentinian elites (political, economic, military, religious and judiciary) watched the emerging fascist movements all over Europe with fascination. They had a lot in common with these regimes: not only the disregard for democracy, but also shared views regarding the danger of communism and the alleged Jewish threat to their nationalist and Christian culture. During those decades, Argentina was guided by a nationalistic, anti-democratic, anti-communist and antisemitic state policy.

That is the reason why Argentina did not join the other American countries in the war against the Axis powers during the Second World War. On the contrary, Argentina refused to break diplomatic relationships with Germany until January 1944, and did not declare war on the Axis until March 1945.

Furthermore the Argentinian government followed a clearly antisemitic immigration policy: while remaining firmly sealed for European Jewish refugees, they opened their borders to thousands of war criminals from defeated Germany and its allies after the war.

The anti-liberal state policy continued throughout the following decades, especially during the consecutive dictatorships that devastated Argentina in 1955, 1962, 1966 and most brutally between 1976 and 1983.

In this authoritarian environment of intolerance, official educational policy focused on the glorification of key institutions – for instance the army and the church – and aimed at building a homogenous, hierarchical society in which those that were perceived as 'strangers to the community' were treated with prejudice and distrust.

In this atmosphere, Argentina's role between 1933 and 1945 and especially during the Holocaust was not addressed in any pedagogical curricula. For many decades, Argentina was held under an authoritarian rule, in which it was very difficult to teach and learn about the Holocaust. On the contrary, official sources often negated the historic facts and spread revisionist theories about the Shoah. After the military dictatorship collapsed in 1983, this situation began to change along with the development of a commitment to democracy.

The trials against perpetrators of mass crimes in Argentina: an opportunity and a challenge

In 1985, Argentina's democracy conducted a spectacular trial against the leaders of the last military dictatorship. The trial was exemplary in many ways. It was extremely important because it publicly acknowledged the crimes the authoritarian regime had committed against its political enemies.

But the movement towards deeper levels of justice and truth in the young, and therefore unstable and weak, democracy was soon replaced by a policy of impunity for the perpetrators, hidden behind a facade of forgiveness and reconciliation. This policy was followed until 2002.

In the last ten years, the parameters changed again and a human rights policy was implemented at the centre of the political system. The consolidation of Justice, Truth and Memory became top priorities in public affairs. For the first time in our nation's history, a **State Policy** with the goal of coming to terms with our recent past of state terrorism and its mass violence, was decided upon and is being implemented by all public entities.

Since 2002, legal procedures have begun all over the country, especially in the major cities. Hundreds of members of the military and security forces, from leaders to low-level agents, were put on trial for their crimes and thousands of victims were recognized as such. These attempts to confront the past are leading to a satisfactory reparation process.

The public trials were documented by the mass media, so that during these last ten years the public had the opportunity to realize what really happened during those years of darkness under the military rule: thousands of people were kidnapped, tortured and disappeared; homicides were committed systematically.

Along with the changes in the judiciary and the political system, the Argentinian educational system has also undergone a deep and historical change. Thanks to the strong efforts and permanent dedication of teachers and activists, the educational curricula of the past have been replaced.

Holocaust teaching is a key element in this process, not only because of the enormity and importance of these historical events, but because the legal processes are demonstrating the links between methods and systematic practices of the Argentinian military dictatorship and those of the Nazi regime. Furthermore, Holocaust studies have proved to be indispensable if we want to obtain a deeper comprehension of our recent past of mass violence. And finally, the historic events of the Holocaust play a crucial role in putting Argentina's state terrorism and its crimes into perspective. We will briefly touch upon these three aspects of how Holocaust education sheds light on Argentina's political history.

The shadow of Nazi methods against Jews and other minorities in Argentina's political repression in the 1970s

During the legal processes to discover the truth about the military dictatorship in Argentina, a terrifying institution was put on trial: the clandestine kidnapping and torture centres. These places existed all over Argentina and especially in the major cities between 1976 and 1977, with the goal of defeating the political enemies of the regime.

The government hid the horrible practices that they enforced at these centres from the public. The victims of the centres were systematically dehumanized and subject to degrading treatment: they were deprived of their names, blindfolded and forbidden to speak. They were deprived of food and clothing and forced to sleep in inhuman conditions. In addition to suffering unbearable living conditions, the victims endured torture.

When court trials and other investigative work revealed information about these methods, the public made comparisons with other places of institutionalized terror, such as the Nazi concentration camps.

Today we know that the objective of the clandestine kidnapping and torture centres was to turn people into non-persons, to strip them of any semblance of human dignity.

The reign of torture inside these terror places in Argentina in the 1970s was inspired by Gestapo methods. The insight of Jean Amery, a prisoner of the Nazis in the Auschwitz concentration camp, that torture was at the heart of national-socialist culture, also applies perfectly to Argentina's military dictatorship: everything was centred around torture. Not only was it a terrible method to gather information from the victim, it was also a tool to break the person's resistance and, perhaps even more important, a prelude to physical extermination.

Another connection between the violent methods of both regimes is the strategy of forcing people to disappear (*desaparecidos*). By denying someone's existence or knowledge of their whereabouts, the authoritarian regime can deny any illegal actions while simultaneously perpetrating any crime against the victim's body and soul. The person who has disappeared is completely isolated from his or her circles of belonging, without any rights at all, no defenders, no fair trial, not even due process of law: only a system of 'Police Justice'. The victims are kept in secret and hidden places, where torture is the normal procedure, where existence remains suspended between life and death. These were the same procedures used by the Nazi regime with its infamous decree of *Nacht und Nebel* (night and fog) in occupied France and other territories to persecute members of unwanted minorities.

The study of the Holocaust allows a deeper comprehension of Argentina's recent past of mass violence

I would like to illustrate this argument with the following two examples: a) the antisemitism of the Argentinian perpetrators and b) the mass violence, which had never been observed on such a level in Argentina, or even anywhere in Latin America.

Regarding antisemitism, the recent trials in Argentina have proven beyond any doubt that a large majority of the perpetrators were extremely cruel towards Jewish prisoners and subjected them to extremely violent forms of torture. Jewish victims held in a clandestine centre often disappeared or were killed without mercy.

Argentina's Jewish population makes up approximately one per cent of the total population, but about ten per cent of those disappeared and killed during the last military dictatorship were Jewish, so Jewish victims are ten times over-represented in this unfortunate statistic.

As in the Germany of 1933, in Argentina in 1976 the goal of the official authorities was to annihilate 'undesirable elements' in the country. This policy was inspired by national-socialistic ideology, but had a political and religious base. According to Argentina's authoritarian regime, the 'Jewish-Bolshevik conspiracy' tried to undermine the country with its communist ideology.

This ideology was transmitted in the official speeches of military authorities during that time. But it was also the language used by the torturers and kidnappers in the clandestine centres, in statements such as 'we are not nationalist, we are national-socialist'; or 'Hitler's work is not finished and we must continue with the task until the last Jew has been annihilated from the face of the world.' It was not unusual to hear German military anthems and recordings of Hitler's speeches or to see swastikas and Nazi flags inside those Argentinian centres.

In conclusion: the cultural and educational environment from the 1940s to the 1960s, when the soldiers and policemen were growing up, was filled with intolerance, hate and fear of anyone who didn't fit the strict model of the authoritarian culture nationalistic, occidental and Christian. That intolerance, hate and fear was unleashed with immense power in the last dictatorship of 1976.

The second point is the level of mass violence in this phase of the dictatorship. This mass violence was analysed in depth over the last decades, and today it's possible to state that in 1976 the military leaders, and their civilian collaborators inspired again by the Nazi persecution of the European Jews – decided to implement a domestic 'Final Solution', in this case of the 'subversive' or 'extremist' question.

Indeed, the military and police forces had fought against left wing military organizations that continued to persevere in their struggle against oppression. Despite the perpetrators' efforts, the 'subversive' question continued to exist. So, inspired once again by the Nazi regime, a radical option emerged, an obviously criminal option, impossible to realize under conventional state institutions and mechanisms: the physical extermination of all 'extremists', and also of their collaborators or sympathizers. Once they had finished the work, Argentina's military leaders declared that 'the subversive question is definitively solved from now on'. At the cost of writing the darkest page in the nation's history.

These two examples show clearly that both aspects of Holocaust studies and education – learning about antisemitic ideology (especially linked with anti-communism), and the genealogy and implementation of the logic of the 'Final Solution' – are essential in order to better comprehend what happened in Argentina in those years.

The crucial role of Holocaust studies in putting Argentina's state terrorism and its crimes into perspective

Holocaust education plays an important role in comprehending Argentina's recent past of mass violence. A deeper knowledge about the Holocaust allows us to put all our different points of view, our established truths and our language, our way of defining and expressing what happened to us as a society, into perspective.

I would like to elaborate more on this with a few thought-provoking examples.

Inside the Argentinian clandestine centres I mentioned before existed a rule of torture, and the depersonalization of the inmates was its primary function. On the basis of this characteristic, a number of intellectuals, historians, journalists and survivors, whose work centred on the historic facts of these centres, called them 'concentration camps'. Some even went so far as to describe them as 'extermination camps'.

This is not the place to argue against these definitions and the use of these terms. Nevertheless it seems obvious that if we get a deeper understanding about the concentration camp system, and even more about extermination camps under the Nazi regime, we will inevitably seek a different definition, a special term, to differentiate Argentina's centres, despite the fact that some similarities exist between them.

Another discussion between sociologists and jurists dealing with Argentina's recent past examines whether it is possible to define the events in Argentina as genocide. In political circles, in the media coverage of the issue, in the language used by human rights activists, and in the voice of many survivors, it is very common to use the word *genocide* to refer to Argentina's case.

In addition, some judges defined the crimes committed as perpetrated in the context of *genocide.* At this point it becomes clear that the use of Holocaust terminology to describe other events makes it necessary to create a definition of genocide to name the unnamed: a definition able to comprehend those extraordinary situations where a totalitarian regime decides to eradicate a whole people, distinguished by a racial or other arbitrary reason, forever from the face of the earth.

Holocaust studies allow us to understand the deep and special implications of the concept of genocide: If humanity is a tree, the perpetrators want to cut off one of its branches forever; their intention is not only to physically exterminate the persecuted minority (including old people, women and children), but also to erase any trace of their existence from history and culture.

Hence, in Argentina, learning more about the implications of the Shoah, especially the consideration of the scale of the perpetrators' objectives, might lead to a more cautious application of the term *genocide* to the history of our mass crimes. It was proven widely in our judiciary process that the motives of Argentina's authoritarian regime were guided mainly by *political reasons*; the military wanted to exterminate the left wing organizations, their members and their allies, but not the parents or the families of the leftists, nor their extended communities. That they did not care about their religion, or any other factor or motive is key to Raphael Lemkin's concept of *genocide*.

As a judge who deals with the terrible facts of Argentina's past, I'm convinced, especially when comparing them to the history of the Shoah, that the term *genocide* is not suitable for the Argentinian case. In the last three years, the majority of the criminal courts, including the National Cassation Chamber – the highest criminal court – refused to use it and defined what had happened as *crimes against humanity*.

Conclusions

One conclusion we can draw from Argentina's experience is that when a society with a state policy that prohibits review or discussion of an authoritarian past lies in the shadow of other historic eras, like the Nazi period and the Holocaust, this history in turn remains unexplored and is not understood. For many decades Argentinian society lived with a forced collective amnesia, dealing only with an immutable, impenetrable past and a superficial present, where Holocaust survivors in Argentina had to remain in silence because no one wanted to hear or believe that truth.

Fortunately, since the last decade, those days are over.

In the challenging field of searching for justice, truth and memory, Argentina's experience over these last ten years shows how an environment favourable to revisiting the past, with the goal of consolidating the democratic process and preventing the authoritarian culture, also allows for a better understanding of the past and favours teaching about the past. It teaches what happens when citizens have neither rights nor guarantees against a devastating military state power: concentration camps, or the clandestine centres, with massive killings and disappeared people.

Despite the fear that concentrating on Argentina's recent past of state mass violence could lead to ignoring other terrible experiences, just the opposite has happened. Never before has there been such widespread interest in the Holocaust and its origins as in recent years. Now there are many more opportunities to introduce teaching about the Shoah into Argentinian public education. New initiatives in Argentina's universities abound, such as official chairs, seminars, or open courses which address aspects of the Shoah.

There are two explanations for this phenomenon: one is the undeniable connection between the Nazi totalitarian procedures and strategies and those of Argentina's military perpetrators. This includes the shared perception of a Jewish-Bolshevik conspiracy, the use of facilities recreating the concentration camp universe, and the logic of the Final Solution against their internal enemies. The second explanation is a general awareness of the importance of in-depth knowledge of past experiences for the present. This link between the past and the present remained closed in Argentina for a long period. It seems the open view of the past illuminates not only the domestic past, but also the Shoah. The interest in both phenomena is growing, bringing about fruitful mutual feedback. We are taking advantage of these extraordinarily positive circumstances and have focused on working especially with the new generations.

In conclusion, as a Latin American country with a past submerged in the authoritarian culture through most of the twentieth century, Argentina is finally giving itself the opportunity, perhaps for the very first time in its history, to look honestly into its recent past. In this process, Holocaust remembrance has a key role, not only as a crucial episode of modernity, but also as a source of knowledge and essential studies for a better comprehension of what happened to Argentina as a society. Teaching about the Holocaust also helps to reinforce our still developing democratic system, in order to guarantee – for the next generations, fully educated in a democratic atmosphere – a future that supports one universal goal: never again.

Educating about the history of genocides in Rwanda

François Masabo

Located in the African Great Lakes Region, the Republic of Rwanda covers an area of 26,338 square km, with a population estimated at 11 million in 2011. It became a German colony after the Berlin conference of 1884 and fell under the Belgium mandate after the First World War. After the Second World War it became a United Nations Trust territory still under the rule of Belgium. The country gained its independence on 1 July 1962.

Rwanda's population is composed of three social groups, namely Hutus, Tutsis and Twas. All these social groups live together in the same villages without any separation of areas belonging to a specific group, sharing the same culture, beliefs and institutions. However, the colonial rule considered social groups (Hutu, Tutsi, and Twa) as different social classes, tribes, casts, and races. All anthropological definitions such as castes, tribes, social classes and groups do not apply to the Rwandan case.[65] Unfortunately, the colonial rulers, in the first republic (1962–1973) as well as in the second (1974–1994), built their leadership on the basis of these wrong interpretations of the Rwandan identity.[66]

The first republic set up a discriminatory regime by institutionalizing 'ethnic racism' through a de facto mono-party system[67] based on 'ethnic majority', which eventually got radicalized by the second republic through the so-called democracy of an 'ethnic and regional quota' system[68].

During the time of the two republics, periodic ethnic massacres against the Tutsi group were organized, in 1963, 1966, 1973, 1990 and1992, finally culminating in the 1994 genocide against the Tutsi.[69] Within three months, from April to July 1994, one

---

65 A. Shyaka, *The Rwandan Conflict, Origin, Development, Exit Strategies*, Kigali, NURC.

66 C. Braeckman, 1994, *Rwanda, Histoire d'un Génocide*, Paris, Fayard.

67 The single party was the *Mouvement Démocratique Républicain pour les Hutu* (MDR-PARMEHUTU).

68 This time the single party was the *Mouvement Révolutionnaire National pour le Développement* (MRND)

69 C. Braeckman., *op.cit.*

million Rwandan Tutsi were cruelly killed by **Interahamwe** (those who fight together) militias, assisted by the national army and many members of Hutu groups under the command of the genocidal government of the so-called **Abatabazi** (rescuers). The survivors (casualties, women who were raped and infected by HIV, numerous widows, widowers and orphans) are seriously affected and psychologically traumatized by the genocidal atrocities committed against them.

More than one million Hutu people have been sentenced by the Gacaca jurisdictions for their participation in the genocide against the Tutsi[70]. It was planned by Rwandans to kill other Rwandans. But it was also stopped by the Rwandans themselves. Moreover, it was stopped by those who were targeted by the genocide ideology. The education about genocide in Rwanda is linked directly to the specific situation created by the 1994 genocide against the Tutsi.

Educating about genocide as an obligation in Rwanda.

In the aftermath of the genocide, the Rwandan society feels the importance of teaching the history of this genocide on a large scale. On various occasions, many Rwandans have demanded the development and dissemination of knowledge related to the concept of genocide. In 2001, the umbrella organization of survivor associations organized an international conference on the theme 'Life after Death'. One of the recommendations at the conference made to the Ministry of Education was to develop a curriculum on the history of genocide appropriate for different levels of education in primary, secondary and tertiary schools. The main objective of the teaching material is to provide young generations with relevant knowledge about genocide and to empower them with prevention mechanisms[71].

At the same conference, secondary school teachers stated that they face various questions from students in their history courses, who want to know exactly what happened during the genocide in Rwanda in 1994. They need to know the significance of the genocide for Rwandan society and why all adult Rwandans perceive it as such

---

70   National service of Gacaca Courts, summary of the report presented at the closing of Gacaca courts activities, Kigali, 2012, p. 36-37. According to the report, the number of suspects tried by Gacaca courts is 1,003,227.

71   Association IBUKA, *Rapport synthétique et préliminaire de la conférence internationale sur le génocide : La vie après la mort. Rétablissement de la vie des survivants du génocide, défis et opportunités,* preliminary report from the international conference 'Life after death', Kigali, 25 30 November 2001, p.31 (unpublished).

a horrible crime. Educating about genocide has become an obligation in a society torn by genocide.

The government of the Republic of Rwanda has shown its determination to fight against genocide by stating in its Constitution (1) the commitment to oppose genocidal ideology (art.9), and (2) the creation of a National Commission to strive against genocide, with a dual mission: to institute a research and documentation centre on genocide, and to coordinate all activities pertaining to the perpetuation of memory of the genocide against Tutsi (art.176).

The theme the government chose for the eighteenth anniversary to commemorate the genocide against Tutsi in 2012 was 'Learning from the past and building a bright future'. It captured the relevance of the history of genocide to foster prevention mechanisms.

From this background, it is clear that there is a real need in Rwanda to relate the post-genocide reconstruction of the country to the teaching of the history of genocide. Otherwise, it can be very difficult to address the various consequences of genocide visible within Rwandan society.

However, there is some resistance by both survivors and perpetrators to teach about the genocide within Rwandan society. The Tutsi genocide was planned and executed by Rwandans against other Rwandans. Survivors and perpetrators are still living together. Remembering the horror may be unbearable for survivors because it refreshes the memory of their own suffering. At the same time, perpetrators declare that addressing this past reminds them of the crimes they committed, frustrates them, and opposes the process of reconciliation.

Some people consider teaching about the genocide harmful and useless. But we have to be aware that downplaying the unpleasant past has consequences. After all, since it happened once it could always happen again.

Despite the resistance, there are many reasons to advocate for genocide education in Rwanda: fostering human rights, conveying knowledge about the concept of genocide, and creating preventive measures.

Fostering human rights

Teaching genocide history in Rwanda is a way of fostering human rights, tolerance and mutual respect. It is a means of building unity and reconciliation in the society after the 1994 genocide against the Tutsi. Teaching about genocide reminds us that such violence is not spontaneously generated. It is planned and executed in an organized way, and it occurs when the mechanisms to regulate society are overturned by genocidal ideology, and human rights and civic values – the very rights and values at the centre of living together in the community – are no longer respected or enforced.

In every country where genocide or other atrocities have occurred, historians noticed a preceding flagrant violation of fundamental rights of citizens; segregation mechanisms, and other stigmatization and discrimination measures in various aspects of life. All these practices culminate in the dehumanization and extermination of target groups. In Nazi Germany, for example, Hitler's accession to power coincided with legal measures excluding Jews from public service, denying citizenship to all Jews, stigmatizing Jewish citizens by marking their passports with a 'J' (Jude), destroying their synagogues and businesses. The systematic denial of rights to the Jews culminated in their murder[72]. The same happened in Rwanda during the first and second republic on the basis of the ideology of ethnic segregation. The Tutsi were denied full citizens' rights. They served as scapegoats for the regime. During the first republic all opponent parties affiliated to Tutsi parties were suppressed without any reason. Their members were threatened, imprisoned, killed or forced into exile. During the second republic an 'ethnic quota system' was established that aimed at limiting the number of Tutsi children in schools, and Tutsi in public service. Around 1990, only one Tutsi was in the cabinet out of 25 ministers, only one was the governor of a province out of 10 and not one was a mayor out of 107 throughout the country.

The crime of genocide involves a process of different phases, with the objective to desensitize people to the violation of the target group's basic rights. Teaching the history of the Holocaust and genocides can help raise awareness of those different phases and prevent all kinds of injustice and unfairness. Holocaust education can also foster the rule of law, in which all citizens can cooperate to gain the full enjoyment of their fundamental rights. This cannot happen in country that subscribes to genocide ideology.

Finally, it empowers the whole society to promote tolerance and democratic practices such as the civic right to participate in public affairs, fair and transparent elections, tolerance, and reinforcement of institutional capacities.

---

72   W. L. Hewitt, 2004, *Defining the horrific*, Pearson Prentice Hall, New Jersey, p. 143.

Providing knowledge and skills

From my own experience of teaching in the field of genocide studies, I know how difficult understanding genocide can be. First, the concept of genocide is complex because its definition has so many constitutive elements. Second, there are many schools of thought in the field of genocide studies that challenge the United Nations definition. These schools 'contest the importance of particular facets of the crime to understanding its fundamental nature, and which of the multitude of atrocities in the last century can truly be called genocide'.[73] Thirdly, the denial of genocide is one of the core components of its planning and execution. Perpetrators of these atrocities make huge efforts to mask the reality.

Teaching about the Holocaust and genocide must respond to a series of questions, such as: Which specific elements constitute the crime of genocide? What is its specific nature? What distinguishes it from other related crimes such as war crime, ethnic or identity-based conflicts, etc.? Who are the victims? Who are the perpetrators? What is genocidal ideology? How does it express itself in a given national context? As stated by Deborah Harris: 'An appropriate definition of genocide is a crucial tool through which to understand and interpret both specific instances of genocide and the phenomenon more generally.'[74]

Holocaust education provides us with a well-researched and documented conceptual framework that allows us to define genocide and to differentiate it from other related crimes such as war crime, crime against humanity, mass killings, etc. As such, it can be used as a starting point to understand other forms of human violence in other contexts.

Creating preventive measures

Most of the time, the crime of genocide is perpetrated within a context of classic and conventional warfare. This leads often to some confusion between genocidal crimes and other related crimes. Rwanda faced the same challenge with the genocide against the Tutsi. Until now, we have faced denial and revisionism based on the same confusion. The planners of genocide talk about the ethnic conflict or double genocide because it happened directly after a conventional war between the

---

73   Idem, p. 29.

74   Ibid., p. 29

government of Rwanda and the RPF rebellion, even though it ended with the Arusha peace agreement of 4 August 1994. This confusion can be cleared up by skilled people who are capable of deconstructing and reconstructing the real nature of the crime of genocide. Thus they can take appropriate measures to prevent it.

The Great Lakes Region especially is characterized by genocide-related ideologies, some of which even deny the genocide against the Tutsi. Genocide education is a tool that can bring support to educators and researchers who are committed to opposing these negative ideologies. As stressed by Deborah Harris: 'The definition of genocide has the power to influence how the history of genocide is written, and even which parts of history are written.'[75] The best way to prevent genocide is to stop the spread of its ideology. This cannot be achieved without enabling skilled people in the field to identify and trace it through speeches and writings[76]. Ignorance in this matter may lead to denial, lack of remembrance, or repetition of the crime.

Engaging with Holocaust education in post-apartheid South Africa

Richard Freedman

This paper will examine both the history of and rationale for the integration of Holocaust history into the national South African school curriculum, as well as the challenges and opportunities the inclusion has presented in the context of post-apartheid South Africa. It will investigate the question of how it came about that the study of the Holocaust was included in the National South African Schools Curriculum. In what way has this served as a catalyst for grappling with South Africa's own history of a racial state? These questions will be explored in the course of this article.

---

75 D. Harris., 2004, Defining Genocide: Defining History? in W. L. Hewitt (ed.), *Defining the horrific. Readings on Genocide and Holocaust in the twentieth century*, pp. 29–37.

76 H. Fein., 2002, Genocide: a sociological perspective, in Alexander Laban Hinton (ed.), *Genocide: an anthropological reader*, pp. 74–90.

The first Holocaust centre in Africa

The South African Holocaust and Genocide Foundation (SAHGF) is the first of its kind in Africa. Through its three centres in Cape Town, Durban and Johannesburg, it is uniquely positioned to respond to the challenge of creating a space for dialogue around social cohesion in a multicultural society, especially as it plays out in the formal education environment in South Africa. To mark International Museums Day 2010 in Cape Town, South African heritage practitioner Wandile Goozen Kasibe argued that: 'In post-conflict societies such as South Africa, museums are beginning to grasp the urgency of assuming responsibilities as catalysts of socio-cultural change and inclusivity. ... Fostering social cohesion is a founding principle of South Africa's new democratic dispensation. ...We must heed Paulo Freire's comment, "We must never provide the people with programmes which have little or nothing to do with their own preoccupations...." This question could not have come at any better time than when the citizens of South Africa's fledgling democracy and its institutions are collectively seeking ways of fostering an inclusive society, where people can no longer fear the nature of their differences. South African museums have begun to assume a leading role in opening a *space for this dialogue through education and public programmes.*' [77]

In this context of new dialogue, while it may be tempting to compare the Holocaust and apartheid, this would not be an accurate reading of the historical exhibitions of the SAHGF and the entire enterprise of Holocaust education in post-apartheid South Africa. Whilst there are distinct parallels between the racial laws of apartheid South Africa and Nazi Germany between 1933 and 1939, the period following the beginning of the Second World War bears no comparison. Yet the points of intersection between these two racial states, and the timing of the opening of the Cape Town Holocaust Centre in 1999, paved the way for the successful inclusion of the study of the Holocaust into the national school curriculum.

On the eve of the first democratic elections in South Africa in 1994, the Anne Frank Centre in Amsterdam, breaking its boycott of South Africa during the apartheid years, accepted an invitation to send over the exhibition 'Anne Frank in the World'. The exhibition toured eight major cities and was seen by thousands of South Africans from all backgrounds and strata. To underscore the message of the exhibition and its plea for greater understanding and acceptance of differences, a smaller ancillary

---

77   Africom News, 20210/11, Issue 9, p. 19

exhibition 'Apartheid and Resistance' was devised by the Mayibuye Centre of the University of the Western Cape. This exhibition helped to contextualize the story of Anne Frank in South Africa's own history of racial discrimination and oppression.

The impact of the eighteen-month-long travelling exhibition was profound. It opened a new discussion about racism. For most South Africans who saw the exhibition, it was the first time they were exposed to the concept that racism is not a black/white issue alone, but is rooted in prejudices experienced across the globe. A teacher who brought a busload of school children to visit the exhibition in Cape Town made the following revealing remark:

'You have no idea how important this experience has been for the self-esteem of my students. You see, this is the first time that my students have understood that a person can be discriminated against even if he does not have a black skin.' [78]

Such visitor feedback clearly demonstrated the potential for Holocaust education in the new South Africa to challenge conceptions of racial prejudice and the abuses of extreme power. This provided a context for fulfilling the vision of the founding committee of the Cape Town Holocaust Centre: the creation of a powerful tool for social transformation. The study of Holocaust history provides a prism through which South Africans are able to engage with human rights violations. The study of the past provides a framework for confronting the many forms of prejudice that still today remain latent challenges within South African society.

Dealing with prejudice in the context of South African history remains difficult because of its immediacy and legacy in both time and space. However, the history of the Holocaust, so removed from the South African experience, helps people gain distance from their own predicament. This helps them to engage not only with the past but also the pressing needs of a still deeply wounded society. Thus, the first panel of the Holocaust Centre exhibitions in South Africa illustrates the legacy of racial theory with particular reference to the apartheid experience. The use of visual cues through artefacts and photographs in the exhibition establishes strong parallels to the later panels in the exhibition that deal directly with Nazi Germany. This may be seen through the display of identity documents that black South Africans were forced to carry, photographs reflecting the separation of public amenities such as benches, and the inclusion of legislation that served as the building blocks of apartheid laws, which were reminiscent of the Nuremberg Laws. For any South African with

---

78   In a comment to Myra Osrin, Founder of the Cape Town Holocaust Centre, when the exhibition was shown at the Iziko South African National Art Gallery.

knowledge or memory of their national history, the exhibition experience therefore becomes profoundly personal.

Engaging with the formal education structures

From the outset, the Cape Town Holocaust Centre's education team worked hand in hand with the Western Cape Regional Department of Education to develop a school programme that would incorporate the exhibition as a teaching tool. This was a crucial decision, reflecting the understanding that the Centre could not serve only as a memorial, but also had to be a place of learning. There is no doubt the existence and impact of the Cape Town Holocaust Centre profoundly influenced the decision of the national school curriculum designers to include the study of the Holocaust.[79]

The manipulation of the education system had been a key component in the apartheid regime's process of creating a racial state. Schools reflected the broader South African society: they were divided along racial lines defined in terms of colour into four separate Departments of Education. The group to which you were assigned impacted the quality of the education you received and the resources the State allotted to your education. The majority of the population – those classified as black – received totally inadequate and inferior facilities in overcrowded conditions, taught by underqualified and poorly trained teachers. It is clear the content of the curriculum, which differed according to the racial classification, was carefully designed to perpetuate the divisions in society and not to fulfil the expectations and aspirations of pupils.

It is no wonder therefore that one of the key tasks confronting the first democratically elected South African government in 1994 was to dismantle both nearly fifty years of apartheid education and nearly three centuries of colonial education that had gone before. This was an enormous challenge, informed and underpinned by the new South Africa's Constitution and Bill of Rights. The resulting curriculum is one that has human rights at its core.

The school curriculum

The curriculum designers felt the inclusion of the Holocaust as a case study of human rights abuse was very important, given the curriculum was to be based on the Constitution and Bill of Rights. This in turn was directly influenced by the Universal

---

79   Interview with Gail Weldon, former Chief Curriculum Advisor (History) WCED,19 April 2012.

Declaration of Human Rights, which had arisen out of the Second World War and the knowledge of the Holocaust. The protection and enhancement of human rights informs the central philosophy of the Constitution, to 'heal the divisions of the past and establish a society based on democratic values, social justice and fundamental human rights.'[80]

The resultant curriculum is one 'ensuring that the educational imbalances of the past are redressed, and that equal educational opportunities are provided for all sections of our population', promoting 'human rights, inclusivity, environmental and social justice' and 'infusing the principles and practices of social and environmental justice and human rights as defined in the Constitution of the Republic of South Africa.' [81]

The commitment of the South African post-apartheid government to Holocaust education is evinced by the fact that learners in Grade 9 are obliged to study it. This is most likely because completion of Grade 9 provides a possible exit point from the education system and those who continue to Grade 10 are required to make a narrower subject choice selection. There is thus no guarantee that learners will study history beyond this point. Hence, since 2007, all South African history teachers have been required to teach the Holocaust in their schools across the country. Fifteen hours have been allocated to the study of the Holocaust, second only to the amount of time given to the study of apartheid. The impact of the programmes and classroom support materials entitled *The Holocaust: Lessons for Humanity*,[82] developed by the education team at the Cape Town Holocaust Centre, played an important role in the decision-making processes of the national curriculum designers.[83]

The challenges in the national education arena

Certain anomalies in the South African political and educational arena pose particular challenges to the teaching of the Holocaust in the South African context. Teachers often have little or no knowledge of the Holocaust. Many South Africans may approach any European history with a degree of scepticism as it is often viewed in terms of the devastating impact of colonialism.

---

80   The Constitution of the Republic of South Africa, Act 108 of 196, preamble, p. 1.

81   National Curriculum Statement and Assessment Policy Statement for Social Sciences, January 2011, p. 3.

82   The materials comprise a DVD with historical overview and survivor testimonies, a learner's resource book, a teacher's manual and a poster set.

83   Interview with Gail Weldon, former Chief Curriculum Advisor (History), WCED, 19 April 2012.

Other hindrances towards effective implementation of the Holocaust history syllabus are the most profound and enduring effects of apartheid inequalities that are to be found in education, including inadequate infrastructure and amenities, especially in poor communities, inadequate training for teachers, high levels of poverty and unemployment, and the debilitating effects of illness and premature death (especially as a result of HIV and AIDS). The SAHGF, as the major service provider of teacher training in Holocaust education in the country, has had to find ways to work even in the most affected rural communities.

South Africa has eleven official languages. The language of instruction, English, is often the second or third language for teachers and learners. Workshops for teachers and learners are usually conducted in English, but where possible, the SAHGF makes use of mother tongue speakers to augment the discussion. The SAHGF's education team now includes facilitators who are proficient in, or are mother tongue speakers of, Xhosa, Afrikaans and Zulu.

Holocaust education in South Africa

'In line with the guidelines of the National Department of Education, the SAHGF's approach to teacher education is based on the notion that, while content knowledge of the Holocaust is vital, providing educators and learners with content alone is not enough. Workshops run by SAHGF teachers reflect upon the creation of identity, assessing societal influences on the individual that sow the seeds of prejudice, ignorance and racism. A key question addressed is why people choose to act out their prejudice. What conditions encourage such behaviour? What are the consequences of these choices? This approach to Holocaust education operates from the belief that exploring these questions is essential in helping participants see themselves as agents and shapers of their world, capable of making a difference.'[84]

'The curriculum underlines the choices and responsibilities faced by everyone in their personal capacity, and looks at a spectrum of human behaviour as envisaged through Holocaust history; this includes the perpetrators, bystanders and resistors, and elicits an appreciation that this is not predetermined, that there are always choices. It is hoped in this way to create an understanding that participants do have

---

84 T. Petersen, 2010, *Holocaust education in post-Apartheid South Africa: impetus for social activism or a short-lived catharsis?* Paper presented at inaugural conference of FIHRM, Liverpool, p.1–2.

the power to make an impact on their world and that they have a moral and ethical responsibility to act in order to protect and promote human rights.'[85]

The SAHGF is viewed as a major resource in the country for teacher training and classroom materials, but it is not the only source and neither should it be. Yet there is cause for concern if the locus of control for teacher education and resource materials falls outside of the SAHGF. There has been a frenzy of textbook writing and all those devoted to social sciences and history cover the Holocaust. They vary in both the range of material covered and levels of accuracy. Where some provide merely a footnote to the Second World War, as it was in the former curriculum, others have gone into more detail. However, there is little or no control over the accuracy of information or degree of trivialization of the historical specificities that appear in the textbooks. Ultimately, the creators of educational resources material have minimal influence over the decision of an individual teacher to use inappropriate material in the classroom.

At the core of the SAHGF's classroom support material is the examination of the Holocaust in order to confront issues facing contemporary society. For example, in the pages that document the flight of Jews from Nazi-occupied Europe in the 1930s, the questions directed at the learners include the following:

Should governments help refugees from countries where there are severe human rights violations? And how are refugees in South Africa viewed and treated?

Unfortunately, questions like these do not in themselves lead to changes in attitude. This largely depends on the effective facilitation of the educator in the classroom. The challenge is that teachers have to address their own attitudes before they are able to bring awareness to the learners.

Because it is so removed from the experience of both teacher and learner, the Holocaust, as a case study of human rights abuse, has the potential to draw out personal attitudes and prejudices such as xenophobia that otherwise remain repressed. Only when these issues are exposed can they begin to be addressed and overcome.

There are many unresolved issues in South African society and a great need for healing. This was revealed in a recent independent external evaluation of the SAHGF's

---

85 Ibid., p. 2.

teacher training programme.[86] The study also demonstrated that the emotional preparation of educators is central to Holocaust education. It would appear that learning about the Holocaust 'created the emotional space for educators to speak frankly about their own experiences.'[87] Thus, by moving first into the extreme history of the Holocaust, they were more prepared to begin examining their own painful history. The SAHGF programme, because it engages with contemporary issues of prejudice and racism, invariably evokes a response from educators in which they relate their own stories of prejudice and discrimination experienced during the apartheid era. In this sense, the encounter with Holocaust history has given permission for this frank self-examination and revelation.

There were never a great number of Holocaust survivors who made South Africa their home after the war, and thus Holocaust education in South Africa has not depended on personal interaction with survivors. The successful inclusion of the Holocaust into the curriculum has depended on the commitment of government through the National Department of Education to the inclusion of the subject in the national curriculum in a substantial and significant way. This has included increasing access to materials designed specifically for the South African context and the endorsement of effective teacher training programmes facilitated largely by the SAHGF.

The road ahead

Much investigative work still needs to be done on the impact of the introduction of Holocaust education into schools and on whether there has been a measurable change in the ethos of the schools where the subject has been taught successfully. It remains the goal of the SAHGF to use the study of Holocaust history to produce learners who are motivated and empowered to recognize their potential to be effective agents of positive change and who will choose not to be bystanders in the face of injustice.

Whilst the inclusion of Holocaust history has presented enormous challenges, it is clear that through effective teacher training and classroom teaching the study in South African schools of this particular area of history has the very real possibility of

---

86 An Evaluation of the South African Holocaust and Genocide Foundation's Teacher Training Programme from 2007 to 2011, Final Report, April 2012. Mthente Research and Consulting Services.

87 T. Petersen, 2010, Holocaust education in post-apartheid South Africa: impetus for social activism or a short-lived catharsis?,. Paper presented at inaugural conference of FIHRM, Liverpool, p.3.

catalysing our emergent democracy into becoming a more caring and just society, respecting diversity and healing the injustices of our past. Now more than ever, the value of including the study of the Holocaust in South Africa's school curriculum has assumed a new urgency and relevance.

References

The Constitution of the Republic of South Africa, 1996, Act 108.

Department of Basic Education Republic of South Africa, 2010. Curriculum and Assessment Policy Statement (CAPS).

Freedman, R.,2008. Teaching the Holocaust to non-traditional audiences: the South African experience. Association of Holocaust Organisations Conference, Yad Vashem. "Teaching the Holocaust to Non-Traditional Audiences: Results and Applications".

Mthente Research and Consulting Services, 2012. *An Evaluation of the South African Holocaust and Genocide Foundation's Teacher Training Programme from 2007 to 2011.*

Nates,T. May 2009. Teaching the Holocaust in post-apartheid South Africa: issues and challenges. UNESCO conference *Combating Intolerance, Exclusion and Violence through Holocaust Education.*

National Department of Education, *C2005 Revised National Curriculum Statement*

National Department of Education, 2006, *The National Policy Framework For Teacher Education and Development in South Africa.*

Petersen, T. 2006. Lessons for Humanity. South African History Teachers Conference.

Pollack, L. 2009. *A Place of Memory, a Place of Learning: The first ten years of the Cape Town Holocaust Centre.* Hands-On Media

Sigabe, M. and Mphithi, E..1999. JET Education Services, The President's education initiative research project. *A descriptive study of the nature and effectiveness of in-service teacher training and support in the implementation of OBE.* University of the Witwatersrand.

Silbert, M and Wray, D. 2010. *The Holocaust: Lessons for Humanity, Learner's Interactive Resource Book*, 2nd edition.

South African Human Sciences Research Council, 2006, *Education Hearing Report Part II.*

A new frame to reinterpret China's past: Holocaust studies in China

Xu Xin

Holocaust studies/education is a unique programme in China. China is a country without an antisemitic tradition and the Holocaust happened in places thousands of miles away. Is Holocaust education necessary in a country such as China? What is the importance of promoting Holocaust education among the Chinese? Chinese experiences indicate that the development of Holocaust education is linked closely to Judaic studies in China. It is necessary to encourage the study of the Holocaust in order to promote Holocaust education. The paper attempts to analyse the uniqueness and importance of Holocaust studies/education by providing the background and accounting on some of the major activities of Holocaust studies in China.

Historical background

In order to address the issue of Holocaust studies/education in China, it seems necessary to examine briefly the background of the issue.

The Chinese public knew very little about the Holocaust at the time because there were relatively few reports in China about what was happening to the Jews in Western countries between 1933 and 1945. The Chinese were facing the invasion of Japan at that time, their country was in dire trouble and they were focused on their own problems. But this does not mean that all Chinese were totally ignorant about the situation, and particularly not the intelligentsia. A few events are worth mentioning.

Chinese intellectual circles became aware of the persecution against the Jews shortly after the Nazis came to power in Germany. For instance, when the news that Germany was burning books reached China, a protest against Nazi persecution of Jews was organized on 13 May 1933 in Shanghai by the China League for the Protection of Civil Rights, a non-governmental organization of Chinese intellectuals and social activists headed by Song Qingling, better known as Madam Song, wife of Dr Sun Yat-sen (Dr Sun was considered the founder of the republic of China and a supporter of the

Zionist movement [88]). This is the first recorded event of a protest against the Nazis in China.

Secondly, once Hitler came to power in Germany in 1933, the Chinese, especially those who lived in cities such as Shanghai, Tianjin or Hong Kong, where Jewish communities had existed for many decades, began to learn about the ill treatment of German Jews, mainly through the arrival of Jews from European countries. Many Jews who escaped antisemitic persecution in Germany came to Shanghai for safe haven and brought with them stories of the horrors committed by the Nazis. From 1937 to 1940, when persecutions got worse in Europe, more than 20,000 Jews sought refuge in Shanghai. Chinese newspapers began to describe them as Jewish refugees and informed Chinese readers about their fate.

In general, Chinese people as well as the Chinese government were very sympathetic to Jewish refugees and took action to assist the Jews in China, even though the Chinese people were then enduring Japanese oppression. The Chinese government set about helping Jews in Europe. Sun Fo, son of Dr Sun Yat-sen and Chairman of the Chinese legislative body, proposed to establish a settlement in Southwest China for those who were suffering in German-occupied countries in 1939. Newly-discovered documents show that his proposal was officially approved by the Chinese Administrative Council and the government.[89] Though the resolution was regretfully not implemented due to the complicated situation of the Second World War, it serves as strong evidence that the Chinese government and people did not stand by in silence. Sun Fo's proposal makes it clear that at least he and the Chinese government were fully aware of the sufferings of the Jews in Europe.

The significance and importance of that action stands out even more when one considers the situation in China at the time. In 1939, as the persecution of the Jews in Germany was intensified, the Chinese were suffering greatly from the Japanese invasion and its atrocities. Half the territory of China was under Japanese occupation, and millions of Chinese died. The brutality of the Japanese war against China was truly horrific. For instance, during the full-scale war against China, the Japanese

---

88 Sun wrote in his letter to N.E.B. Ezra, Secretary of the Shanghai Jewish Community on 24 April 1902: 'All lovers of Democracy cannot help but support the movement to restore your wonderful and historic nation, which has contributed so much to the civilization of the world and which rightfully deserves an honorable place in the family of nations.' *The Selected Works of Sun Yat-sen*, 1985, Beijing, Vol. 5, pp. 256-257. See also *Israel's Messenger*, a Jewish publication in Shanghai, November 4, 1972.

89 'Chungking National Government Programme for the Placement of the Jews in China', *Republican Archives*. 1993. No. 3, , pp. 17-21.

conducted the Nanjing Massacre in 1937, which in about six weeks left some 300,000 people dead.

It is worth mentioning that the Chinese communists, who were few at the time, also denounced fascism (both the Nazis and the Japanese). They considered the Jewish people a component of the Asian oppressed nations. In October 1941, a gathering on anti-fascism was held in Yan'an, site of the headquarters of the Communist Party of China at that time.

However, the attention given to the issue by the Chinese was not widespread. Only a limited number of Chinese, mainly scholars, politicians, diplomats and social elites, were aware of the Holocaust and were able to express their concern. [90]

Post-war period

Reports of the horrible consequences of the Holocaust reached China early on, almost as soon as the Second World War ended in Europe, because of the presence of Jewish refugees in China. They were eager to learn about the fate of their loved ones who had remained in Europe and a Jewish network passed the information to China. We have evidence that lists of those who died in concentration camps and elsewhere were posted on Chinese streets in Shanghai. Affecting only a limited number of Chinese, this news did not draw substantial public attention. The situation in China continued to be difficult, and the attention of the Chinese remained almost entirely on their own fate. [91]

The earliest more general awareness of the Holocaust during the post-war period was perhaps the publication of the Chinese version of *The Diary of Ann Frank*. It is estimated that many hundreds of thousands of copies were sold. It was through the *Diary* that a majority of the Chinese learned for the first time about the Final Solution and the atrocities committed by Nazi Germany.

The topic of the Holocaust was barely raised after the Chinese Communists took power in China in 1949. It does not mean the Communists entirely dismissed the issue. Rather they followed the Soviet Union's line on the Holocaust and viewed the destruction of the Jews as merely a small part of racist fascism's murder of millions of European civilians. Since fascism was considered the ultimate form of capitalism,

---

90   There were from time to time a few articles appearing in various Chinese magazines and newspapers reporting or commenting on the persecutions during World War II.

91   It is estimated that more than 30 million Chinese died during the war.

capitalism was blamed as the root cause of the massive killing. According to this perception, nothing was different or special about what had happened to the Jews.

As Communist China was (and is) a highly politicized country, politics and ideology have played a decisive role in all fields, including academia and education. The ultra-leftist policies adopted in Chinese social and academic circles since the1950s made it almost impossible to conduct serious academic research on the Holocaust. On top of that, the discussions in the early 1950s on establishing formal relations between China and Israel were fruitless, even though Israel had recognized Red China in January 1950, the first country in the Middle East region to do so. China adopted an anti-Israel foreign policy in the mid-1950s after it established diplomatic relations with three Arab countries (Egypt, Syria, and Yemen). The nature of the relations between China and Israel obstructed the study of the Holocaust. Even the trial of Adolph Eichmann in the early 1960s did not break the silence[92]. Indeed, China became more and more separated from Israel as it aligned with the Arab states in foreign policies and Middle East affairs. The Holocaust was hardly mentioned in Chinese textbooks about the Second World War.

A changed situation since the 1970s

The relations between China and the West changed in the beginning of the 1970s, and the country opened up to the Western world. As a result, books and movies about the West were introduced to the Chinese public, and strict control over academic activities was relaxed. As a result, a few Western books which mention the Holocaust were translated into Chinese. Among them were *The Rise and Fall of the Third Reich* by William Shirer [93] and *The Winds of War* by Herman Wouk.[94] These books, which dealt mainly with the Second World War and Nazi Germany, became very popular, and gave Chinese readers a chance to learn about the antisemitic policies of the Nazis. The wartime atrocities and genocide of the European Jews then began to appear frequently, in numerous other books. Chinese scholars began to pay attention to the issue.

---

92 The book by Simon Wiesenthal about hunting Adolf Eichmann and other Nazis was finally translated into Chinese and published in 1991 by Beiyue Art and Letters Press.

93 First published by Beijing Sanlian Shudian in 1974. There are numerous editions by various publishers in China.

94 First published by the People's Literature Publishing House in 1975. Many editions by different translators exist.

Mass awareness

A change in the relations between China and Israel occurred in the late 1980s and early 1990s, which ultimately led to the establishment of full diplomatic relations. Chinese attitudes toward Israel began to change dramatically. A number of related public events took place around that time, which helped the Chinese learn a great deal about the Holocaust. For example:

Genocide, a documentary about the Holocaust produced by the Simon Wiesenthal Center, was aired on Chinese TV in 1991.

The exhibition 'The Courage to Remember: the Holocaust 1933 1945', also prepared by the Simon Wiesenthal Center, was shown in a few Chinese cities including Shanghai, Beijing and Nanjing from 1991to 1993. In Nanjing, the exhibition caught the attention of the public when it was displayed deliberately at the Memorial Hall of the Nanjing Massacre; it was widely covered by the city's media and attracted as many as 80,000 visitors in a period of seven weeks.

Other events further increased awareness of the Holocaust. One was a documentary entitled *Sanctuary Shanghai—Jewish Refugees in Shanghai,* which aired on Chinese television in 1998. Another was Chinese President Jiang Zheming's visit to Israel in 2000. His visit to Yad Vashem was widely reported on prime time Chinese television, so that tens of millions of Chinese learned about the Holocaust when they tuned in to the news. The film *Schindler's List* reached a large audience in China as well.[95] It was thus in the 1990s that the grim revelations of Nazi atrocities were widely exposed in China.

Academic Studies

Education depends largely on scholarly research. Holocaust education is no exception. Therefore, it is very important to address Holocaust studies in Chinese academia.

Since the late 1980s, Chinese scholars have begun to examine the Holocaust. Books on the Second World War written by Chinese authors started to include sections on the Holocaust. *On Hitler's Antisemitic Policies* by Zhang Qianhong is perhaps

---

95　At the same time, quite a few novels such as *The Holocaust* were translated into Chinese and movies such as *Life is Beautiful* were shown in China.

the first academic essay in Chinese focusing on the issue.[96] Though its emphasis is on Hitler's policies and it does not trace the deep roots of Hitler's antisemitism, the article nonetheless provides a fairly good analysis. Zhang presents a 'three-phase' theory in her scrutiny of the Holocaust process: First, legal persecutions from 1933 to 1939; mass expulsion and segregation from 1939 to 1941; and the 'Final Solution' from 1941 to 1945.

Jewish studies, which started in the late 1980s and early 1990s in China, accelerated after the normalization of the diplomatic relations between China and Israel in 1992. Besides conferences, exhibitions and courses, a large number of books[97] and articles on various Jewish and Israeli subjects appeared in Chinese.

In 1995, two books specifically on the subject of the Holocaust were published in Chinese, marking a turning point in Holocaust studies in China. They were Yang Mansu's *Catastrophe for Jews—Records of the Holocaust*[98] (which sold more than 100,000 copies in a few months) and Zhu Jianjing's *The Death of Six Million Jews in Europe.*[99] These publications provided Chinese readers with a much fuller and more concrete picture of the Holocaust than any previous books. Though both present a narrative description, and not a strictly academic analysis, they played an important role in informing Chinese people about the Holocaust. The two books have many similarities. Both describe the history of the Holocaust chapter by chapter and try to analyse Nazi policy towards Jews at different stages. Both give accounts of the hunting of Nazi criminals after the war. Both underline that no one must ever forget the Holocaust and all should do their utmost to prevent it from happening again.

Anti-Semitism: How and Why,[100] my book examining the issue of antisemitism from a historical perspective, gives a deeper analysis of the causes of the Holocaust. Examining the root of the Nazi antisemitic policy, it cites not only the Germans' long tradition of antisemitism and the role of the Christian tradition and the church in generating antisemitism among Germans; it also points out that antisemitism became a popular viewpoint in modern Germany. This approach aimed to help Chinese readers understand why very few Germans stood up to condemn Hitler's policies against Jews.

---

96 Zhu W. and Jin Y. (eds).1992. *Chinese Judaic Studies in the 1990s*, Shanghai Sanlian Shudian.

97 More than 60 books published in Chinese by 1994. For details see *Catalogue of the Chinese Books about Israel and Jewish Culture*. 1994. Xu X. and E. Propper (eds).

98 Published by China Social Sciences Publishing House, 1995.

99 Published by Shanghai People's Publishing House, 1995.

100 Published by Shanghai Sanlian Shudian,1996.

The book also explores the post-war influences of the Holocaust on ideological and political concepts; the way in which the world regards the Jews and the Jews regard themselves in the post-war period; the treatment of the Holocaust in historiography; and the repeated attempts to deny the Holocaust or to distort its meaning. The book's attempt to analyse antisemitism and relate the Holocaust to the history of antisemitism in Europe is perhaps its unique aspect.

In 2000, Pan Guang, a scholar of Jewish history, published 'The Nazi Holocaust and its Impact on Jewish People and Jewish Civilization' in **World History**,[101] a well-known Chinese journal for world history studies. The article may mark the beginning of the development of Holocaust studies in China.

Holocaust education

Holocaust education appears in Chinese colleges and universities with the deepening of Holocaust studies and the awareness that 'the Holocaust fundamentally challenged the foundations of civilization and the unprecedented character of the Holocaust will always hold universal meaning'.[102] Nanjing University has played a leading role in Holocaust education in China.

Under the leadership of the Glazer Institute of Jewish Studies at Nanjing University, a 'learning Jewish culture' project was launched in 1990 to promote the study of Jewish subjects among Chinese college students. Though at the very beginning the Holocaust was only a small part of the regular courses on Jewish culture, students' interest in learning more about it grew. In 2000, the centre started to offer an entire course, entitled 'The Holocaust through Videos'. The syllabus was prepared jointly by Xu Xin and Dr Peter Black, a senior historian at the United States Holocaust Memorial Museum. Through a combination of lectures and videos, the course covers not only the roots of the Holocaust, its process with details of persecutions and atrocities, and its consequences; it also presents its lessons for humanity, the human rights issues involved, its messages to the Chinese, and how to prevent it from happening again.

In order to introduce Holocaust education throughout China, a teacher's training seminar was held at Nanjing University in 2005[103], co-sponsored by the Task Force of the European Union, the Fondation pour la mémoire de la Shoah, the London Jewish

---

101 *World History*, 2000, No. 2, pp. 12–22.

102 Cf. 'Declaration of the Stockholm International Forum on the Holocaust'.

103 A second one was held at Henan University in July 2006 with over 100 participants.

Cultural Centre, and Nanjing University. Over eighty people from seven countries participated in the seminar. The project included participants from Yad Vashem; the United States Holocaust Memorial Museum; the Anne Frank House (Amsterdam); the Shoah Memorial; the Centre of Contemporaneous Jewish Documentation (France); the Imperial War Museum (London); the Chinese Academy of Social Sciences; the Memorial Museum of the Anti-Japanese War of China; the Centre for Nanjing Massacre Studies; the Shanghai Academy of Social Sciences; and others.

As Chinese scholars learned about the Holocaust and how to teach it, they also shared their expertise on the Nanjing massacre with the non-Chinese participants. Parallels were drawn between the two atrocities. The seminar sparked considerable interest from the Chinese side and helped promote education, remembrance and research about the Holocaust in colleges throughout China. Seminar participants learned not only the facts but the necessary skills to disseminate their knowledge at their universities. Holding a seminar on the Holocaust with the background of the Nanjing Massacre proved to be effective and useful for presenting unprejudiced and accurate knowledge of the Holocaust to Chinese scholars who teach and study world history or western civilization at Chinese universities. This context helped the Chinese to recognize the unprecedented characteristics of the Holocaust and made the Holocaust real for the participants. Moreover, it provided a unique opportunity for Chinese scholars to study the Holocaust in a systematic way without having to go abroad, and to learn how to teach Holocaust-related courses in China.

Chinese educators have also been going abroad to attend Holocaust educational programmes since 2000. Professor Lihong Song, Deputy Director of the Glazer Institute of Jewish Studies at Nanjing University, reflected during the 2005 seminar on a workshop he attended in the US: 'I heard for the first time in my life the first-hand accounts from four Holocaust survivors and one liberator. Their stories and experiences are the unforgettable episode of the workshop.' Song is currently editing a volume in Chinese of international papers on the Holocaust, some of which are from the *Occasional Papers Series* published by the United States Holocaust Memorial Museum.

In 2010 and 2011, groups of young Chinese scholars and graduates from various universities and colleges attended a Holocaust education seminar organized by Yad Vashem. The participants of this programme will surely go on to play an important role in promoting Holocaust studies/education in China, since many of them are instructors in Chinese higher education.

Uniqueness of Holocaust studies and education in China

Holocaust studies in China are unique. They are closely linked to and appeared with the advance of Judaic studies in China, which exposed many scholars to Holocaust issues. Hence most scholars who have published or translated books or articles on the subject are involved in Judaic studies in China. Yang Mansu, Pan Guang, and I, for instance, are all leading figures in the field.

Summarizing the development of Holocaust studies in China, we note an invariable trend: Judaic studies leads to the study of antisemitism, which leads to Holocaust studies. With the growth of Judaic studies, Holocaust studies will surely grow in China as well.

Holocaust studies/education becomes a valuable reference for the Chinese because it provides a reference for examining the Nanjing massacre. The unspoken purpose of Holocaust studies in China is to establish that reference between the Holocaust and the Nanjing massacre. We cannot say the interest in Holocaust studies in China stems only from the Chinese's attempt as a tactical measure to highlight their own sufferings. But Holocaust studies certainly help the Chinese to focus on these sufferings and to find different ways of examining and remembering the Nanjing massacre in particular and the persecutions of the Chinese during the Second World War in general.

Moreover, Holocaust studies/education provides useful lessons for the Chinese to combat the denial of the Nanjing massacre. Like the Holocaust denials in the West, some Japanese historians attacked the authenticity and objectivity of evidence and testimony regarding the historic events.

Holocaust studies/education highlights human rights issues in China. What Hitler did is considered a crime against humanity and it raises a number of questions: How could one group of human beings commit these crimes against another group? Why did the rest of the world stand by in silence when the Holocaust took place? What is human nature? Why did the preservation of human rights disappear during the Second World War? Those questions are raised and discussed in the Holocaust courses, helping to bring out more human rights debates among the Chinese.

Conclusion

Looking back, Holocaust studies/education in China has made great progress since it began about ten years ago. Interest in this field among scholars and young people is growing. More and more scholars are involved in Holocaust studies/education. However, compared to the situation in many other countries, Holocaust studies/education in China is in its infancy. China still needs a national institution or a national programme for Holocaust education. Textbooks, especially for elementary and secondary school students, mention almost nothing about the Holocaust. There is no single Holocaust museum in China. Though some thought has been given to planning a workshop or seminar on the Holocaust for instructors at Chinese colleges and universities, action is needed.

The vast majority of the Chinese still have difficulties comprehending the Holocaust. Many issues concerning the Holocaust such as questions about the guilt of the German people, complicity and collaboration in the countries under German occupation, the failure of non-Jews to attempt to save their Jewish neighbours, etc. are rarely touched upon by Chinese scholars. Therefore, there is still a long way to go and much to be done. It is certainly my wish that, with the advancement of Judaic studies in China, more Chinese scholars take on this topic and deepen their study of the Holocaust. It is imperative for Chinese scholars to improve their research to meet international standards, and to produce fruitful results of value to their colleagues in Holocaust studies/education all over the world.

Promoting human rights and democratic values

Holocaust, democratic values and Jewish-Arab dialogue: The work of the Center for Humanistic Education at the Ghetto Fighters' House Museum

Anat Livne and David Netzer

The Center for Humanistic Education (CHE) was founded in 1995 by Raya Kalisman as an autonomous institution within the Ghetto Fighters' House (GFH). It has developed a particular approach to Holocaust education in terms of its content, methodology and target groups. The distinctive feature of CHE programs is the pedagogical connection between learning history and cultivating democratic values and a pluralistic dialogue. The history of the Holocaust is learned as a conceptual platform for humanistic discourse and in-depth Jewish-Arab dialogue oriented towards democratic coexistence in the Israeli context.

The CHE approach to Holocaust education deserves a conceptual analysis for two reasons. One is the pivotal role of Holocaust memory in Israeli society: it is not an overstatement to say that the legacy of the Holocaust still has a formative impact on Israeli collective identity. The second is the unconventional integration of the Holocaust with Jewish-Arab dialogue. The two issues are commonly perceived in Israel as oil and water – they do not mix. At CHE, however, the Holocaust is the departure point and *leitmotif* of the entire educational process. The location is no less important than the content: Ghetto Fighters' House is a publicly established Holocaust commemoration institution, a sort of Holocaust-related brand name, and CHE does not attempt to play down this association.

Holocaust Education in Israel

An analysis of Holocaust education should start from a conceptualization of history teaching in general. Historical perception is always a socio-political product. Examining a historical representation of any subject requires an understanding of the social context and of the motivations, goals and aspirations underlying pedagogical decisions. 'History', we know, is not an absolute or objective entity – it is an expression of a worldview, a narrative, a story.

In a comparative study of school history textbooks published in Israel in the years from1948 to 2006, Kizel writes 'The textbooks serve the educational establishment as a tool to provide a selective structuring of events, to categorize and shape the content, and also to hide and erase parts of history. Since the texts hold the status of official authority in the eyes of the students...they form a collective "We", particularly vis-à-vis "the Other"", and prevent stepping out of line to know and accept that "Other"' (Kizel, 2008).

Since the early 1980s, the state's educational leadership has sought to mobilize the memory of the Holocaust to strengthen Jewish identity. A law enacted in 1980 by the Knesset that made it mandatory for every Israeli high school student to study and pass an examination about 'The Holocaust and Heroism' (*HaShoah vehaGevura*) was explained by the need 'to make the Holocaust a cornerstone of the identity of Israeli youth' (Porat, 2004).

Zevulun Hammer, the influential education minister of the 1980s and 90s, pointed to three elements of modern Israeli identity: Judaism, Zionism, and the Holocaust. The latter 'plays a vital role in our ongoing physical and spiritual struggle to live in our homeland' (Knesset protocols, quoted in Porat, 2004).

These ideological goals were buttressed by publication of a new textbook, which became dominant: Gutman and Schatzker's *The Holocaust and its Meaning* (note the singular), which clearly and openly emphasized the uniqueness of the Holocaust in both Jewish and global history as a singular event that should be studied by itself, on its own merits.

Another book that appeared at the same time was Arie Carmon's *The Holocaust: A History for the Upper Grades*. Totally different in concept and structure, this text was rarely used in schools and never approached the popularity among teachers of Gutman and Schatzker's text. Keren (1998) described it as an attempt to revolutionize the historical and educational perception of the Holocaust: 'For the first time, a historian and pedagogue dared to present Nazi conduct as a process that might occur in any society and that might cause other national groups to dehumanize their rivals, to engage in systematic violent and even murderous behavior.' Carmon explicitly challenged the mainstream linking of the Holocaust with Zionist postulates, and refrained from highlighting the Zionist youth-led ghetto uprisings in his narration of the Holocaust.

Carmon's non-conformist book was a meaningful inspiration for the founders of the Center for Humanistic Education.

CHE Approach to Holocaust Education

Since 1995, CHE has specialized in teaching the universal meanings of the Holocaust, and educating in light of the moral issues it raises.

The humanistic vision rests on two pillars. One : instilling the notion of the ethical priority of the individual over the society, obliging the latter to provide the individual with the conditions required to fulfil his or her potential. According to this notion, human dignity and wellbeing top the value-scale, above any social ideology – religious, national, or economic.

The second pillar is the socio-political implementation of this ideal: namely, pursuing a progressive, enlightened, democratic society based on equality, moral sensitivity, and social solidarity.

The educational programmes bring together both an historical and ethical dimension, seeking to instil humanistic ideals, attitudes and behaviour:

The historical dimension revolves around the Holocaust, focusing on human behaviour in extreme situations. Social and political processes in Germany of the 1930s – the collapse of German democracy and the swift Nazification of German public life; the persecution of Jews, Sinti and Roma, homosexuals, political opponents, those with mental or physical disabilities, and other groups; the evolving marginalization of non-Aryans and finally the initiation of the 'Final Solution' – these are some of the issues probed to elicit relevant insights across time and place.

The ethical dimension deals with the concept of democracy as a set of values, conceptualizing human rights as an ethical framework for relations between individual and state, the 'I' and the 'We'. In this context, there is a critical analysis of racism; the socio-psychological mechanisms of stereotyping, exclusion, and conformity; the moral choice between not getting involved and intervening; the moral dilemmas of officials and soldiers who encounter immoral orders. Other cases of genocide in the twentieth century are analysed in order to enhance knowledge and enable educated criticism of human social and moral behaviour.

It must be acknowledged that this approach faces criticism by both historians and pedagogues. The major arguments can be summarized along two themes: the instrumentalization and the trivialization (or banalization) of the Holocaust.

Instrumentalization: Schatzker, cited above, wrote that enlisting the Holocaust for ends other than itself carries the risk of emptying the Holocaust of its unique and singular meaning in human history – which is a moral error. 'Using the Holocaust as an exercise in moral education is futile', wrote Schatzker. 'Everyday behavior should draw from everyday examples, not from extreme, unprecedented dilemmas imposed on the victims' (Schatzker, 1999).

We disagree, and believe a rigid presentation of contextual knowledge provides the student with tools to make sound connections. Referring to genocide, for example, Yehuda Bauer wrote, 'While the Holocaust is the most extreme case of genocide, it still belongs to the same general kind of human activity. Nazi conduct was cruel, but not inhuman' (Bauer, 2008). When confronting our students with moral dilemmas, we refrain from encouraging them to make judgments, which have little to draw upon from their personal experience. Rather, we promote an understanding of the situation, the considerations, the options or lack of them. Our goal is to shed light on the complexity of the situation and its moral variables, and thus help change a simplistic, one-dimensional perspective into a complex, multi-dimensional one.

Trivialization: The risk of reducing the Holocaust to one more example of human cruelty is a pitfall we are aware of and careful to avoid. We acknowledge our responsibility toward the special place of the Holocaust, and we labour to balance properly the general with the specific. 'The only way to construct definitions and generalizations is through comparisons. If we want to know more about social pathology, the question of whether the Holocaust constitutes an incomparable case of genocide in history is a very important one' (Bauer, 2008).

Our experience is that when done properly and consciously, placing the Holocaust alongside other cases of genocide does not diminish its particularity, but, on the contrary, provides the student with the tools to understand it in a broader context. In their feedback, our students point to these associations as significantly different from their school learning.

A universalist approach in Holocaust education – still a challenge

The difference between the State and CHE in terms of the rationale for teaching the Holocaust relates to both the type of historical interpretation and the educational-social goals.

With regard to the historical interpretation, the difference is manifested in the particularistic Jewish versus the universal approach. The former maximally isolates the Holocaust from other historical and social contexts in other times and places with the goal of creating a Jewish story that has no counterpart. In the universal approach, we take the opposite tack – the Holocaust is connected to a range of contexts in an effort to illustrate that it could have happened in another place or circumstance.

Bauer puts it this way: 'What happened before can happen again. We are all potential victims, potential perpetrators of crime, potential bystanders...If there is one chance in a million that reason and the desire to survive can prevail, we have the moral obligation – as in the ethical imperative of Immanuel Kant – to make the effort' (Bauer, 2008: 75).

The educational-social goals address different issues. When the Holocaust is used to construct and sustain a collective national identity, non-Jews are unable to participate in the evolving Israeli ethos. The CHE seeks to harness this historical event for broadening the common denominator among all segments of society.

CHE's educational activity channels the perception of the Holocaust as a universal event into the realm of multicultural and bi-national dialogue. Empathy with the victims of Nazism and revulsion from racist theories and the persecution of minorities are bound to a humanistic worldview, creating an emotional and moral bond among diverse groups in Israeli society. Reflection upon moral and human issues shapes a discourse of tolerance and empathy, which allows for a productive discussion about contemporary problems in Israeli society and Jewish-Arab relations.

In Israel, mainstream teaching of the Holocaust in schools with a Jewish majority still uses the particularistic approach, in which the memory of the Holocaust reaffirms the Jewish-Zionist lesson. The trend that began in the 1980s continues to dominate, and we find ourselves trying to persuade school principals and teachers who are not much different from those in the early years of CHE. Israeli society, in general, has increasingly turned inward and isolated.

Jewish-Arab dialogue – and talking about the Holocaust as part of this quandary - has not become easier. Since 2000, with the Israeli-Palestinian conflict alternately raging and deadlocked, Jewish and Arab citizens of Israel are drawing further apart from each other. Mutual hostility has not eased, but rather become even more virulent, as has the refusal to acknowledge the Other or the Other's narrative. In this reality, many perceive humanistic, universal values to be naive or irrelevant.

In 1995, the founders of CHE were sure they were blazing a trail that would in short order become a well-travelled highway. These were the 'Oslo days', when new approaches and new melodies were in the air about fundamental Israeli issues such as its identity, internal relations among its groups and external relations with its neighbours.

At the dawn of the second decade in the twenty-firstcentury, this vision still seems distant. Some say the weakness of educators is their optimism. Perhaps this is the secret of their strength?

References

Aloni, N. (ed.). 2008. *Empowering Dialogues in Humanistic Education*. Tel Aviv, Hakibbutz Hameuchad, pp. 18–45 (Hebrew).

Bauer, Y. 2008. *Thinking about the Holocaust*. Jerusalem, Yad Vashem (Hebrew).

Carmon, A. 1980. Teaching the Holocaust as education for values, in *Halakha Lema'aseh Betikhnun Limudim*, (3), Tel Aviv, pp. 96–110 (Hebrew).

Keren, N. 1998. Preserving memory within forgetting: the struggle over teaching the Holocaust in Israel *Zmanim* (64), pp. 56–64 (Hebrew).

Kizel, A. 2008. *Subservient History: A Critical Analysis of History Curricula and Textbooks 1948–2006*. Tel Aviv, Mofet Institute (Hebrew).

Netzer, D. 2008. *The Work and Impact of the Center for Humanistic Education*. UK, University of Sussex (PhD thesis).

Porat, D. A. 2004. From the scandal to the Holocaust in Israeli education. *Journal of Contemporary History*, Vol. 39 (4), pp. 619–36.

Schatzker, C. 1998–99. Problems in contemporary Holocaust teaching. R. Feldhay and I. Etkes (eds.). *Education and History: Cultural and Political Contexts*. Jerusalem, Zalman Shazar Center for Jewish History, pp. 447–56 (Hebrew).

Facing History and Ourselves

Leora Schaefer and Marty Sleeper

*...let's think about the history we learn. It is important that
we learn the uncomfortable parts. It is from the uncomfortable
parts that we really learn. It is there that we can find the conflicts
that help us to understand ourselves.*

These are the words of a 17-year-old high school student reflecting upon her
Facing History and Ourselves class. For nearly four decades, Facing History and
Ourselves has been providing junior and high school classes with resources for
the 'uncomfortable parts' of history, encompassed within a model of educational
intervention and professional development that helps teachers and their students
make the essential connections between history and the moral choices they confront
in their lives. Through an in-depth study of the years leading to the Holocaust as
well as other historical cases of mass atrocity and genocide, Facing History engages
teachers and students of diverse backgrounds in an examination of racism, prejudice
and antisemitism, as well as courage and compassion, to promote development of
student capacities for active, responsible participation in a pluralistic democratic
society.

In Facing History and Ourselves classrooms, middle and high school students learn
to think about individual and group decision-making and to exercise the faculty of
making moral judgments. Drawing on the seminal work of developmental theorists,
including Dewey, Piaget, Erikson and Kohlberg, the pedagogy of Facing History
and Ourselves speaks to the adolescent's newly discovered ideas of subjectivity,
competing truths and differing perspectives, along with the growing capacity
to think hypothetically and the inclination to find personal meaning in newly
introduced phenomena. Facing History recognizes that adolescents are budding
moral philosophers who come to their schooling already struggling with matters of
obedience, loyalty, fairness, difference and acceptance, rooted in their own identities
and experience. They need to build the habits, skills and knowledge to help them
find the connections to the past that will inspire their moral imaginations about their
role in the future. By exploring a question in a historical case such as why some
people willingly conform to the norms of a group even when those norms encourage

wrongdoing, while others speak out and resist, Facing History and Ourselves offers students a framework and a vocabulary for thinking about how they can make difference in the world.

The intellectual and pedagogic framework of Facing History and Ourselves is built upon a synthesis of history and ethics for effective history education. Its core learning principles embrace intellectual rigor, ethical reflection, emotional engagement and civic agency. Its teaching parameters engage the methods of the humanities: inquiry, critical analysis, interpretation, empathic connections and judgement. Facing History and Ourselves teachers employ a carefully structured methodology to provoke thinking about complex questions of citizenship and human behaviour. Building upon the increasing ability to consider alternative scenarios and imagined options, they stretch the historical imagination by urging consideration of what might have been done, choices that could have been made and alternative scenarios that could have come about.

The framework not only focuses on how history informs the present, but also helps young people look at difficult events and find connections to their own lives. It encompasses concepts and vocabulary that are familiar to adolescents: identity, membership, stereotyping, conformity, peer pressure, leading and following, in-groups and out-groups, judgment and responsibility. Having students use such terms as an entry into history and as a lens through which to confront its complexities helps illuminate universal themes and also encourages them to make connections between these particular historical moments and the choices they make in their everyday lives. For our students in North America, the Holocaust happened on a different continent in a much different time from the one in which they live. For this reason, students can feel disconnected from the content. However, the Facing History approach to the teaching of history, and specifically to the study of the Holocaust, invites students to make meaningful connections that engage them cognitively, ethically and emotionally to the content that they are studying. The student whose words open this article, for example, later recalled that, as a recent immigrant from Brazil when she studied Facing History in high school, she could barely speak English. But as part of that study, 'I not only learned to read and write, I gained a language for dealing with what has happened in history and in my life. Words like bystander, prejudice, exclusion, choice. I did not just learn these words– I learned to understand through them.'

The focal case study of Facing History and Ourselves is an in-depth analysis of the failure of democracy in Germany and the steps leading to the Holocaust—the most documented case of twentieth-century indifference, de-humanization, hatred, racism, antisemitism and mass murder. It goes on to explore difficult questions of judgment, memory and legacy, and the necessity for responsible civic participation to prevent injustice and protect democracy in the present and future. The materials used draw on content from history, literature, art and science. Students examine such resources as propaganda posters that demonstrate the power of labelling and the use of words to turn neighbour against neighbour. They make connections to other situations past and present of collective violence based upon hatred and discrimination. Throughout the unit, students learn and practise the skills of in-depth historical thinking and understanding, including knowledge of chronology, analysing historical context, evaluating evidence, determining causality and confronting multiple perspectives.

Students learn that violence and injustice begin with small steps of indifference, conformity, accepting one's environment uncritically. They discuss what words like perpetrator, *bystander* and *upstander* can mean in the context of both everyday and extreme situations. First person narrative, from writings, video testimonies and guest speakers, constitutes a compelling core to the programme. Holocaust survivors tell of their experiences and talk about the need to confront and bear witness to history. 'When you talk about the Holocaust, you're talking about six million people. You can't even fathom that many,' noted one Facing History teacher after a Holocaust survivor spoke to her class. 'But when you talk to one person and talk about his experience – how members of his family died and the hiding he went into – you have some details about the individual that make a history come alive.' Students also hear about individuals whose actions reflect courage and resilience and whose determination to stand up for human rights have influenced subsequent public policy.

While the failure of democracy in Germany and the years leading to the Holocaust comprise the core case study of Facing History and Ourselves, other examples of de-humanization, hatred, discrimination, mass violence and destruction, such as the histories of the eugenics movement, apartheid in South Africa, and the civil rights struggle in America, broaden and deepen these themes. Each component of these histories is linked to issues and decisions in the present and the constellation of individual and group choices, decisions and behaviours that comprise 'Ourselves'. Teachers provoke the intellectual, ethical and emotional impulses of their students to draw the connections between past, present and future. Examining the collapse of democracy in Weimar Germany, the rise of the Nazis, the role of propaganda, conformity and obedience in turning neighbour against neighbour, and examples of courage, compassion and resistance, for example, provide the needed perspective to talk about both the past and the present. Using a case study of another time and place, in which universal themes of human behaviour, choice and decision making are embedded, facilitates analysis and reflection about resonant historical patterns while avoiding false comparisons and simplistic parallels. By learning the particulars of each history, Facing History students are provided with the necessary tools with which they can begin to make connections to other historical moments and current events, as well as to their own life experiences.

Throughout their Facing History 'journey', students continually return to the question of participation and its meaning within the framework of a democratic society Democracies are fragile enterprises, and can only remain vital through the active, thoughtful and responsible participation of its citizens. Education for democratic citizenship means encouraging students to recognize that responsible participation grounded in ethical judgment can make a difference in the present and future. To that end, they should not only engage with examples of what Facing History calls 'upstanders', but must also develop such social-emotional skills and competencies as self-awareness, empathy, perspective-taking, conflict resolution and ethical decision-making. By ending with participation, Facing History and Ourselves helps teachers and students explore those moments in history and today when individuals, acting with courage and compassion made a difference in achieving social justice.

For many educators, the experience of learning and teaching Facing History and Ourselves resonates with the deepest aims and goals that brought them to the profession. Teachers are usually introduced to the programme through workshops offered in school and community settings or online. Professional development seminars, all including face-to-face interaction and online components, provide intensive sessions in the latest scholarship and in the methodology of teaching sensitive issues in the classroom. Content is interwoven with pedagogy to engage participants in fundamental issues of teaching: how to come to grips with the prejudices and preconceptions teachers and students bring to difficult and controversial subject matter; how to address moral decisions with students without preaching or evasion; how to build a classroom environment of trust and respect for diverse opinions; how to orchestrate discussion in which students truly talk and listen to one another; how to use journals and personal writing and reflection; how to ask the additional question that complicates the simplistic answer and provokes critical thinking. In essence, the pedagogy aims to create a classroom climate of respect and inclusivity, foster student participation, encourage diverse viewpoints and engage students with different learning styles. Through their own confrontation with the issues of history and human behaviour that the seminars raise, teachers think together about the meaning and the challenge of bringing those issues to their classes. They consider the need to evoke and honour student voice to build together a reflective learning community, where teaching and learning take place in a climate of respect, multiple perspective-taking, acceptance and understanding of difference.

Numerous studies have documented the positive impact of Facing History and Ourselves on teachers and students. In the most comprehensive evaluation to date, a two-year study using an experimental design provides significant evidence that Facing History and Ourselves helps create effective teachers who improve their students' academic performance and civic learning. The study was designed to assess the programme's impact on these teachers and on the academic performance (e.g. skills for analysing history), social and ethical awareness, and civic learning and engagement of their students. The report concluded the Facing History and Ourselves professional development services engage teachers and increase their effectiveness. Those teachers who received Facing History and Ourselves services, compared to those who did not, demonstrated a statistically significant increase in efficacy in promoting community and learner-centred classrooms, deliberative skills, historical understanding and civic learning. The study's findings for students were equally encouraging: Facing History students reported more positive classroom climates, and demonstrated greater historical understanding and civic skills and dispositions, including tolerance, awareness of the power and danger of prejudice and discrimination, and a belief in their power to make a difference.

Facing History and Ourselves classrooms are both marketplaces of ideas and laboratories for democracy. The conversations are neither simple nor tidy; a Facing History classroom does not offer formulaic answers. But, as one Facing History educator said, 'When students walk into a Facing History classroom, they know that not only is it a safe space, but there is an expectation that they will be critical thinkers.' They think about the habits of head and heart that build institutions, the practices necessary to prevent discrimination and injustice and sustain democratic society, and the responsibilities they bear toward those goals. 'To really understand yourself,' as another student put it, 'you really do have to understand that you have to face *his-tory*, and it is not just *his-tory*, it is *our* story. Until you understand that, you can't move forward.'

Holocaust education and the promotion of democratic ideals – The United States Holocaust Memorial Museum

Jennifer Ciardelli

As the events of the Holocaust fade from living memory, educators are faced with ensuring the history remains vivid and real – and rather than simply dates and statistics, the events evoke images of individual human beings living through some of the most enormous challenges a society can face. The scale and scope of the Holocaust, its abundant documentation and legacies, have made the event a touchstone in many arenas, including genocide and mass atrocity studies, human rights, medical ethics, and international law. With study and discourse about this history becoming more global, audiences learning about the event are increasingly diverse, with many having no personal, family or national connection to the history. A good number encounter the topic through popular culture. Some come to the Holocaust from the perspective of other experiences of persecution. Others have been exposed to Holocaust denial and propaganda. These widely diverging entry points present challenges to educators as they seek to promote meaningful engagement with this history. Why study a history that didn't occur on one's home soil, or appears at first glance to have no immediate connection?

With over 35 million on-site visitors and with educational outreach that has touched more than 270,000 youth and adult professionals since its opening in 1993, the United States Holocaust Memorial Museum has had ample opportunity to reach audiences seemingly unconnected to the events of the Holocaust. Traditionally, the American public comes to the history with exposure to the experience of first-hand witnesses both the survivors of the atrocities who resettled in the United States and the soldiers who witnessed the death and destruction when they encountered the camps at the end of the war. However, as the number of eye-witnesses declines and the US population becomes increasingly diverse, it is less and less likely those who study the Holocaust will have a personal connection to the event, raising challenges of relevance and meaning.

This article will highlight the Museum's educational outreach to two groups in particular, youth and adult professionals, and consider how it addresses these challenges. The discussion of outreach to youth will focus on educational experiences for Washington, D.C.-area teens united by geography yet diverse in most other respects. This programming reinforces democratic principles and the importance of an active citizenry. These themes also prevail in the professional development opportunities offered to those in institutions with significant responsibility for protecting individual rights and the health of society, in particular law enforcement, the military, and judges, all with significant power over the life and liberty of civilians. In the case of military officers, this work moves beyond issues of leadership and professional responsibility to address the prevention of genocide and mass atrocities. Outreach to all groups is rooted in the examination of the Holocaust as a specific historical event that was not inevitable. Because it was the result of human choice and human action, it could happen again. Examination of the Holocaust prompts reflection on what is required to ensure the health of a democratic society as well as how susceptible all humans can be to abusing power, believing the 'other' is inferior, and justifying any behaviour – including inaction.

The approach is rooted in the Museum's foundational philosophy, articulated from its inception by the Presidential Commission charged with examining how the Holocaust should be memorialized in the United States. The 1979 President's Commission on the Holocaust, convened by President James Carter and chaired by Elie Wiesel, acknowledged that Nazism was 'facilitated by the breakdown of democracy' and affirmed that 'a democratic government must function and perform basic services and that human rights must be protected within the law.'[104] For many, the crimes of the Holocaust illustrated the fragility of democracy and underlined what happens when a citizenry, either actively or passively, allows democratic freedoms to be eroded in the name of national unity, economic growth or national security.

Acknowledging the unique components of the Holocaust, in particular the Final Solution's targeting of Europe's entire Jewish population, the Commission stated that the 'universal implications of the Holocaust challenge Western civilization and modern scientific culture.'[105] A federal institution that served as a memorial to the victims while educating about the history would 'allow the presentation of a more complete picture of civilization, a greater vision of its promises and dangers' by adding a 'somber dimension to the progress of humanity celebrated'[106] by the

---

104 *President's Commission on the Holocaust Report, 1979*

105 Ibid.

106 Ibid.

Smithsonian Museums located in the nation's capital.[107] In addition to memorializing so many lost lives, this 'living memorial' would be responsible for raising an 'institutional scream' to alert the world to contemporary dangers that threaten to repeat the crimes of the past. [108]

The Museum is first and foremost a memorial to honour the victims of the Holocaust. Doing so with dignity leads to a belief that an important way to honour the victims is to work to prevent such atrocities from occurring again. Embedded in the Museum's vision is the mission to work to combat hatred, prevent genocide, and promote human dignity. It is through this lens that the U.S. Holocaust Memorial Museum has prioritized its educational outreach to society's leaders, including youth, who are our future leaders, and those professionals whose day-to-day decisions are at the crux of many competing values, including the need for security and freedoms.

Bringing the lessons home: youth

Launched in 1994, Bringing the Lessons Home (BTLH) is a foundational programme for the Museum. BTLH provides Washington, D.C.–area youth the opportunity to become actively involved with the Museum while learning content and skills that will bolster their abilities to be leaders in their communities. Through the programme, the Museum has developed long-term partnerships with more than thirty middle and high schools, enabling more than 100,000 students, teachers, and parents to participate. Hundreds of students have completed the ambassador programme and serve as docents and local leaders for their peers.

The students who come to the Museum for the ambassador programmes are diverse. They are African-American, Latino, Arab, Asian and Caucasian. They are Muslim, Jewish, and Christian. They arrive with varying degrees of Holocaust knowledge; some come with ancestral legacies of slavery, some as descendants of Holocaust survivors and some as new immigrants to the United States. What these high-school students have in common is their geographic proximity to the Museum, and that they come primarily from public schools. Beyond that, the common ground is provided by two core principles of the programme – principles that in actuality apply to all of

---

107 Founded in 1846, the Smithsonian is the world's largest museum and research complex. Its mission and vision is 'Shaping the future by preserving our heritage, discovering new knowledge, and sharing our resources with the world.' (http://www.si.edu/About)

108 Op.cit.

the Museum's programmes: the history and lessons of the Holocaust are relevant to today's world, and participants should be actively engaged in their own education.

Always grounded in the history, small group sessions and opportunities for conversation allow students to learn about the events of the Holocaust while considering its implications. What does the Nazi party's ability to transform a democracy into a dictatorship say about the vulnerabilities of a democracy? What role did law and legislation play in increasingly marginalizing and ultimately excluding the Jews, formerly full-fledged German citizens, from society? How did trusted institutions facilitate this process? What was the effect on individuals and their families? What was the human cost? What are the Holocaust's legacies?

Creating a learning environment in which the insights and opinions of young people are taken seriously is essential to the programme and is embedded in the expectations of outcomes: After completing the twelve-week series of intensive classes, students lead their parents, peers and other members of their communities on tours of the Museum. These tours demand that students, with support and guidance from Museum staff, design a narrative of the history that remains historically accurate while featuring aspects of the history that resonate today. One may discuss antisemitic legislation that imposed racially-based segregation and recognize a reality all too familiar to the US. Another may discuss the Evian Conference that dealt with refugee issues and think about today's struggles with immigration. Another may point out artefacts created by Warsaw ghetto residents who risked their lives to document their day-to-day persecution and note the importance of individuals speaking truth under extreme duress. The tours enable students to find their own personal voice and connection in articulating the history of the Holocaust.

Learning about the singularity of the event prompts considerations about the challenges we have yet to resolve as a society. The learning is never about comparing suffering and is always about the experiences of humans as individuals and as part of their various communities. The ability to think critically, clarify the values they want to live by, and articulate strengths and weaknesses of a society are important skills for emerging leaders. As programme participant Sade Gowens expressed: 'Being an ambassador means that I accept full responsibility for every action within my community. By combining my voice with others' we can become leaders and make a difference in the world.'

Law, justice, military, and society: Professionals

While working with youth is essential for the future of society, we are remiss if we do not provide opportunities for those currently in positions of leadership to reflect on the values at the core of their service. For over a decade, the Museum has provided professional development experiences to those in professions essential to maintaining the health of a democratic society. The history shows that successful implementation of the Nazi's racial ideology depended upon the cooperation of a range of professionals: civil servants to keep the bureaucratic infrastructure running; lawyers and judges to prosecute so-called offenders and uphold discriminatory legislation; police to enforce unjust laws; doctors to carry out unethical medical procedures; and the military to wage aggressive war and to participate in the murder of civilians. Countless individuals, members of professions traditionally relied upon to protect the public good, became participants in gross violations of human and civil rights and even mass murder. They often became complicit in small steps, in day-to-day decision-making that failed their fellow human beings and violated the values of their profession. Examining this past provides a window for their counterparts today to think about the importance of their role and how their actions can serve to either uphold or to subvert the civic ideals that are the backbone of a free and just society.

As with the youth, understanding of the Holocaust for these professionals varies. Some may have a personal connection. Some may have never studied the history before. Framing is vital. The emphasis is on the progression of events that involved tens of thousands of ordinary people and reveals the importance of day-to-day actions and choices. Many participants comment that Germans were brainwashed or would have been shot for not complying. Museum programmes complicate this notion through examination of historical context that reveals these assumptions to be inaccurate. What might have motivated German citizens to support or acquiesce to the Nazi platform? What economic, social or national needs did the political party fill? Were German professionals executed for resistance or opposition to Nazi policy and practice? Programmes use cases studies that feature individuals making decisions to break down and personalize the challenging context and reveal the variety of choices and options available to individuals during the period.

For example, Wilhelm Krützfeld worked as a police officer in Berlin. Praised by his superiors for his professionalism, Krützfeld was promoted to commander of District 16 in the heart of Berlin. During Kristallnacht (the state-sanctioned, anti-Jewish pogroms in Germany that occurred in 1938), Krützfeld confronted Nazi storm-troopers who had set fire to the New Synagogue located in his district. While police had been ordered to let the destruction and burning of Jewish property go unstopped, Krützfeld saved the Synagogue by producing documentation confirming the architectural importance of the building and an old imperial law requiring its protection. He chased off the Nazis at gunpoint and ordered the fire department to put out the fire. Nazi officials and the Berlin's police director learned of this event, and they took no formal action against Krützfeld. The police director chided him for acting against 'sound popular instinct.' Krützfeld replied that the duty of the police is to uphold peace, order and respect for the law.[109] Even before the mass killings had begun, Krützfeld saw that this targeting of a whole community was not right; he sought to blunt the policy, where possible, through the enforcement of professional values. He retired at his own request in 1943 but returned to policing in Berlin after the war. He passed away in Berlin in 1953.

Then too, we might consider the situation of the 691st Infantry Battalion stationed in occupied Belarus in October 1941. As part of an effort to pre-emptively contain a perceived partisan threat, a German major issued to three company commanders an order to kill the Jews under their jurisdiction. In essentially the same context, the commanders provided three different responses. One carried out the order without delay; the second hesitated, received confirmation, and assigned a subordinate to carry it out; the third refused completely, claiming 'Good German soldiers do not dirty their hands with such things.'[110] The records show the third company commander experienced no repercussions for his refusal. The purpose in this case study is not to judge what people in the past did or did not do. Rather, the examination illuminates the situational and motivational dynamics at play in challenging circumstances. What influenced each individual to behave differently? How did their choices impact the treatment of civilians?

Classrooms must allow space for in-service professionals to respond to the history in ways that resonate for them. Because they come with their colleagues, the professionals raise points of relevance specific to their professional expertise. Participants will often raise examples from their own work where dilemmas can occur as they work to match mission agency with actual implementation, while considering the impacts on individual lives. One programme participant, Rebecca White Berch, the Chief Justice in the state of Arizona, articulated: 'The Museum's

---

109 2011. *Behind the Badge: Police during the Holocaust,* United States Holocaust Memorial Museum.

110 Lange, T. 2005. Lernziel Gerechtigkeit? Zum didaktischen Umgang mit juristischer Vergangenheitsbewältigung *Geschichte in Wissenschaft und Unterricht,* Vol. 56 No. 11, p. 629.

thought-provoking programmes challenge participants to examine the pressures facing judges, prosecutors, defenders, and police those who are charged with the duty not only to uphold the justice system but also to protect individual liberty. All who participate come away with a renewed commitment to ensuring that the rule of law is not used as a tool of oppression.'

In addition to examining the failures of leadership during the Third Reich, Museum programmes for military professionals provide an opportunity to examine the Holocaust in the context of early warning indicators necessary to recognize genocide unfolding. This approach stems from interest expressed by military training academies and the Obama administration's effort to promote a whole-of-government approach to genocide prevention. President Obama has identified that 'Preventing mass atrocities and genocide is a core national security interest and a core moral responsibility of the United States.'[111] After completing a Museum programme, one active duty officer noted that 'Genocide can and still happens today. Sometimes I fell into the trap of thinking genocide was a "thing of the past". [I now see the] importance of early warning and really understanding the situation.' Educating military professionals about early warning indicators informs their understanding of how genocides unfold   knowledge which contributes to their potential to prevent future genocides.

Working to promote these understandings, whether related to genocide prevention or the preservation of democratic ideals, Museum programmes strive to honour the victims of the Holocaust by examining the context that allowed the events to occur. Personalizing the history via case studies that illustrate human involvement provides points of entry that engage because people can relate. Examining the 'why' prompts conversations that address implications for today. The Museum's new special exhibition, 'Some Were Neighbors: Collaboration and Complicity in the Holocaust' will further this conversation. Launched in April 2013, the new exhibition shares with broader audiences the content and case studies that reveal the all-too-human motives and pressures that influenced individuals' actions – or inactions. Our democratic society depends upon an active citizenry that remains vigilant in ensuring that its leaders and its institutions uphold the democratic values espoused in the nation's founding documents. The Holocaust is an essential means to examine these most challenging prospects, for as one participant expressed: 'This is our past; this is humanity's past and what we did to each other.'

---

111 August 2011. President Obama, Presidential Study Directive-10..

4

Final reflections: The moral and political issues ahead

The civic and political challenges of Holocaust education

Georges Bensoussan

Translated from French

'The real story of this Nazi-constructed hell is desperately needed for the future. Not only because these facts have changed and poisoned the very air we breathe, not only because they now inhabit our dreams at night and permeate our thoughts during the day, but also because they have become the basic experience and the basic misery of our times,' wrote Hannah Arendt in September 1946.

Although we have the impression that the pivotal nature of the event is only now being discovered, in view of the thoughts expressed immediately after the war by Dwight McDonald in the United States of America, Georges Bataille in France and, above all, Hannah Arendt in her articles between 1943 and 1946, it is rather being rediscovered.

The event – the destruction of Europe's Jews – gives cause for anxiety. It upset established patterns and language and set at naught the great liberating narratives of humanism, progress and science. To reflect on that pivotal event, customary benchmarks must be disregarded, new cognitive tools must be devised, and many factors that are often overlooked in history, such as the role of fear, the irrational, the Devil and resentment, must be taken into account. In short, an effort must be made to understand, without projecting the new onto the old, and, as Michel Foucault wrote in his preface to *The Use of Pleasure*, to think our innermost thoughts, silently.

Why should we raise questions about an event that occurred seventy years ago? Well, we should, not because it is yet another genocide in what Michelet called 'the sad and violent history of humankind', but because it constituted an anthropological break, with a before and an after, and thus the very definition of an 'event'. Simply stated, 'Action T4'[112] and the destruction of Europe's Jews were two intimately linked crimes that, after the Great War and the mass murders, ushered in the era of 'superfluous humanity.'

---

112 'T4' refers to the secret mass killing programme of people with mental and physical disabilities in the Nazi Reich (Ed.).

If the Holocaust is the expression of 'radical evil', to quote Hannah Arendt (who defined it as such in 1952 'because it can no longer be deduced from humanly comprehensible motives'), then the 'radical evil' in this case was that human beings, who had been stripped of membership in the world, were made 'superfluous as human beings.'

That historical fact has therefore become a cultural event of prime importance in the West and transcends Jewish communities. But that event should be understood first and foremost as a historical fact *while disregarding* the subsequent course of history.

Think of 1942 while disregarding 1943, while breaking with all teleological views of history such as 'history and progress' and 'history and reason', while breaking with academic optimism that turns history into a substitute faith and a kind of civic religion. Use history, on the contrary, as a tool for seeing things differently rather than as accumulated and sterile knowledge ossified in 'astonishment' at the extreme violence unleashed in the twentieth century, even though all human history is tragic, as noted by so many European thinkers (in particular after 1918), from Paul Valéry of France to José Ortega y Gasset of Spain.

Consider history, in particular cultural history, as past achievements in order to understand the path that led to Auschwitz: we are the products of the history of our predecessors. Because there is no 'first man', Nietzsche wrote that the future belongs to those with 'the longest memory'.

To understand ultimately entails avoiding all-purpose concepts that trivialise the event, starting with the concept of totalitarianism, which equated Nazism with Communism and lost sight of the distinctive quality of Nazism, namely the destruction of a people for the crime of birth.

What links culture to barbarism? Can the Holocaust be deemed a resurgence of 'age-old barbarism'? But in fact 41 per cent of the Schutz Staffel (SS) officers were higher education graduates and two thirds of the Einsatzgruppen leaders held doctoral degrees.

Barbarism, as a concept, does not account for the Treblinka and Belzec factories for producing corpses. That radically new development was part and parcel of a world order far removed from pogrom violence. When the process of civilization of a developed nation such as Germany leads to the annihilation of part of the human race, extreme violence does not run counter to, but is consubstantial with, civilization. In such a case, 'barbarism' and 'civilization' are mutually sustaining. The spurious barbarism-civilization opposition is laid bare, however, on examination of the technique, which was not only a means, but also a thought system, a world vision and an end in itself.

Was the destruction of Europe's Jews an unrepeatable event? Was it unique? These descriptions are both self-evident and tactless in a time of competition between victims.

The fact in itself was unprecedented: from Chelmno (December 1941) to Treblinka (July 1942), within seven months, humanity was plunged into a new era. No such event had ever been recorded in history. Likewise, the motivations of murderers were without precedent: there was no religious, territorial or economic incentive. They were existential motivations, combined with the millenarian passion of some medieval strands of Christianity, drawing on the most atavistic fears of the human race and on the most delusional paranoid beliefs, starting with conspiracy theories.

To claim the event was unprecedented, we must necessarily compare it with others, while remembering that comparison does not mean amalgamation. If no comparisons are drawn, then this historic event will stand as a fact of religious nature and the remembrance of the event then appears to be a revealed truth or even a dogma. The more the tragedy of the Holocaust is compared with other catastrophes, however, the more its singularity will be highlighted. When situations are weighed against each other, discrepancies are exposed. Comparisons preclude trivialization, whereas an elective approach will foster historical relativism in the future.

The destruction of Europe's Jews was not the means to achieve a policy, but a policy in itself. Therein lay the difference between the crime of Auschwitz Birkenau and those of Hiroshima and Nagasaki. The atomic bombing of the two Japanese cities in August 1945 was a war crime, a barbaric means of achieving a policy. It was not a policy in itself. There was no question of the United States of America committing genocide against the Japanese people, and the bombings stopped as soon as Japan surrendered (15 August 1945).

The barbarism of the German plans for Eastern Europe (GeneralplanOst, 1941 1942) was the means of a racist policy, although its aim was not genocide against the Slavic people. The Holocaust, however, was an end in itself, the deliberate and planned resolve to exterminate all Jews from the surface of Europe first, and from the face of the earth if possible. This radical specificity is evident in its disastrous human toll, for 60 per cent of non-Jews deported from France (mostly political deportees) returned in 1945, but fewer than 3 per cent of the Jewish deportees did. Jews accounted for 54 per cent of Nazi deportees Europe-wide, but only 6 per cent of the survivors.

One and a half million Jewish children under the age of 15 (a quarter of the death toll) were killed during the Holocaust. No other population group targeted by Nazi Germany, including the Slavs, who were hardest hit, was slaughtered on such a scale.

Can the cultural roots of the event be identified? In particular, does it stem from a biological conception of humanity, which is characterised by the transition from sentient beings to living subjects, by the primacy of instrumental (technical) reason and by the shift towards a zoological conception of the human race owing to scientism and social Darwinism? After all, the Enlightenment had been the idea behind the development of the blueprint for the overhaul of human nature, based on the concept of a useful, productive and young body politic, while pushing 'useless mouths' to the margins. This reactionary modernism, a blend of disenchantment with modernity and exaltation of technology, held sway in the West before 1914.

Counter-Enlightenment thinkers contributed to the desacralization of the human person in the name of science. Biology became the only source of truth about the human race, supplanting the ancient political vision of a government of subjects defined primarily as **sentient beings**. This intellectual school of thought, which thrived in the 1900s, led to negative eugenics and racial hygiene, in addition to the setting of 'thresholds of humanity'. Owing to the biologization of politics, people were regarded as a population whose life and death were managed in the same way as a breeder ensures the survival of his livestock and the farmer ensures the growth of his crops, eliminating the dross if need be. Nature (the struggle for existence) was therefore transposed to culture (humanity). Europe in the 1900s was marked, in some intellectual circles, by the exaltation of war as a redeeming experience, in that it disposed of 'waste'. It was also marked by the pre-eminence of race and the disavowal of otherness inherent in the rejection of the three 'dangers' of modernity — Jews, women and the city.

Racism flourished as an ideology in the second half of the nineteenth century. It was not confined to the purported existence of races, which negated the unity of humankind, or of racial inequalities, which were used to justify the separation between the dominant and the dominated. Rather, it was the biologization of social considerations, in which humanity was viewed only as a species living a life that was a mere Darwinian struggle for existence in a hierarchical and violent world. Racism brings up the issue of the primacy of biology over politics. It also leads us to reflect on the counter-Enlightenment thinkers who defined what was 'inherently human', thereby establishing an exclusive norm: 'One does not dictate norms to life', wrote the French philosopher Georges Canguilhem.

The idea of race as an absolute invariant rose to prominence in the second half of the nineteenth century when the natural order was shaken, social ranks became blurred and divine transcendence no longer seemed to recognise the faithful in an increasingly secular world. Race then became the explanation of the world. And racism became a means for the transcendence of the destitute, the revenge of a rooted life against a wandering existence, the revenge of the intangible against removal by time and the seemingly ever quickening pace of history. In short, race relieved identity-related anxiety in troubled times, for rejection of others confirms identity and dispels doubts. However, anxiety soon turned into hatred, ever ready to set its sights on a real enemy. Between 1850 and 1945, that enemy in Europe was 'the Jew', who functioned as the cursed element in the collective unconscious during those times of disillusionment and who had previously been stigmatised for centuries by the Christian world, which had made anti-Judaism a cultural hallmark of the West.

The Holocaust was therefore an ideological crime committed against the backdrop of Judeophobic fervour in Europe. Even if it can be subsumed under other historical processes, in particular that of all-out war – the corollary of the mass society – in the general transition from conventional warfare (crushing the enemy and signing a peace agreement) to all-out war (annihilating the enemy with no agreement being possible), and from the enemy-adversary to the drive for annihilation. The genocide of the Jews therefore raises not only questions of antisemitism, that lethal passion characteristic of regressive societies (former Nazi Germany and Austria), but also of modern societies' anomie that encourages the commission of acts of murder owing to inaction by the majority, groupthink and fear of rejection, the sense of service and, lastly, of obedience.

Genocide is not the return of the ancient right to kill. Quite the contrary, it is linked to the modern power to manage life and to the shift in medical discourse through which the concept of 'person' is superseded by that of an ailing body that must be repaired. Far from being the return of 'barbarism', genocide becomes a permanent temptation for modern political powers as soon as nature is transposed to culture. As nature is pitiless to the weak, humanity is anti-nature. Consequently it is also *responsibility* (answerable for others) and *thought* while the dignity of the oppressed lies ultimately in their ability to understand what is destroying them.

Paradoxically, therefore, the politics of life (biopower) as exaltation of nature ultimately instituted a culture of death that crushed the weak and strengthened the strong. The destruction of Europe's Jews, related to the Action T4 biological and political crime, formed part of the counter-Enlightenment trend. As such, the Holocaust was no 'lapse into barbarism' but, on the contrary, an aspect of 'modernity'.

In Belzec, Sobibor, Treblinka, Chelmno and Birkenau, more than elsewhere in the killing fields, the Holocaust brought the attack against the concept of the human person to new heights, hence the political centrality of the Holocaust today and the recognition of its significance as marking an anthropological break and cultural upheaval.

This destruction of humanity in each human being was ultimately made manifest through the desecration of the bodies and the mixing of the ashes. Admittedly, only the Jewish people fell victim to that 'nameless crime', but only the myopic would fail to see that, through them, the very principle of human life has been weakened forever, as noted in 1947 by Georges Bataille, the French writer, who wrote that 'by now the image of man is inseparable from that of a gas chamber'.

The Holocaust was the outcome of a certain strand of contemporary nihilism. But it is because our present, haunted by that nihilism, is cause for anxiety that it raises questions about the Holocaust. The inverse, however, is not the case. The genocide of Jews, therefore, was not a dreadful interlude but a foundational event. Can the clock be turned back to the pre-1940 years as if nothing had happened at Treblinka? Can people today remain faithful to the spirit of the Enlightenment without questioning the counter-Enlightenment idea of progress? Can people embrace science and technology without thinking about the links between Nazism and techno-science? We do not live in a world free of Nazism; we are immersed in post-Nazi societies.

Holocaust education and the prevention of genocide

Yehuda Bauer

What is the purpose of teaching the Holocaust, the genocide of the Jews at the hands of Nazi Germany and her allies and supporters, worldwide? Why concentrate on this particular genocide, and not on others? Can Holocaust education be of any help in advancing the prevention of genocides and genocide-like events?

The central reason for teaching the Holocaust, in both formal and informal frameworks, in high school and higher education, lies, it would seem, in the fact that here we deal with the most extreme case of a mass annihilation of a targeted population known to us so far. When we say 'extreme case', we do not mean that the suffering of the Jews was in any sense greater than others' in similar circumstances, or that the number of Jewish victims, or their percentage of all Jews, was higher than in other cases. Suffering cannot be measured, and the suffering of Tutsi, or Fur, or members of Congolese ethnic groups in today's Democratic Republic of the Congo, or indeed of anyone caught up in instances of mass murder, is not in any sense different, lesser or greater, than that of the Jews in the Second World War. By 'extreme', we mean that the Nazis aimed at killing every person defined as being Jewish by the perpetrators all over the globe. Every such person was to be identified, registered, marked, dispossessed, humiliated, concentrated, transported and killed. Also, this was to be done against all principles of pragmatic, economic or political, logic; for the Jews had no territory, no army, they did not control any country's economy, and had no united political representation. The motivation for the mass murder was purely delusionary, ideological in the sense it bore little or no relation to the factual situation of Jews or others. In all these regards, the motivation was opposed to modern principles of economic interest, and of political expediency. Nazi Germany could have used the Jews for its purposes, for instance it could have employed them as slave labourers, but even when Nazis did so, they then murdered those very slaves who were working for them. There is no precedent for all the above. The statement that the Holocaust was the most extreme form of genocide is based on this structural analysis.

It is a good idea to teach the Holocaust as an introduction to the problem of genocide generally, precisely because it is, arguably, the most extreme case of this human illness. But that does not mean other instances of genocide, in the more distant or more recent past, or the present, should not be addressed – quite the contrary. The problem for the educator, however, is always a very practical one: she/he has very little time at her/his disposal, and on top of that has to deal with other topics as well. In most cases, the teacher does not have the kind of training that would make him/her capable of dealing with the Holocaust or any other genocide. Training of teachers is therefore an integral part of any effort to teach the Holocaust and other genocides. Yet the problem is not only how to overcome these serious obstacles, but first of all to determine whether the effort to do so is justified.

The justification for teaching the Holocaust is not difficult. Genocide and mass violence are with us all the time and we should educate young people (and their parents) to realize that in order to fight against these phenomena they need to be aware of them, recognize them for what they are, and devise ways and means to influence the political world to respond to them. And, as the most extreme form of genocide was the Holocaust, there is every justification in the world for people in Kenya, Mongolia, Thailand and Ecuador to know what happened in this extreme case, and why. The problem then arises of how to provide education.

One of the obvious answers is to use contemporary technology – internet, video, applications and all the rest. This is certainly essential, but these are tools, and they do not deal with the content. We should realize, first of all, we deal here with human lives, and statistics and dry facts alone will not penetrate into the minds of our students, whatever their age. We might well start with authenticated stories of real individuals in situations of mass violence, in this case the Holocaust, stories that will bring home to the listeners the fact that this might happen to them if we do not recruit all our talents to prevent such things from happening. There are many thousands of individual stories from the Holocaust, on video, in many archives, and they can be used. One cannot teach only horrors, because that will be rejected by our students. The survivors of the Holocaust are not many, but they tell the story of their survival and, importantly, of the rescuers – again, the rescuers were a small minority, but they existed, and they proved there was a way of resistance, not only by means of arms or force, but by unarmed actions of rescue. In other words, their stories are life-affirming, and they must be used, although it should always be emphasized how few the rescuers were.

Any kind of teaching the Holocaust must always be related to the particular culture and historical experience of the audience. It is best, perhaps, to start with that local culture and historical experience. Thus, if we teach in, say, a South American country, we might be well advised to start with the dictatorship of the Argentinian Junta in the seventies of the last century, or the genocidal murders of the Maya in Guatemala, and proceed from there to the danger of genocide generally and then concentrate on the Holocaust as the specific example.

The question arises whether this kind of educational effort contributes to the possible prevention of genocide generally. It is, of course, highly unlikely that children of current or even future perpetrators will attend courses on the Holocaust, but that is not the aim of Holocaust education in any case. Rather, the aim is, or should be, to prompt as much of the general public as possible to prevent and not to be indifferent to mass violence and genocidal acts. The direct impact on genocide prevention is not possible, but then, education in any case is by its very definition a prolonged process, and the purpose of Holocaust education, on this and other issues, is long-term impact. Holocaust education is possible, mostly, in democratic or half-democratic societies, although it is possible in certain non-democratic regimes as well, in limited forms. It is totally impossible in ideologically-directed authoritarian or dictatorial regimes. Its purpose in all the cases where it can be done will be to influence all those who can be reached to realize the threat they, as part of humanity, are facing, wherever they live.

Students of whatever age who live in societies in which they have the possibility to influence public officials, whether by electoral processes or in any other way, should be encouraged to make it clear to people of political influence that prevention of mass violence and genocidal threats are important to their constituents. Prevention of genocide and of similar events is a matter of practical politics, although without a deep moral conviction that the preservation of human lives must be at the basis of all such action, no prevention is likely to succeed.

What prevents prevention? In practically all cases, economic, political, military or ideological (often religious) interests stand in the way. A major power whose politicians are convinced that without energy sources – oil, minerals, chemicals, etc. – it cannot maintain its position will refuse to act against forces that control such vital resources and that have an interest in annihilating a human group as such, in whole or in part. Alternatively, a major power may have no interest whatsoever in a certain area or a certain place, where mass violence or genocidal massacres take place or may take place, and will not act to prevent them. Or, again, a radical ideological movement will seek the annihilation of a group or groups that it sees as enemies, and other powers may be reluctant to endanger their own interests in preventing that movement from acting out its annihilatory wish. In all such and similar cases, the crucial element is that local, regional, or all-embracing ideological interests may seem more important to these actors than the prevention of massive loss of human lives.

Humans are creatures who, in certain circumstances, kill other humans. They have been doing so since time immemorial. Is it then hopeless to try to change a type of behaviour that recurs again and again, throughout history? No – because humans are also capable of the opposite type of action, namely of saving and preserving lives, even of people they dislike. They are capable of showing sympathy, love and cooperation with others. It is safe to say that humans have both possibilities of action in their make-up: murder, and rescue from murder. The choice between the two is, in many ways, a political choice. While, as stated above, moral conviction is essential for any kind of what we call genocide prevention, it is not very useful to engage in preaching moral sermons, convincing as they may sound. To repeat endlessly that it is bad to murder individuals or groups of humans does not help to oppose economic, political or ideological interests. What is needed is to combine moral conviction with practical political wisdom. Education is a basic, long-term way to raise generations of people who will be willing and able to do that. Holocaust education will zero in on the central issue to be faced.

Can international law help us reach this goal, and can Holocaust education be relevant to the enactment of international law directed against the perpetration of genocidal acts? Over the past several decades, there has been an impressive development of international law designed to prevent mass violence. The problem is not that we lack international legal tools to prevent genocide, but that their practical application is usually prevented by the fact that states, whether big or small, refuse to obey them. In other words, international law is extremely important, but its force is not yet sufficient to overcome the complete disregard for such legal norms by a large number of states. The conclusion is not we should abandon international law – quite the contrary, we should do everything in our power to strengthen it. Again, education of future politicians, other public figures, lawyers and the population at large is one of the best ways to move forward in this regard. Holocaust education is about the denial of the basic human right, the right to life, to a group targeted for annihilation. To say the Holocaust was an extreme form of an attack on international legal norms even seventy or so years ago is an understatement. Holocaust education should lead students to realize that the strengthening of international law is a basic requirement for her/his own life and survival.

Holocaust education is not the only way all these aims can be accomplished. A wrong approach to it could lead to the opposite: the student, especially the young one, will identify with the perpetrators. We need to avoid that at all costs. We can do this by eliciting empathy, and through empathy for the victims of that particular genocide we can create empathy for all victims, all threatened groups, and in the end, for our immediate neighbours as well, wherever we live. We should then move from empathy to analysis and understanding, and then the facts of history may begin to make some sense. Holocaust education, finally, is one facet, though a very important one, in a general attempt to create a world that will not be 'good', but possibly slightly better than the one we live in now.

> **Notes on editors**

> **Notes on authors**

Notes on editors

Karel Fracapane

Karel Fracapane started his professional career at the French Ministry of Foreign Affairs, as a Policy Officer. In 2003, he was hired by the Task Force for International Cooperation on Holocaust Education, Remembrance and Research (now International Holocaust Remembrance Alliance, IHRA) and was appointed its first Executive Secretary in 2005. In this capacity, he worked successively for the governments of the United States of America, Italy, Poland, Hungary and the Czech Republic. In late 2007, Karel Fracapane became Head of a newly established Department of International Relations of the Shoah Memorial in Paris, coordinating many activities pertaining to Holocaust and genocide studies in several regions of the world. He was also a member of the International Committee of Memorial Museums in Remembrance of the Victims of Public Crimes, 2011 Chairman of the IHRA Memorials and Museums Working Group and a fellow of the Salzburg Global Seminar. Karel Fracapane joined UNESCO in 2011 as a Senior Project Officer, Focal Point on Holocaust Education.

Matthias Haß

Matthias Haß, Ph.D., works as a consultant, educator and researcher in the fields of memory politics, European integration, and international exchange programmes. He served as the director of the US programme of Action Reconciliation Service for Peace in Philadelphia. He also taught at the Free University in Berlin and York University in Toronto, and worked at several memorial sites dedicated to the Nazi past, including the Topography of Terror, the House of the Wannsee Conference and the US Holocaust Memorial Museum. Among his publications are *Gestaltetes Gedenken. Yad Vashem, das U.S. Holocaust Memorial Museum und die Stiftung Topographie des Terrors* (Frankfurt/Main, New York, 2002) and 'The Politics of Memory in Germany, Israel and the United States of America' (Working Paper Series of The Canadian Centre for German and European Studies No.9, Toronto, Montréal, 2004).

Notes on authors

Yehuda Bauer

Yehuda Bauer is Professor of Holocaust Studies (Emeritus) at the Hebrew University, Academic Advisor of Yad Vashem, Member of the Israeli Academy of Science, and Hon. Chair of the International Holocaust Remembrance Alliance. He is also internationally involved in efforts at the Genocide Prevention Advisory Network. He has published fifteen books, almost all on the Holocaust, and most were translated into several languages. He has published some 100 scientific articles in various journals. His best-known books are *Jews for Sale?* (Yale University Press, 1994), *Rethinking the Holocaust* (Yale UP, 2001) and *Death of the Shtetl* (Yale UP, 2009).

Georges Bensoussan

Georges Bensoussan, historian, former professor of history in secondary schools, is Director of Publications of the Shoah Memorial in Paris. He is Editor-in-Chief of *Revue d'Histoire de la Shoah*, the only francophone journal dedicated to the history of the genocide of the Jewish people. He is the author of numerous books about the Shoah, Zionism, and the end of Judaism on Arab lands, including: *Histoire de la Shoah* (PUF, 1996, 5th edition 2012), *Auschwitz en héritage? D'un bon usage de la mémoire* (Fayard-Mille et une nuits, 2003) and *Histoire intellectuelle et politique du sionisme 1860-1940* (Fayard, 2002). In 2008, he was awarded the prize of the Fondation du Judaïsme Français (French Judaism foundation).

Jennifer Ciardelli

Jennifer Ciardelli develops and facilitates educational programmes for US and foreign military officers and federal executives at the United States Holocaust Memorial Museum. Approaches to examining the Holocaust include considerations of leadership and genocide prevention. She is involved with institutional initiatives that involve special exhibitions, the Museum's web presence and institutional planning. She has presented in both national and international settings. Prior to joining the Museum, she taught high school and graduate education workshops on topics including the Holocaust and genocide studies, European history, critical thinking, and curriculum design. She holds undergraduate degrees in history and English and a Master's degree in education.

Sophie Ernst

Sophie Ernst is a teacher of philosophy. She is currently working on the teaching of 'morale laïque' (secular morality), soon to be implemented in French schools. She worked previously as a researcher at the French Institute of Education of the Ecole normale supérieure of Lyon, where she contributed to numerous teacher training programmes for primary and secondary schools. She also created a research group on the challenges created by the growth of memorial claims, conveying moral exigencies and political demands. She is associated with the Auschwitz Foundation in Brussels and ran a seminar at the Collège international de philosophie on 'History traumas, memory and education: ethical and political challenges'. Ms Ernst is the author of *Quand les mémoires déstabilisent l'école. Mémoire de la Shoah et enseignement* (IFE-ENS [ex-INRP], Lyon, 2008).

Richard Freedman

Richard Freedman serves as the Director of the Cape Town Holocaust Centre and of the South African Holocaust and Genocide Foundation, which is the umbrella body to the three Holocaust centres in South Africa, situated in Durban, Johannesburg and Cape Town. He was active in South African independent schools, having served as principal of Herzlia Weizmann School from 1990 to 2005, chairman of the Association of Principals of Jewish Day Schools of Southern Africa, and a member of the executive committee of the Independent Schools Association of South Africa (Western Cape). He is a council member of the Federation of International Human Rights Museums. He is a fellow of the United States Holocaust Museum and the Salzburg Global Seminars and has been a guide on the international 'March of the Living'.

Konstanty Gebert

Konstanty Gebert is scholar-in-residence at the Taube Center for Jewish Life and Culture in Warsaw, associate fellow at the Warsaw office of the European Council on Foreign Relations, and an international reporter and columnist at *Gazeta Wyborcza*, Poland's leading daily newspaper. A dissident activist in the 1970s and 1980s, he helped organize the Jewish Flying University and worked as an underground journalist. He went on to found *Midrasz*, the intellectual Polish Jewish monthly. He also serves as an advisory board member of the Einstein Forum in Potsdam, Germany and of the Dutch Jewish Humanitarian fund. In addition to essays and articles, Mr Gebert has published eleven books on twentieth-century Europe, Israel, Polish Jews and other topics.

Zehavit Gross

Zehavit Gross is the head of the graduate programme of Management and Development in Informal Education Systems at the School of Education, Bar-Ilan University, Israel. Her main areas of specialisation are Holocaust Education, Human Rights Education and Peace Education. She is currently involved in international projects in Europe, Australia, New Zealand, Singapore and Hong Kong. She was invited with Doyle Stevick of the University of South Carolina to edit two special issues for *Prospects* (UNESCO International Bureau of Education quarterly review) on Holocaust education. She is also the author, with Lynn Davies (Birmingham University) and Khansaa Diab, of a book entitled *Gender, Religion and Education in a Chaotic Postmodern World*, published by Springer.

Matthias Heyl

Matthias Heyl has served as Educational Director of the International Youth Encounter Center Ravensbrück and Director of Educational Services of the Ravensbrück Memorial Site/ Brandenburg Memorial Site Foundation since 2002. He was previously Director of the Hamburg Research and Study Centre for Holocaust Education (1998-2002). He studied history, educational science, and psychology at Hamburg University. He has authored, co-authored and co-edited several publications in the field of Holocaust Studies and Holocaust Education, including *Thema Holocaust – ein Buch für die Schule* (1996), *Erziehung nach Auschwitz. Eine Bestandsaufnahme* (1997, a comparative study on the development of Holocaust Education in West Germany, the Netherlands, Israel and the US) and a monograph on Anne Frank (2002), also published in Japanese (2003). (For further information: www.heyl-online.eu.)

Wolf Kaiser

Wolf Kaiser is the Deputy Director of the House of the Wannsee Conference and Head of its Educational Department. He has worked at this memorial and educational site since its inauguration in 1992. He is a member of the German delegation to the International Holocaust Remembrance Alliance and on the board of advisors to the International Centre for Education about Auschwitz and the Holocaust in Oświęcim. Mr Kaiser has recently published on human rights education and education at memorial sites, and specifically on a concept for teaching about the

Wannsee Conference and its historical context, as well as teaching the crimes committed by the German police during the Nazi period.

Anat Livne

Anat Livne earned her BA in History and Philosophy, together with a teaching certificate, from the Hebrew University (1981), and her MA (1991) and PhD (2006) from Tel Aviv University in Jewish History and Jewish Studies. She taught and advised students at Oranim College from 1998 to 2010. In the years from 1996 to 2010 she was Pedagogical Director at the Ghetto Fighters' House Center for Humanistic Education. In 2011 Dr Livne was an educational consultant at the Educational Department of the United States Holocaust Memorial Museum, Washington, D.C. Since 2011 she has served as Executive Director of GFH.

Peter Longerich

Peter Longerich is the Director of the Research Centre for the Holocaust and Twentieth-Century History at Royal Holloway, University of London. He has served as chair of the Expert's Committee on Antisemitism since 2009 and of the International Academic Board at the Vienna Wiesenthal Institute since 2010. He worked on his biography about Heinrich Himmler while he was at the United States Holocaust Memorial Museum as the J.B. and Maurice Shapiro Senior Scholar in Residence at the Center for Advanced Studies (2003–2004). The biography *Heinrich Himmler: A Life* (Oxford University Press, 2011) is one of his many publications on the Holocaust including *Holocaust: The Nazi Murder and the Persecution of the Jews* and *The Unwritten Order: Hitler's Role in the Final Solution, and The Systematic Character of the National Socialist Policy for the Extermination of the Jews*.

François Masabo

François Masabo is an Associate Professor and a senior researcher at the Centre for Conflict Management (CCM) at the National University of Rwanda. He is also a Lecturer in two Master's Programmes run by CCM, entitled Genocide Studies and Prevention and Peace studies and Conflict transformation. Prof. Masabo holds a PhD in Sociology of Change, Crisis and Conflict. His research focuses mainly on genocide remembrance and prevention, peace building processes, social transformation and meeting new challenges in post-conflict development.

Angelika Meyer

Angelika Meyer graduated in political science from the Free University of Berlin. She is currently a staff member of the Educational Department of the Ravensbrück Memorial Site/ Brandenburg Memorial Site Foundation. Ms Meyer was previously involved in extracurricular education projects with the Topography of Terror Foundation (1997–2007) and with the Anne Frank Centre in Berlin. She designed educational materials for the exhibition 'Aschwitzprozess 4ks 2/63 Frankfurt am Main' of the Fritz Bauer Institute (Berlin 2004), curated the exhibition 'Varian Fry /Berlin-Marseille-New York' (Aktives Museum & Berlin Academy of Arts, 2007), and was a research assistant for the sourcebook *Subcamp of the women's concentration camp Ravensbrück* (2001). She also directed the construction of a memorial of the Ravensbrück sub-camp Retzow-Rechlin located in Mecklenburg-Vorpommern (1999).

David Netzer

David Netzer is a lecturer on pedagogy and teacher training at Oranim Academic College for Education, Israel. He is also a writer of educational programmes and an instructor of students and teachers at the Centre for Humanistic Education in Ghetto Fighters House Museum, Israel. His publications include: *The Work and Impact of the Centre for Humanistic Education*, 2008, University of Sussex (PhD thesis); and 'Painful Past in the Service of Israeli Jewish-Arab Dialogue: The Work of the Centre for Humanistic Education at the Ghetto Fighters House in Israel'. 2008. Factis Pax 2 (2) pp. 282–291. (http://www.infactispax.org/journal/).

Falk Pingel

Falk Pingel, Ph.D., Associate Research Fellow of the Georg Eckert Institute for International Textbook Research in Braunschweig, Germany, served as the Institute's Deputy Director for several years. In 2003–2004, he was the first director of the Organization for Security and Co-operation in Europe's Education Department in Sarajevo, Bosnia and Herzegovina. He is an editor and co-author of a German history textbook. He taught contemporary history as well as theory and didactics of history at Bielefeld University and served as guest lecturer abroad, in particular in Israel, South Eastern Europe and Shanghai. Comparative approaches to the teaching about the Holocaust have been a core issue in his scholarly activities. Among his publications are the *UNESCO Guidebook on International Textbook Research and Textbook Revision* (2010) and 'From Evasion to a Crucial Tool of Moral and Political

Education: Teaching National Socialism and the Holocaust in Germany' (2006, *What Shall We Tell the Children?* Foster/Crawford, eds).

Daniel Rafecas

Federal judge, advisor to the Shoah Memorial Foundation of Buenos Aires, Argentina, Daniel Rafecas is a criminal law professor at the University of Buenos Aires. In his capacity as federal judge of the criminal court in Buenos Aires since 2004, he investigates crimes against humanity committed in Argentina during the last military dictatorship. His investigations have included crimes committed by the Primer Cuerpo Ejército, and specifically the perpetrators of crimes at the Olimpo, Vesubio and Mansion Sere clandestine centres. Rafecas is also academic advisor to the Holocaust Museum in Buenos Aires. He has published several works, the most recent of which is *Historia de la Solución Final (History of the Final Solution)* (2012, Buenos Aires, Siglo XXI Editores).

Paul Salmons

Paul Salmons is the Programme Director of the Centre for Holocaust Education at the Institute of Education, University of London. While at the Imperial War Museum in London, he devised Holocaust education programmes that work with the Museum's permanent collection, established the IWM's Fellowship in Holocaust Education, and published *Reflections: The Holocaust Exhibition – A cross-curricular resource pack for teaching about the Holocaust*. He has represented the UK at the International Holocaust Remembrance Alliance since its foundation, where he currently chairs the subcommittee on Holocaust, Genocide and Crimes against Humanity. Salmons has also consulted on various international projects, including the UN International Holocaust Remembrance Day.

Leora Schaefer

Leora Schaefer has served as the Director of the Facing History and Ourselves Toronto Office since its inception in 2008. In this role, she oversees the organization's Canadian programme, which includes professional development opportunities for teachers, curricular initiatives and educational events for the greater community. Schaefer oversees and facilitates summer seminars for educators in Canada as well as workshops on teaching practice and pedagogy. She has written study guides to accompany films, most recently for a new documentary on the life of Hannah Senesh. She has been a member of adjunct summer faculty at several institutes of higher learning and has presented at conferences throughout North America. Leora has a BA degree in education from the University of Winnipeg and an MA from Brandeis University.

Marty Sleeper

Martin Sleeper is the Associate Executive Director of Facing History and Ourselves. His undergraduate degree is from Williams College in history and he holds masters' and doctoral degrees in teaching and curriculum development from the Harvard University Graduate School of Education. He has extensive experience in teaching at the secondary and college levels as well as in curriculum design and museum education. From 1979 to 2000 he was Principal of the John D. Runkle School in Brookline, Massachusetts. He is the author of numerous articles on history education and adolescent development.

Doyle Stevick

E. Doyle Stevick is Associate Professor of Educational Leadership and Policies at the University of South Carolina, where he directs the Office of International and Comparative Education. A Fulbright Fellow to Estonia in 2003 and 2013 - 2014, he has researched Holocaust education for more than ten years. Special issues appear in the journals *European Education*, *Intercultural Education* (edited with Deborah Michaels), and *Prospects* (with Zehavit Gross). Gross and Stevick are completing a book of new empirical research in the field which will be published soon. His previous books, with Bradley Levinson, are *Reimagining Civic Education* and *Advancing Democracy through Education?*

Xu Xin

Xu Xin is the Director of the Institute of Jewish Studies at the University of Nanjing and the Founder and President of the China Judaic Studies Association. Xin became interested in Jewish studies through his scholarship on American literature. He taught for two years at Chicago State University in the mid-1980s then continued his research as a visiting scholar at Harvard University's Center of Jewish Studies in 1996. He has studied and taught in various institutions worldwide, including Tel-Aviv, Yale, Notre Dame and York universities. Among other publications, he contributed to and edited the Chinese edition of the *Encyclopaedia Judaica*.